Embodiment Theory and Chinese Philosophy

Also available from Bloomsbury:

Cultivating a Good Life in Early Chinese and Ancient Greek Philosophy,
edited by Karyn Lai, Rick Benitez, and Hyun Jin Kim
Interpreting Chinese Philosophy, by Jana S. Rošker
Material Objects in Confucian and Aristotelian Metaphysics,
by James Dominic Rooney
Self-Cultivation in Chinese and Greek Philosophy, by David Machek
Skill in Ancient Ethics, edited by Tom Angier and Lisa Raphals

Embodiment Theory and Chinese Philosophy

Contextualization and Decontextualization of Thought

Margus Ott

BLOOMSBURY ACADEMIC
LONDON • NEW YORK • OXFORD • NEW DELHI • SYDNEY

BLOOMSBURY ACADEMIC
Bloomsbury Publishing Plc, 50 Bedford Square, London, WC1B 3DP, UK
Bloomsbury Publishing Inc, 1359 Broadway, 12th Floor, New York, NY 10018, USA
Bloomsbury Publishing Ireland, 29 Earlsfort Terrace, Dublin 2, D02 AY28, Ireland

BLOOMSBURY, BLOOMSBURY ACADEMIC and the Diana logo are
trademarks of Bloomsbury Publishing Plc

First published in Great Britain 2024
This paperback edition published 2026

Copyright © Margus Ott, 2024

Margus Ott has asserted his right under the Copyright,
Designs and Patents Act, 1988, to be identified as Author of this work.

For legal purposes the Acknowledgments on p. viii constitute
an extension of this copyright page.

Cover image: Fortis Design/Adobe Stock

All rights reserved. No part of this publication may be: i) reproduced or transmitted in any form, electronic or mechanical, including photocopying, recording or by means of any information storage or retrieval system without prior permission in writing from the publishers; or ii) used or reproduced in any way for the training, development or operation of artificial intelligence (AI) technologies, including generative AI technologies. The rights holders expressly reserve this publication from the text and data mining exception as per Article 4(3) of the Digital Single Market Directive (EU) 2019/790.

Bloomsbury Publishing Plc does not have any control over, or responsibility for, any third-party websites referred to or in this book. All internet addresses given in this book were correct at the time of going to press. The author and publisher regret any inconvenience caused if addresses have changed or sites have ceased to exist, but can accept no responsibility for any such changes.

Library of Congress Cataloging-in-Publication Data
Names: Ott, Margus, author.
Title: Embodiment theory and Chinese philosophy : contextualization and decontextualization of thought / Margus Ott. Description: 1. | London : Bloomsbury Academic, 2024. | Includes bibliographical references. | Summary: "This book analyses some of the seminal texts of the Chinese tradition and shows how they exemplify aspects of embodiment theory: the Analects of Confucius, the Zhuangzi, and the Treatise on Music. Margus Ott also develops far-reaching possibilities of an embodied philosophy. The embodied understanding did not go unchallenged in Ancient China. There were important counter-currents, most notably the Mohists and the so-called Legalists. By using embodiment theory Ott demonstrates how these ideas can be seen as a decontextualizing tendency of thought that plays an important role in human affairs"– Provided by publisher.
Identifiers: LCCN 2023058337 (print) | LCCN 2023058338 (ebook) |
ISBN 9781350424142 (hardback) | ISBN 9781350424173 (paperback) |
ISBN 9781350424166 (epub)
Subjects: LCSH: Human body (Philosophy)–China. |
Legalism (Chinese philosophy) | Philosophy, Chinese–To 221 B.C.
Classification: LCC B105.B64 O88 2024 (print) |
LCC B105.B64 (ebook) | DDC 181/.11–dc23/eng/20240318
LC record available at https://lccn.loc.gov/2023058337
LC ebook record available at https://lccn.loc.gov/2023058338

ISBN: HB: 978-1-3504-2414-2
PB: 978-1-3504-2417-3
ePDF: 978-1-3504-2415-9
eBook: 978-1-3504-2416-6

Typeset by Integra Software Services Pvt. Ltd.

For product safety related questions contact productsafety@bloomsbury.com

To find out more about our authors and books visit www.bloomsbury.com
and sign up for our newsletters.

Contents

Acknowledgments — viii

1 Introduction — 1
   1.1 Contextualizing and Decontextualizing Thought — 1
   1.2 Roots of Embodiment Theory — 3
   1.3 Chinese Traditions and ET — 4
   1.4 Content Summary — 5

2 Embodiment — 9
   2.1 Tenets of Disembodiment — 9
   2.2 Embodiment — 10
   2.3 Embeddedness — 13
   2.4 Enactment — 14
   2.5 Extendedness — 15
   2.6 Affectivity — 17
   2.7 Emergence — 19
   2.8 Self-relation — 21
   2.9 Other-relation — 22
   2.10 Implicitness — 23
   2.11 Guidance by Example — 24
   2.12 Singularities and Intensities — 25
   2.13 Embodied Disembodiment — 27
   2.14 Meaning of Disembodiment — 28
   2.15 Conclusion — 30

3 Background — 31
   3.1 Greek Sociopolitical Background — 31
   3.2 Chinese Sociopolitical Background — 34
   3.3 Ritual Background — 36
   3.4 Rituals as Contextualizing — 39
   3.5 Kurankos — 40

	3.6	Hasidic Tradition	43
	3.7	Ritual Knowledge	45
	3.8	Conclusion	47
4	Embodied Foundations: Confucius 孔子		51
	4.1	Embodied	51
	4.2	The Singular and the Intensive	53
	4.3	Embedded	54
	4.4	Flexible	57
	4.5	Enacted	58
	4.6	Extended	60
	4.7	Other-relation	63
	4.8	Emotive	66
	4.9	Implicit	67
	4.10	Emergent	68
	4.11	Ease and Joy	69
	4.12	Self-cultivation	72
	4.13	Conclusion	74
5	Mohist Disembodied Reaction: Mozi 墨子		77
	5.1	Introduction	77
	5.2	Disembodied Standards	79
	5.3	Extension of Subjectivity: All-Inclusive Care	82
	5.4	Meritocracy	83
	5.5	Explicitness	85
	5.6	Conclusion	90
6	Legalist Disembodied Reaction: Han Feizi 韓非子		91
	6.1	Introduction	91
	6.2	Laws (*fa* 法)	92
	6.3	General and Explicit	96
	6.4	Generality of Basic Preferences	98
	6.5	Staying Cool	100
	6.6	Decontextualized Civic Morality	102
	6.7	Objectivity, Quantity	105
	6.8	Conclusion	107

7	A Confucian Development of Embodiment: Record of Music (*Yueji* 樂記)	109
	7.1 Mencius	109
	7.2 Xunzi	112
	7.3 Record of Music	114
	7.4 Emotions	115
	7.5 Returning to One's Body: Individual Transformation of Emotions	117
	7.6 Social Embeddedness: Collective Transformation of Emotions	118
	7.7 Ontology of Energy and Veins	121
	7.8 Self-cultivation According to Energy and Veins	123
	7.9 Enacted Knowledge	125
	7.10 Music and Rituals: Integration and Differentiation	129
	7.11 Free Space	131
	7.12 Simplicity and Ease	134
	7.13 Cosmic Purport	136
	7.14 Conclusion	138
8	A Daoist Development of Embodiment: Zhuangzi 莊子	141
	8.1 Introduction	141
	8.2 Knack in Performance	141
	8.3 Stages of Practice	146
	8.4 Danger of Mechanical Mind in Extended Cognition	151
	8.5 Other-relation	152
	8.6 Sitting and Forgetting	157
	8.7 Transformation	160
	8.8 Free Roaming	166
	8.9 Knowing with Non-knowing	170
	8.10 Zhuangzian Ideas as Reflection on a Skill	175
	8.11 Zhuangzi and Decontextualization	177
	8.12 Conclusion	179
9	Conclusion	183
Notes		185
References		205
Index		216

Acknowledgments

This book is the outcome of several courses given at Tallinn University on rituals, embodiment, music, and the history of Chinese philosophy. I received a grant from the Taiwan Fellowship to write an article covering this subject matter (research grant MOFATF20160021), but the topic kept expanding and ramifying, until it eventually became this book. The research was also supported by the Estonian Research Council (grant PRG319).

I would like to thank Siegfried Fau for an initial impetus into skill research. I am very grateful to Dr. Lee Hsian-chung 李賢中, Dr. Xie Xiaodong 謝曉東, and Rita Niineste for their help during my research. Special thanks to Jordan Jackson for his immense help in improving the draft.

1

Introduction

1.1 Contextualizing and Decontextualizing Thought

The improvement of knowledge can take two directions: toward contextualization or decontextualization. Contextualization and decontextualization are each aspects of every act of knowledge. On the one hand, every act of knowledge is grounded and situated in a context, and it has meaning relative to it. On the other hand, to know something means that one is not identical with the context but distinguished from it and extends beyond it. The improvement of knowledge can move in either direction, and some fields of experience seem to better exemplify one or the other.

Contextualization more closely engages the situation and materials and agents involved, including one's own body. Examples include skills and crafts: when we learn to dance, to do carpentry, etc., we learn how to better understand the context and the givens of the activity. For instance, in the case of dance, a dancer interacts with gravity, their abilities and limitations, other dancer's bodies, the environment around where they dance, and the characteristics of the floor, room, lighting, etc. In the case of carpentry, the carpenter must deal with the peculiarities of the material they work with, the type and the grain of the particular piece of wood, the characteristics of the tools, the way body interacts with wood and tools, etc. This all brings the practitioner closer to the material and intersubjective context.

Decontextualization refers to a kind of disengagement from the situation. Examples of this include mathematics and physics. In these sciences, students learn to abstract entities: addition involves abstract objects like "one" and "two," not a particular apple or chair; and those "ones" can be combined through certain rules (addition, multiplication, etc.). In this example, not only is there abstraction from the particular givens of an apple (what kind of apple, where was it grown, how big it is, how does it feel under touch, etc.) but even abstraction from its being an apple, leaving simply an entity, a "one." Operating with symbolic tools, like numbers and formulas in mathematics, is one of the clearest examples of decontextualization.

Two comments are warranted immediately. First, when we look closer, we find these two directions to be present in each act of knowledge. On the one hand, our dancer and carpenter are not machines that would be utterly unaware of what they are doing; they monitor their behavior and are able to modify their actions, interrupt them, or even wonder what they are doing, or why. They may marry closely with the context, but they can loosen this grip and move out of the context. On the other hand, every type of abstract knowledge needs to be somehow grounded and situated. For them to have any meaning in general, they must be related to the life-projects of some agents who are interested in their environment. Scientists may be detached from immediate contexts, but in the end what they are doing must have some meaning to them being in their environment.

Second, it is possible that moving in one direction (contextualization or decontextualization) one may inadvertently at the same time move also in the other direction. On the one hand, if one works toward the contextualization of knowledge, one becomes more and more familiar with the different aspects, behaviors, and affordances of one's own body, of other bodies and materials, and of the environment. This may give the person a certain freedom not only in the context of that particular art but in her life in general (i.e., in all contexts). This is an important point that we will discuss more closely later, especially in the last chapter about Zhuangzi: even a humble craft like butchering oxen or catching cicadas can be an emancipating and liberating practice. On the other hand, decontextualization may become contextualized in an indirect way. For creative mathematicians, mathematics may receive its meaning not only from its applications to everyday phenomena but they may experience mathematical entities as part of their lifeworld, so that these entities *are* aspects of their world context. It would be direct, intuitive knowledge, and not simply mediated and abstract as it is for most people.

Since the Modern Era, decontextualization has been valued much more highly than contextualization. It is the principle of the "royal science" (Deleuze and Guattari 1987; DeLanda 2002: 219; DeLanda 2004). Royal science is "the science of the royal societies and academies at the service of the state preoccupied above all with the discovery of abstract general laws" (DeLanda 2004: 15). It is distinct from a contextualizing type of knowledge (that Deleuze and Guattari call "minor" or "nomad science") used by engineers who build instruments for "testing the validity of those laws in concrete physical situations" (DeLanda 2004). Royal science, as it was conceived in the Modern age, dealt mainly with homogenized substances, linear equations, and near-equilibrium processes.[1]

The "royal" way of abstraction, decontextualization, homogenization, and symbolization also penetrated treatments of human mind. A large and influential branch of philosophy was formed, starting from Frege, the main preoccupation of which was to deal with a disembodied mind, using abstractions, symbols, and logic. It was reinforced by the Western tradition that, from early on,[2] had strong decontextualizing tendencies. But in this process, important aspects of knowledge were discarded or downplayed. Mind and thought were investigated for and in themselves, with little regard to their embodiment in a situation, a context, through certain bodily activities and tools, in interaction with other subjects. This is the motivation behind the development, in recent decades, of Embodiment Theory.

1.2 Roots of Embodiment Theory

Embodiment Theory (ET) is a current of research that has developed in recent decades within several different fields of study. It is a motley collection of different research projects with only family resemblances, making it difficult to unify its different expressions into a single theory. The central idea of ET is that body shapes our cognition in important ways, and one of its main targets of criticism is an abstract, disembodied account of knowledge. It often entails a criticism of a clear-cut mind-body dualism and representational understanding of cognition.

Some of the earliest expressions of ET are found in Spinoza[3] and Nietzsche,[4] but its more direct ancestor is Husserl's phenomenology: Husserl distinguished between objective body (*Körper*) and subjective body (*Leib*) and investigated how our perceptual and motor apparatuses structure our experience.[5] Heidegger (1996) also made contributions to ET with his analysis of things ready-to-hand (*Zuhanden*) in contrast to things present-at-hand (*Vorhanden*): one is the hammer that I hold in my hand in order to drive in nails, and the other is a hammer with a broken handle that I look at in frustration. Investigation of embodiment was important for another follower of Husserl, Jean-Paul Sartre (1956), but the most thorough work on ET was done by Maurice Merleau-Ponty, whose "Phenomenology of Perception" (2012 [1945]) investigates in detail several key aspects of embodiment. In the wake of Husserl, he distinguishes body as object and body as my own (*corps propre*) and explores the spatiality and temporality of the own-body, its sexuality and relations to others, language, etc. (see Thompson 2007: 312–59; Gallagher 2014: 9–12). Merleau-Ponty's book can be considered as the founding text of modern embodiment theory.

One important branch of ET traces its origins to Jakob von Uexküll (1864–1944), a Baltic German biologist, who made important contributions to the investigation of animal and plant lifeworlds (*Umwelten*), and how these lifeworlds are determined by their sensory and motor organs (see Uexküll 1926, 1957). This line of thought has been continued most importantly in biosemiotics (see Hoffmeyer 1996; Stjernfelt 2007: 257–73; Emmeche 2011: 91–111, 113–28; cf. also Buchanan 2009).

ET was brought together with non-Western traditions early on. In their seminal book *The Embodied Mind* (1991), Francisco Varela, Evan Thompson, and Eleanor Rosch make an explicit connection between their theory of embodiment and the Buddhist tradition. Yet, since then the connection between ET and non-Western traditions has been somewhat neglected. This book attempts to tighten and broaden these links.

Contemporary Embodiment Theory is a vast constellation of different research projects throughout different domains: cognitive science, neurology, psychology, linguistics, robotics, artificial intelligence, etc. General interest in different aspects of ET has spread in recent decades (for an overview, see Gallagher and Schmicking 2010: 181–252; Shapiro 2014; Wilson and Foglia 2015; Durt et al. 2017; Newen, Bruin, and Gallagher 2018; Gallagher 2023), although it cannot be said to have become mainstream.

1.3 Chinese Traditions and ET

While ET is a recent development of Western metaphysics, in the Chinese traditions, the "embodied" approach has been dominant from the beginning (with some opposing currents that we are also going to explore). The embodied understanding of knowledge and existence was expressed by Confucius in his *Analects* and later developed by other Confucians. This view was also shared by Daoists, who developed certain of its implications even further. Although some countercurrents (like Mohists and Legalists) gave important contributions to the Chinese tradition, the embodied understanding of knowledge became the mainstream.

Several intuitions toward the conception outlined in this book were expressed early on during the Western encounter with the Chinese tradition from nineteenth century onward. But they often suffered from the fact that Chinese philosophy was subjected to Western concepts that did not match important articulations of the Chinese tradition itself. Notably, Chinese thought has been described as "concrete" in contrast to "abstract," "practical" in contrast to "theoretical," "aesthetical" in contrast to "scientific" (or "religious" or "ethical") (cf. Nakamura 1964; Hall and Ames 1998a, b; Li 2010; Jung 2011). These descriptions capture the intuition that the Chinese tradition was more contextualized, but the distinctions of concrete-abstract, practical-theoretical, and aesthetical-ethical-religious-scientific are ill suited to describe it adequately. These distinctions come from Western preoccupations that arise from disembodied accounts of knowledge. I argue that the ET developed in recent decades can give more useful tools to shed light on important aspects of Chinese philosophy. For example, the description of Confucius' behavior in the *Analects* Book 10 does not express a preference to the particular and a disregard for the universal; or the assessment of factors of war in the *Sunzi* does not manifest an attachment to practice and an ignorance of theory. Rather, they involve a different ontology and epistemology that is more embodied and "situationist," and that sees reality as unfolding between an interpenetrating or soft phase and juxtaposing or hard forms.

In Sinology, there is a growing interest in embodiment viewed from different angles and concerning its different aspects.[6] One of the researchers who has made the most direct link between Chinese philosophy and ET is Edward Slingerland (2003b, 2008, 2013, 2018; Slingerland and Chudek 2011), who has forcefully argued against the idea that embodiment would involve a lack of distinction between mind and body: mind is indeed embodied, but mind-body dualism arises spontaneously. In the present book, this discussion is reframed in the terms of contextualization, decontextualization, and recontextualization (mind is the de- and recontextualization of the body). Embodiment theory, refreshed by Chinese materials, leads us beyond a simple revalorization of body.[7]

1.4 Content Summary

This book is divided into nine chapters. In the second chapter, I present some basic ideas of embodiment theory. First, I list a number of tenets that it criticizes, that is, cognition as disembodied, decontextualized, contemplative. Then, I proceed to present key topics of ET—that cognition is embodied, embedded, enacted, emergent, affective, extended. It also necessarily has a self- and other-relation, is extendable, is largely implicit, and requires guidance by example.

The features mentioned first are more common and central in the ET literature; those mentioned later are also present in the ET, but are not so central in the discussions. But they are important features in the Chinese tradition, and through its lens can be noticed in the ET literature (and perhaps also enlarge ET's purview). At the end of the second chapter, I re-analyze the disembodied features mentioned in the beginning of the chapter, and show their meaning and value in reference to an embodied background.

In Chapter 3, I examine background conditions that contributed to the dominance of decontextualization in ancient Greek philosophy and the dominance of contextualization in ancient Chinese philosophy. They are partly due to the sociopolitical factors that drove the Greek to conceive decontextualized and explicit systems and the Chinese to move toward contextualization and implicitness. One very important background feature of the Chinese tradition was ancestor cult and rituals. To show that a reflection on rituals can spontaneously give similar ET-like outcomes in different traditions, I discuss two examples of ritualistic context from two different cultures: the Kurankos of Sierra Leone and the Hasidic tradition from Eastern Europe.

Chapter 4 concerns the seminal book of Confucianism, the *Analects*, and the formation of the mainstream Chinese philosophy with a strong accent on embodiment and contextualization. I discuss the *Analects* in the light of ET themes of knowledge as embodied, embedded, enacted, extended, affective, etc. It also involves topics like "ease and joy" and "self-cultivation" that could be natural parts of ET, but that are not common topics in Western accounts of ET. An ET account of the *Analects* can also shed light on the parts of the *Analects* that otherwise would seem to lack philosophical interest to many (especially Book 10 that was originally probably a ritual manual but was later taken to describe the behavior of Confucius). Hegel said that Confucius is "only a man who has a certain amount of practical and worldly wisdom—one with whom there is no speculative philosophy" (Hegel 1892: 121). He was disappointed because he was looking for a disembodied form of philosophy.[8]

Chapters 5 and 6 involve two "countercurrents" to Chinese embodiment, Mohism and Legalism. The Mohists self-consciously opposed embodiment, focusing on disembodied, decontextualized, general, and explicit understandings of cognition. This had important emancipatory potential: if knowledge is made explicit and disembodied, no one can lay claim to truth by birthright or some "tacit" knowledge. For Mohists, knowledge should have explicit and objective criteria, disembodied from the person who proffers it, not implicit in the action, but separated from it, belonging to an autonomous realm of knowledge.

Chapter 6 concerns another countercurrent, the Legalists, represented by their most famous proponent, Han Feizi. One of the central concerns of Legalists was to devise laws or norms that are explicit and general, and that could in principle apply mechanically without regard to context or to the status of the persons involved. The ruler who "acts without acting" would be like an abstract and depersonalized machine at the top of a meritocratic and decontextualized society. While Han Feizi does not stress moral arguments like Mozi, he does devise a new civic morality that would deterritorialize from old family and clan adherence and reterritorialize on the new bureaucratic society. It should be noted that Han Feizi does not consider the laws or norms as immutable and eternal, but, on the contrary, they have to change and to conform to the needs of the age.

Chapters 7 and 8 concern the "ramifications" of embodiment-based theories in ancient China that take the ET ideas to their furthest consequences. First, in Chapter 7, I discuss the Confucian developments, mainly in the *Record of Music*, but also in Mencius and Xunzi. The *Record of Music* develops an ontology of differentiation and integration, giving us a good example of what kind of ideas and concepts can be developed from an embodied starting point. This does not have only a historic interest but may provide material for a contemporary ontology that wishes to overcome the simple opposition between mind and body, conceived as two separate substances. The *Record of Music* also gives an embodied account of epistemology and affects. Emotions are not solipsistic, experienced only by a certain subject, but shared, communal, social. This involves also the interesting and still relevant idea that if music affects us and creates collective emotions, it is also possible to design those emotions by choosing the type of music.

The second ramification of embodiment in China, discussed in Chapter 8, involves Zhuangzi. The five discussions of the Chinese tradition (Confucius, Mozi, Han Feizi, *Record of Music*, Zhuangzi) follow a broadly chronological order only in the first two of them. Zhuangzi is placed at the end not because it is newer (in fact, its older parts are older than the two previous texts discussed) but because it draws some of the most radical consequences for ET. In the *Zhuangzi*, there are several stories about persons who have perfectly mastered an art: butchers, carpenters, swimmers, wheelwrights, cicada-catchers, etc. At the final stage of mastery, they forget their body, not in the sense of being separated from it but, on the contrary, being completely immersed in it, sensible to all minute articulations of their own body and its surroundings. This fully embodied knowledge is also called "not knowing" in the sense that the obscure ground of knowledge is integrated into the knowing itself. In the conclusion of Chapter 8, I make a connection to Michael Grab, a natural-born Zhuangzian who arranges stones on top of each other and who has, during this process, developed ideas and attitudes similar to those expressed by Zhuangzi's characters, demonstrating that such ideas can arise quite spontaneously from reflection on one's practice.

In the final chapter, I conclude the book with a look back on the itinerary of embodiment (Confucius), counter-embodiment (Mozi and Han Feizi) and the ramifications of embodiment (*Record of Music* and Zhuangzi). I argue that embodiment and disembodiment can be considered as two opposing and complementary tendencies that are both necessary and correspond to different needs and requirements. In my final analysis, I find "embodied cognition" to be a misnomer. Embodied cognition is not just cognition and it does not just happen in the body (Anderson et al. 2012: 727). Radical embodiment that most intimately embraces the transformations of things, and sensitively responds to things, beings, and environments involves also the most radical disembodiment, discarding of bodily and mental forms.

2

Embodiment

2.1 Tenets of Disembodiment

Embodiment Theory often distinguishes itself from a dominant disembodied and decontextualized understanding of mind and cognition. Let us formulate some of the main tenets of that disembodied approach (for more detailed presentations, see Fodor 1975; Bechtel and Graham 1998; Bly and Rumelhart 1999; Bermúdez 2022). The following points form a somewhat loose constellation: they need not all appear together in a theory, and they need not be equally emphasized. I also hasten to point out that decontextualization does have its meaning and value, as mentioned in the beginning of the introduction, and that this meaning comes out namely in conjunction with ET. I will discuss it in the last subsection of this chapter, as well as in Chapters 6 and 7, on Mozi and Han Feizi.

Some of the recurring tenets of disembodiment are:

1. Mind is distinct and separate from body, and cognition is essentially disembodied. Often it is described in terms of manipulation of abstract symbols. There is an abstract(ing), symbolizing machine operating behind our sensorimotor activities.
2. Mind is separated from emotions; in order to achieve "rationality," it may be necessary to suppress or discard emotions.
3. Thought abstracts from concrete contexts. Thinking is namely the endeavor to reach for the "essential" beyond the "accidental," the "general" behind "particulars."
4. Thought is essentially general, and the nobler the thought, the more general it is. This is achieved by the symbolizing and abstracting capacity of human beings. The touchstone of a theory is its capacity to make generalizations, express general laws, and explicate regularities.

5. Thought is explicit, or at least capable of being made so. Behind a thought there may be some intuitions that cannot easily be put into words, but the specifically cognitive processes are explicit.
6. Thought is contemplative, i.e., distinct from action. The computing that takes place in the mind uses input from the surrounding environment (via sensory apparatus) and can give output to the environment (via motor apparatus). This is the "sandwich" model.
7. Thought is representational. Inputs to the computing mind are representations of the outer world beyond our skin (or beyond the central nervous system). The computation works on a mental copy of the physical world.
8. Thought is volitional. If we pay attention to its behavioral output, then it projects or imposes a representation on the world, i.e., the desired state of affairs. Self-conscious and reflective will is responsible for initiating this process and keeping it going.
9. Cognition works in a "top down" fashion: it takes a highly sophisticated representation of the world to work upon and forms another highly sophisticated representation that it projects on the world, in order to realize it in some point of the future. General idea and plan come first; particular implementation comes later.
10. Behavior is essentially based on a code or program and can be reduced to some general laws as its essence.

ET opposes these tenets, characterizing knowledge as Embodied, Enacted, Extended, Embedded, often abbreviated as 4E (see Newen, Bruin, and Gallagher 2018; Gallagher 2023). Sometimes "Affective" is added, which would result in 4EA. In the following, I shall discuss briefly these and some more aspects, and I shall use "Embodiment Theory" or simply "embodiment" as an umbrella term for all those aspects. This list is not intended to be exhaustive, and they are largely implied in each other, so that it is somewhat arbitrary precisely how many different aspects we can distinguish or where we lay the main emphasis.

2.2 Embodiment

Embodiment means that our knowledge and existence in general are essentially shaped by the bodies we have (Clark 1997; Lakoff and Johnson 1980; Shapiro 2014). Embodiment extends beyond the brain and nervous system, and even our skin, to other persons and to the environment. Without body, it is difficult to conceive how anything could have meaning or relevance, as meaning requires paying special attention to something and making it stand out from the background. Something is selected out, and something else is discarded. Without selection there would be no meaning; selecting everything equals selecting nothing. But who or what pays this special attention, if not our body—we as embodied agents with specific needs (see Kull 2000: 339–43)? From the very beginning we make axiological distinctions because of our body, and thus the field of experience is differentiated. We, as embodied and social beings, have positive needs for food, drink, warmth, companionship, etc., and negative needs to avoid excessive stimuli, human aggression, etc. Axiological distinctions and hence meaning exist because we are limited, vulnerable, and mortal.

The ways we are affected by our surroundings and the ways we in turn affect our surroundings are determined by the kind of bodies we have, by our sensory and motor apparatus and its effectivities, corresponding to the affordances of our surroundings (Uexküll 1926, 1957; Turvey et al. 1981: 261; Gibson 2015). This determines, for example, the level and scale of interactions. For instance, a four-inch hard stone affords to be used as a hammer; a forty-foot stone affords climbing; a single silicate grain 10 microns in diameter does not afford anything in for the everyday human world. These same things would afford very different things for an ant or a bacterium. Our body defines the dimensions and nature of things we can interact with and which thus have meaning for us. For instance, we do not perceive ultra-violet light and hence if we are unaided by special devices, UV radiation has no meaning for us in our lifeworld (although it does have to butterflies, and although we ourselves passively undergo its effects on our skin).

Furthermore, our experience is polarized in various and constantly changing ways: we need sleep, and then we want to be active again; we want to eat and rest, and then we want to explore and work. The relevance of each aspect is determined by the state of our body and by certain external conditions. If we are hungry, we are extremely interested in food; if we are full, then we don't care about it. If we perceive an imminent danger to our body, e.g., a fast approaching car, then this aspect of the surroundings becomes urgent to us. The embodied needs[1] create the differences of value which are at the same time potentials for action. The embodied life and its precarity is the basis of meaning.[2]

As Lakoff and Johnson (1980) have shown, the concrete embodied nature of our existence is the basis for even our most abstract language. We structure the world and describe it in terms of "orientational metaphors" like up, down, left, right, before, or behind, all of which are based on the structure of our body in the gravitational field. Up is defined as the direction against gravitation (when we are conscious and happy, we tend to be erect, hence the metaphor UP IS GOOD: "I feel up," "I feel down"[3]). Left and right are determined by our body's two sides which have a distinct prereflective meaning (as most people are right-handed, this side tends to be "better,"[4] "right"). The distinction of before and behind is based on the asymmetry of our sensorimotor structure, where some of our most important sensory organs (especially eyes) are on one side of the body, the "front," and also our hands and feet are mostly directed in the same direction (hence, for example, the English temporal metaphors: "to look forward," "to look back," "to leave aside"). Also the "ontological metaphors" (actually it would be better to call them "ontic metaphors") are defined by our bodily experiences—from manipulating things and moving in the environment we learn their affordances, e.g., their boundaries, so that we form the conception of distinct things (a toy, a plant, a room, a mountain), even where the boundaries may be vague (e.g., we walk on a plain ground that starts to rise, but where exactly starts "a mountain"?). Furthermore, the relations between concepts also come from bodily experience, e.g., the "container metaphors" (that are so important in describing the relation between words and meanings: "to put an idea into words," "to pour an inspiration into a poem," see Lakoff and Johnson 1980: 10–13) come from experiences where we put things into other things or find ourselves contained in limited spaces. To *put* it differently, our embodied being both imposes closures and limits on the surroundings (delimiting things, ontic metaphors) and opens them (aligning them according to orientational metaphors and transferring from one domain to another).

It is important to bear in mind that the "body" in the embodiment theory is not the third-person view on body, but a lived, experienced body. Of course, our body can be investigated from a third-person viewpoint, and measured scientifically, but the scientific activity is a mode that is grounded in a lived body. Scientists have to be embodied, before they can conduct scientific research. Third-person research is part of a first-person world and presupposes it. This means that at the same time the first-person lived experience already contains the possibility to transcend itself, to distance itself from itself—which may develop into the third-person view.

2.3 Embeddedness

Cognition and existence in general are embedded in certain physical, social, cultural, and historical contexts (Damasio 1994: 83–113; Heidegger 1996[5]; Dawson 2014; see also Uexküll 1926, 1957 for a general theory of Umwelt). As we said, the world we are embedded in is not homogeneous and isotropic, but heterogeneous and anisotropic. It has distinctions and preferred directions according to our needs and desires. We do not live in an indifferent 3D space, but the space as we experience it opens up from a certain viewpoint. Space indicates possible movements and interactions; we experience it as affording certain actions and inhibiting others. An experienced space is already a meaningful one. I am engaged in a certain surrounding; I always already project myself toward its articulations.

Let us take an example. I sit in a room behind a desk, writing. The computer I am using implies certain specific interactions with it (how and in what order do I move my fingers, where my gaze is directed, etc.). Next to the computer is a cup, which I can grab at a certain place in a certain way, exerting the force that I anticipate it needs to move given its fullness or emptiness. The desk itself affords certain actions (leaning on it, posing things, etc.). The characteristics of the room I perceive when I turn around and the furniture in it imply certain ways of moving in it (whether the floor is slippery or not, cold or warm, what objects I have to avoid, what things I might want to grab in certain places of it, etc.), as well as the rest of the apartment, the house and the city where it is situated, etc. All of these spatial articulations direct my movements in specific ways. That is why, for instance, city planning creates very concrete bodily feelings and informs the habits and actions of its inhabitants and visitors. Activity, thus, is always embedded in an environment with certain structures and affordances, which consequently also molds my cognition.[6]

We are embedded not only in the physical space but also in a cultural context: embodied existence unfolds itself against a certain cultural background— including language, food, types of clothes, buildings, customs, rituals, etc.— which implies somewhat different bodily experiences. When we learn a language or ritual custom, we train our body in a certain way, either spontaneously as children, or with more conscious effort as adults. Some themes appear to be quite common to all of mankind (and even to some other species),[7] while some are more specific to a particular culture (the habit to speak a particular mother tongue, the extent of "personal space," etc.). Our bodily behavior is always also embedded in a moral background. Our actions are praised or criticized by parents and others. There is no clear dividing line in the ontogenesis between biological and cultural development. Children are keenly tuned to human faces and voices. They already contain moral judgments (implied in different moods) that the infant can detect from very early on.

The cultural context has an inseparable historical and future dimension to it. Even if the temporal horizon of an infant is very limited, it is from the very beginning modeled and informed by the cultural practices that have formed through the historical experience of a community, and that determine specific expectancies and attitudes toward the future. The child is from the very beginning inserted into a wider temporal horizon.

2.4 Enactment

Enactment is present in embodiment and embeddedness. Our cognition, and existence in general, does not take place in a predefined world that we somehow just "observe" and take notice of (indeed, such a distanced attitude requires a special effort). We have to form all of our knowledge in an experiential, enacted way (Varela et al. 1991; Noë and Thompson 2002; Noë 2004). This implies sensorimotor engagement with our environment. Perceiving and acting cannot be separated as in the traditional "sandwich model" (Hurley 1998, 2001), according to which we receive some input (perception), process it (cognition) and give some output (action) (see Ward and Stapleton 2012). Initially, and for the most part, perception is meant to inform our action (Chemero 2009: 106–7). While acting, we create certain perceptions that are fed back into the system, so that the results of our actions can modulate the way we act, and we can become more adapted to our activities. We explore our environment by experimenting with it: we do something in order to see what happens. These two directions—action creating perceptions and perceptions modulating action—are simultaneous. Without active participation in our environment our perceptions do not make sense:

> In a classic study, Held and Hein raised kittens in the dark and exposed them to light only under controlled conditions. A first group of animals was allowed to move around normally, but each of them was harnessed to a simple carriage and basket that contained a member of the second group of animals. The two groups therefore shared the same visual experience, but the second group was entirely passive. When the animals were released after a few weeks of this

treatment, the first group of kittens behaved normally, but those who had been carried around behaved as if they were blind: they bumped into objects and fell over edges. This beautiful study supports the enactive view that objects are not seen by the visual extraction of features but rather by the visual guidance of action. (Varela et al. 1991: 174–5)

Our embodied experience presents us some meaningful distinctions in our environment, but their full meaning is developed only in bodily interaction with those different aspects. From the very start we are driven to interactions (focus our attention to faces, voices, mother's breast, etc.), but without our bodily engagement they are not enacted. We act and perceive something so as to modulate the activity, and in our interactions with other people and surroundings, certain patterns emerge and are reinforced. In fact, bodily movements are part and parcel of perceiving: saccadic eye movements, head movements, etc. (Gallagher 2023: 30–3).

The enactive approach denies the "classical sandwich" model of knowledge development, that we first perceive the surrounding, then mentally process it, and finally act out from that cognitive process. Enactive knowledge does not need representations (see Chemero 2009; Hutto and Myin 2013, 2017). Representations may be tools for a highly developed form of knowledge, but it is not the root. In a nutshell, a mental image (if we would maintain this term) is certainly different from an actual image, for instance, a photograph that we hold before our eyes. In the case of a photograph, we are external to it and the different regions of the photograph are external to each other, they simply lie indifferently one next to another. On the contrary, we are not external to the mental image, because otherwise there should be another observer who looks at it in the brain, just as we look at the physical picture, and the same problem would repeat itself in the case of that homunculus in the head, into infinity. And the "regions" of the mental image are not juxtaposed, but interpenetrating (which is not to say that they are indistinguishable: they are differentiated like attractors in a phase space, but not juxtaposed like a table stands next to a chair) (see Raymond Ruyer's 1946 notion of *forme vraie* and Terrence Deacon's 2011 treatment of homunculi).

2.5 Extendedness

Objects and people cannot be separated from my viewpoint as an embodied agent. They are not objects "in themselves," but objects "for me." This is related to the next aspect of embodiment, namely extendedness (cf. Clark 2008). Cognition and experience are extended in the sense that they extend over a spatiotemporal "place": first of all, over my body. This is the "here" and "now." It is the foundation of all places and times that, in itself, is not situated in a measurable place and time. "Here" and "now" transcend toward "there" and "then." A third-person space and time are abstracted from this transcendence, forming a disembodied, decontextualized space and time, where we can locate things and events without any fixed reference. Again, this objective space-time is grounded in an embodied "here-now" (and you-there) that cannot be situated spatiotemporally. I cannot answer the question "where is my body?" It is simply "here."[8] I can say that it is situated in a cafe in Taipei AD 2016, but these precisions make sense only on the basis of my immediate first-person embodied presence here and now.

The here and now do not have precise borders. Typically, they refer to the presence of my body. I "am" all over my body. In order to raise my cup, I don't have to "travel" inside my body to give order to my hand. Instead, I simply raise it as an embodied whole. I may raise only my hand, but my whole body is implied in it, all of the rest of my body is "behind" my hand, implied in it.[9] My body may shrink, for instance, if one of my limbs is amputated. Then my embodiment is restructured accordingly, my affordances and effectivities are rearranged. My body can also become larger. This is a very typical experience for humans, as many of our daily tools can be interpreted as prolongations of our body. When I hammer a nail, the hammer becomes part of my experienced body (Heidegger 1996 [1927]: 94–7); phenomenologically, I feel with the end of the hammer, not with my hand as receiving signals from the hammer. A blind person will perceive things at the tip of her white cane, not at her hand as receiving "signals" from the cane. When I drive a car, the dimensions of it are incorporated into my body-feeling, so I can intuitively and immediately perceive corresponding affordances: where I can pass, how much space I need to turn around etc. (Merleau-Ponty 1945: 178–9[10]). In the digital and computerized world, spatiotemporal extension of bodily capacities has become even more spectacular; through the Internet my immediate presence is in a sense enlarged to the whole connected planet.

We think to a large extent with the help of the things in our environment, we off-load cognitive work to our environment, where all sorts of cues not only aid our memory and behavior, but also shape them. I don't have to explicitly recall all the details of morning hygiene; it is sufficient that I render myself to the bathroom, and I will find different things there—toothbrush, shaver, bathtub, towel, etc.—that elicit respective actions. Or to take another trivial example, since people increasingly read time from digital numerical displays, such expressions as "half past," "quarter past," "quarter to" may lose ground to telling the exact time, read directly from the display.

Also, several tasks are easier to solve with external props: separate letters on pieces of paper that we can shuffle, in order to create anagrams, instead of trying to do it in our mind; using pen and paper in order to solve a calculation or design problem, or to retain a shopping list. Such external devices may be an integral part of our cognitive system, as Clark and Chalmers argued already back in 1998: if Otto, whose memory has been degraded by Alzheimer's disease, is able to use his notebook and render himself to the Museum of Modern art, and Inga does the same without notebook, the outcome is the same. In Christopher Nolan's movie *Memento*, the use of memory aids is the basis of the whole plot.

It does not mean that external tools and our biological body are exactly the same (de Vignemont 2018): we do encompass tools into our perceptual scope and behavioral capacities, but we cannot, for example, feel the tickle, pain, or itching when hammer is touched, and it is important to have our basic body schema to which we can come back after we have extended or transformed it with some tools, in order to extend or transform it in another way with another tool. Michelle Maiese and Robert Hanna (2019: 22) reject the whole extendedness dimension, because it would cancel the difference between body and its environment. Yet, that the mind does not have a clear and definitive border in its extending toward the things in its surroundings, does not mean that the mind does not have any borders at all. We can still make a distinction between the realm inside one's skin, one's closest surroundings (the "peripersonal space," see de Vignemont 2018), intermediate zones, more distant spaces and things, each of which would have a distinct structure. The only thing is that they are not impermeable. I can become more extensive through tools, and I can contract. This dynamism is crucial in extendedness.

The extension and transformation of subjectivity with the help of certain tools will be very important in the discussions below, see 4.6 and 8.2–4. Especially interesting in this respect is Zhuangzi's idea that through handicraft and other bodily practices, it is possible to attain the highest human way of existence, if one goes beyond mere "technique" and reaches the "Way."

2.6 Affectivity

Affectivity and emotions (see Seok 2013; Colombetti 2014[11]) are important aspects for both ET and for our special interest here in Chinese philosophy.

Embodiment always entails a certain affective background for our life and activities (Damasio 1994: 127–64; Maiese 2014). On a basic level, the needs that structure our world and experience have an intrinsic affective aspect: by definition, a need is something we *feel* as a need. It concerns our bodily existence in a positive or negative way, and we feel it as first-person subjects.

On an even more basic level, we could say that affectivity rises from an even more fundamental relation. In Spinozist terms, every being is characterized by a striving or a *conatus*: everything strives to persist in its existence (*in suo esse perseverare conatur*, Ethics 3p6). Insofar as this striving or *conatus* is conscious, it is called desire (*cupiditas*), that is the most basic affect, resulting from the self-relation of being (about conatus and desire see "Ethics" 3p6–9, Spinoza 2002: 283–4, cf. also Maiese 2011; Colombetti 2014: 4–7). Desire founds our intentionality and brings us into contact with other things and beings. Sometimes the things we encounter help us and sometimes they harm us. Our desiring existence makes an affective differentiation between things that contribute to and favor our temporal project and those that impede it. This is the meaning of pleasure and pain or joy and sorrow (*laetitia* and *tristitia*), that form, together with desire, the three fundamental affects for Spinoza. He defines joy as an enhancement of the power of existing and understanding, and sorrow as the diminishment of that power (see *Ethics* 3p11sch). So, they can be considered as two modulations of desiring existence, toward more and less power.[12] "Emotions call for 'More of this!' or 'Less of this'" (Hanna and Maiese 2009: 238). Joy and sorrow polarize our lifeworld, making an axiological space from it (as we mentioned earlier in 2.2). In modern terms of neurology, a different set of affects may be detected (Panksepp distinguishes between seven basic affects, Panksepp and Biven 2012), but the general idea that our being in world is affective and that this affectivity is polarized, remains the same.

Embodiment gives rise to felt preferences, which is how we are able to make decisions. A purely rational, disembodied creature (an "Emotional Zero," see Hanna and Maiese 2009: 238–54) would be utterly unable to make decisions and to act. Stimuli from the environment would be far too numerous and far too underdetermined (Hanna and Maiese 2009: 231, 237). An imagined Emotional Zero called Bob the Z

> cannot cognize or act intentionally, precisely because he lacks the characteristic affects and feelings that necessarily accompany desire-based emotions, and thus he lacks any ability to focus his attention or focus his goals by means of affective framing. Any movement that Bob the Z makes will be strictly underdetermined by natural stimuli and natural states of affairs. (Hanna and Maiese 2009: 253)

Some forms of autism, where the feeling of one's own body is disturbed, approach the ideal of rationality deprived of adequate emotions; but a savant with some extraordinary mental capabilities may be unable to tie the shoelaces, cross the street or to interact smoothly with another person (cf. Treffert 2009). A completely "cold" rationality would not make our decisions better; on the contrary, they would make them impossible. In Western traditional metaphysics, where rationality has often been praised and feelings disparaged, there is a fundamental self-misunderstanding. The rational that was meant should not in reality mean to *discard* feelings, but to *cultivate* them.[13] There is no dualism of reason and feelings, but rationality is always based on affectivity (felt preferences). And affections always contain their rationality (they imply certain principles in view of promoting life), so that it is all about different *forms* of feeling-reason rather than a choice between these two. These forms are related to different purposes on different tempos: there are impulsive emotions and reasoning that are meant to give quick and powerful answers (like in a fight-or-flight situation), and there are others that operate in a more ample temporal horizon (enabling more nuances to emerge both in feelings and in thinking).[14]

There is one aspect about the emotions that is present in the current ET, but not particularly stressed, namely the joy entailed in a skillful performance of an art or a skill (see Bernstein et al. 1996; Turvey and Fonseca 2009). When one is not constrained by the particulars of the art, they are able to perform them smoothly, gracefully, and effortlessly (the "feeling of flow," see Csikszentmihalyi 2014). In the Chinese tradition this aspect is extremely important, and we shall come back to this aspect in more detail below.

2.7 Emergence

To a large extent, those enactive and embodied patterns are emergent, that is, not fully prescribed in a code (e.g., DNA or a language) or previously given in a program, but they emerge in a self-organizing way through interaction with the environment. For example, Esther Thelen and Linda Smith (1996) have shown that in the case of learning to grasp, if we heed only to the general developmental scheme, then most children seem to go through the same steps in learning how to focus on an object and coordinate the hand in a precise way to reach out for it and grasp it. If we look more closely at individual development histories, however, we see that the same result can be achieved in radically different ways. Thelen and Smith describe two infants, one of whom was motorically very active (moving its limbs a lot) and the other rather passive (moving little). In learning to grasp they had to overcome different problems: the active child had to learn to slow down the motion of the hands, so as to stop it at the desired goal and not to overshoot; the passive child had to learn how to overcome the heaviness of the hands, so as to make a sufficiently energetic reach toward the object (Thelen and Smith 1996: 247–78, cf. Bermúdez 2022: 403–43).

The emergence of forms and its adaptivity to context is true also of the ontogenesis of the body itself. After the discovery of DNA its role has been largely overestimated, and remains so, despite learned criticisms (from a biosemiotic perspective, see Barbieri 2003; Hoffmeyer 2008; Emmeche and Kull 2011). But it is clear that DNA as functionally a 2D entity (in the coding of amino acids it is read sequentially) cannot contain all the information of a 3D entity, viz. the organism. DNA and all the genetic apparatus function more like controllers of development that operates in an emergent fashion. The embryogenesis of a multicellular organism is largely guided by the mutual communication of cells, which mutually induce each other to give some specific outcome (which explains also the flexibility and self-regulating capacity of the embryo that can overcome even some very large interferences and develop normally, as already shown in the classic experiments by Hans Driesch, 1867–1941). The role of DNA is to coordinate the whole process in the fashion of the musical score for an improviser or lecture notes for a speaker.

Most of the developmental processes take place in an emergent way without a fixed plan; the controlling mechanism of DNA has evolved to regulate the complicated biological processes. Just as in a small company one person can be the producer, manager, salesman, etc., but if the company becomes bigger it is necessary to employ a manager that is specialized in keeping the different processes together. The "bottom-up" emergence is primary and the "top-down" regulation is secondary.

Rodney Brooks (1999) has discussed emergence in the case of robotics, with important implications for ET: previous attempts focused on building robots capable of representing the environment and making decisions based on this overview, in a top-down fashion, but such robots were clumsy and expensive. Instead, Brooks built an "insect"-like robot that did not represent anything, but had a simple program for moving around. This robot was much cheaper, it proved capable of emergent behavior, and it was possible to add additional functions to the basic motor operations (see also discussion in Clark 1997).

One important aspect of embodied emergence is that it is basically nonlinear: the results of the interactions between the embodied agent and its surroundings are fed back into the system of interaction, so that input and output of the system are not proportional and the precise outcome or trajectory cannot be predicted. This accounts for the creative power of this kind of interaction and to the fact that the capabilities of the whole system cannot be reduced to the properties of its parts. An irreducible temporality comes to the fore here; the system has to play out and its future program cannot be grasped instantaneously from its present parts or its program.

2.8 Self-relation

A further aspect implied in the previous ones is the self-relation. From the preceding we can see that embodiment essentially is self-related,[15] including pre-reflective consciousness, as well as the psychoanalytic unconscious.[16] In turn, self-relation requires some form of embodiment (that strives to be and creates axiological distinctions). We have said that all of our existence takes place on some emotive or affective background. Emotions, affects, or feelings[17] always have a self-relational aspect. When I feel something, it is related to myself, so that a certain proto-subjectivity is created.[18] On a higher level, when I as a global subject interact with my surroundings, I also feel something. The very concerns and care in my interactions are feelings with an intrinsic self-relation.[19] This immediately experienced feeling or caring is the foundation of our conscious subjectivity. The pre-reflective consciousness implied in our feelings is the basis of our reflective consciousness.[20]

On the other hand, a consciousness that would not be related to preferences and a feeling body is inconceivable. Consciousness always implies a selection and forms an inseparable whole with the unconscious. The light of consciousness is only possible on the background of the obscure unconsciousness. I am all of my body: all my organs, tissues, cells, molecules, and atoms that participate in my bodily processes are part of myself. But most of these processes escape my consciousness. My conscious life implies the functioning of organs, tissues, cells, etc., but it is usually not conscious of them separately. Instead it contracts and concentrates them into an interpenetrating whole that it takes as a background. Consciousness is a contraction. The events of "lower" level (organic events in my body) are contracted and suppressed or constrained,[21] so that the consciousness can operate on a "higher" level (characteristic of my reflective self), which is broader in terms of space, time, and subjectivity.

In the terms of embodiment, if we investigate how we experience other people, surrounding objects and landscapes, we find them inherently imbued with a certain feeling and unfolded from a certain viewpoint. Kant said that a thing taken separately from a subject that experiences it is utterly unknowable—and we could even say that it is impossible. Even the scientific explanation of things, that takes a distanced, third-person view on things, is *somebody*'s view, namely the embodied scientist's view. There is an inherent subjectivity in every objective description. This subjectivity should not be understood in the empirical or everyday sense of the word (meaning "arbitrary"), but in a transcendental sense that every conscious act implies a subjective instance, a viewpoint, a "transcendental ego." Again, the strive for objectivity in science does not equal an endeavor to cancel the transcendental ego, which would equal to cancelling the scientific research itself (as it is done by *somebody*, it means that it is done by some *body*), but as a method to make this subjectivity more nuanced and inclusive. If I arrive at some results at one time in one place, this should not be influenced by some fleeting subjective reasons (e.g., because I am angry or happy); I should discard as much as possible the cruder empirical "subjective" reasons, in order to let the world appear as it does for me as a transcendental ego. In the Western tradition this aspect came to a systematic attention mainly with Husserl's phenomenology, but in the Chinese tradition this view is much older, as we shall see in Chapter 8 on Zhuangzi.

2.9 Other-relation

A special case of extension or transformation of knowledge is through other subjects, especially other human beings. As Husserl (1970) shows, I do not infer other subjects (as being the starting point of an experienced world), but immediately perceive them as such (see also Merleau-Ponty 1945: 403–24; Sartre 1956: 221–431). The discovery of mirror neurons, which fire both when I myself perform an action and when I see another person performing it, has given more credence to the immediate embodied grasp of other subjects (Rizzolatti and Arbib 1998). I experience others as experiencing; my embodiment and emotivity entail the embodiment and emotions of others.[22] Other persons are important "tools" for extending and correcting our knowledge and behavior.

From a phenomenological perspective, Dan Zahavi argues that "no subject … can exist independently of Others" (Zahavi 2003: 115) and that other subjects are the guarantee of objectivity. If the objects can be experienced by others as well, from their viewpoint, it means that these objects are not simply figments of my mind. My experience of objects as independently existing is "mediated by my experience of its givenness for another transcendent subject, that is, by my experience of a foreign world-directed subject" (Zahavi 2003: 115–16). If the object also appears to others, it is not reduced to its appearance to me. Especially for such social animals like human beings, the intersubjective constitution of the world is crucial.

Certain social institutions can do part of the thinking for us, just as in computation we can offload cognitive burden to a calculator. Shaun Gallagher (2013) brings the example of legal systems that are expressions of several minds and fashion the ways people in the legal setting process a situation. All the procedures, formulas, rules for evidence and testimony, etc. extend the person's mind and shape their cognition and behavior (see also the section on social cognition in Newen, de Bruin, and Gallagher 2018: 417–525). Eric Hutton (2018) has tried to apply this idea to Xunzi 荀子 (3rd c. BC). While he finds it problematic, I would suggest that Confucian rituals could be seen as a "mental institution" in Gallagher's sense.

We usually stop short of extending our subjectivity beyond some immediate concerns and incorporating the subjectivity of too many people. Habitually we limit ourselves to the things and tools with which we satisfy our immediate needs, and to some close persons. The preceding descriptive premises, however, can stimulate a prescriptive self-cultivation where this extension is made maximum. This self-cultivation is often not dealt with inside embodiment theories, but it has been an important part of the Chinese tradition, which can supplement ET in this respect (see below, 4.7 for Confucius, 5.3 for Mozi, and 8.5 for Zhuangzi).

2.10 Implicitness

Implicitness is an important aspect of the "personal" or "tacit knowledge" discussed by Michael Polanyi (1962). A behavior always contains more than can be expressed in words or rules. In order to master an art (swimming, sawing, playing the piano, etc.), textbook information is not enough. Instead, one has to acquire personal and experiential understandings of the art. This applies not only to sports and crafts but also to science (how to handle a scientific apparatus, how to read the results, etc.).

Explicating something presupposes an implied state from which it is explicated (literally, "folded out"). The process of making something explicit is far from being unproblematic or mechanical, because when we express something (and if we are not reciting from memory), we at the same time *create* certain articulations. For example, I want to express an idea. I begin with a particular intuition that contains certain interpenetrating articulations, without which it would not come to my mind: for it to appear in my consciousness it must already have certain individuality with its articulations. The unfolding of these articulations takes time and ingenuity; they will not unravel at once and mechanically. As it happens when we wake up in the morning, we know that we had a dream and we have a particular "feeling" of it, but often we are not able to fold it out and thus we cannot say anything about it. When we start to develop an idea or successfully recall a dream, we creatively fold out those articulations, make them explicit, and bring them into clarity. It is a creative process.

In reality, there is always a continuum of implicitness-explicitness or "foldedness," and any extent of unfoldedness or explicitness presupposes a more folded or implicit level. Our whole embodied and embedded existence is implied in every moment of our existence, both "in extension," as the different dimensions of our personality, and "diachronically," as the whole of my previous experience. Every explicit or clear state of mind takes place against the background of this huge implicit reserve.

2.11 Guidance by Example

Embodied knowledge has to be learned through experience, and with guidance: "Connoisseurship, like skill, can be communicated only by example, not by precept. To become an expert wine-taster, to acquire a knowledge of innumerable different blends of tea or to be trained as a medical diagnostician, you must go through a long course of experience under the guidance of a master" (Polanyi 1962: 56; cf. Deleuze 1994: 164 sqq). It has also implications for moral self-development (Jackson 1983; Strejcek and Zhong 2014). It does not mean that a trainer can directly and immediately move us to attain a skill. It requires a certain amount of time, imitation, and guidance. It is possible that we attain a breakthrough in our skill, that after a while we in an instant "get it," but this obtainment builds upon maturation through duration. It is the moment when a musician, an acrobat, a swimmer, dancer, an actor, etc. "forget" their technique and start to perform with ease and grace, so that they have attained the "flow" (Csikszentmihalyi 2014) or "scenic sensibility" (Stanislavski 2010).

The obtainment of enlightenment or "*satori*" (D.T. Suzuki 1996) is related to this phenomenon (cf. below, 7.10).

Implicit and explicit teaching quite often go hand in hand. A trainer usually gives explicit guidance to help an apprentice, although the focus might be on lengthy rehearsals and evaluations of the progress (several interesting cases of dialogical knowledge-in-action are given by Daniel Schön 1983).

On the other hand, and often undervalued or seldom noticed, there is the fact that when we receive explicit teaching, we also learn something by example. At school in mathematics class, we do not learn only how to use mathematical tools, but we also learn something of the teacher as a personality, as a way of being in the world.

2.12 Singularities and Intensities

In disembodied accounts, agency and change are generally attributed to actualized entities, that is, to entities that are distinct and juxtapose each other in spacetime. Common understanding of causality is a good example: A causes B. One separated thing or aspect brings by another. We can point to A that is "culpable" for it (the original meaning of the Greek word *aitia*, "cause"; and the Latin *causa* meant a court case). We then detect the changed state B and say that change happened "between" them.

In terms of embodiment, however, aspects and participants of the situation interpenetrate each other to an important degree, they are in mutual tension, and it is not possible to "accuse" just one aspect or participant of being the cause. By separating that aspect or participant we would already have changed the situation, resolved the tension.

For example, if we analyze the practice of carpenter, we can move in two directions. One direction would be to individuate cultural, social, biological, chemical, and physical factors involved. Why she produces a table of a particular shape? What biochemical processes actuate her hand and body? What are the physical and chemical properties of the tools and wood? Etc. We can move to great detail in such analysis, pinpointing further "culprits" in the observed practice.

Another direction is involved when you yourself want to learn to work wood. The previous analysis may offer you some support in what to pay attention to in your practice but learning itself means that those different aspects must interpenetrate: the wood, the chisel, your fingers and hands, your body, the room you work in, and other people you interact with in your practice (there is no outer limit to such expansion of purview). The question is not to make just one aspect the culprit or cause of something but to learn the behavior of the whole system or situation. And as we saw in previous sections, there are so many minute details and nuances that are implied and that cannot all be made explicit.

In this embodied direction what one discovers are not simply causes but singularities: not juxtaposing and abstracted entities responsible for certain phenomena but nodes in the interpenetrating nexus of aspects and participants. They form an intensive field of tendencies. When the carpenters intuitively "feel" how the wood behaves under their chisel, they understand the incipient tendencies that they can modify already before these become clearly manifest and actualized. They work "upstream" from the actual, juxtaposed level of a piece of wood and a chisel. They detect singularities, the articulations of the situation that give rise to incipient intensive tendencies.

This description overrides the distinction of form and matter, physical and psychological, cultural and biological, living and inert. All these different factors can contribute to the distribution of singular nodes of the situation: the shape of the table that the carpenter fashions, the wood, the tools, carpenter's mood and physical strength, aesthetic preferences, etc. The more expert the carpenter becomes, the better they can make those aspects interpenetrate and the better they feel the important singularities, "how the situation wants to evolve," "what does this piece of wood want to become." The word "want" does not refer to some crude anthropomorphism, but expresses important aspects of the situation itself, of which the human person is just one participant.

In mathematical terms, the disembodied juxtaposed account is metric, and the embodied account is topological. The contiguities of points in the metric space are defined by fixed lengths that show how close or distant the points are. In a topological space the exact lengths are not important, but only the property of "being nearby" (DeLanda 2002: 15). Metrically, a square and a circle are very different figures, but topologically they are equivalent, as the contiguities remain the same and one can transform continuously into the other.

When the Greeks conceive of form, then whether it is transcendent as in Plato or immanent as in Aristotle, it is still metric. The *idea* of a chair is a mental image or representation physical chair that is "repeated" or "copied" to the mental sphere. It is an actual chair, but simply immaterial or mental. It has all the metric differences between its parts.

On the other hand, an embodied understanding of a situation does not rely on any image that would repeat the actual one but expresses the distribution of singular points of the situation and the incipient intensive tendencies of it. They interpenetrate each other to some extent, and as they unfold, the situation changes its nature at every step. While the disembodied account is situated only on the level of actuality and juxtaposition, the embodied account moves through different levels of actualization and interpenetration.

2.13 Embodied Disembodiment

Having discussed different aspects of ET, we may now come back to the disembodied tenets mentioned in 2.1. We can see that the problem is not so much that they are false but rather that their claims are misplaced. They do not describe the essence of mind or knowledge, but manifest one aspect or one tendency of knowledge, namely toward decontextualization, and it must be treated together with the other tendency, the one that moves toward contextualization.

The two tendencies are grounded ontologically: in my being an individual, on the one hand, I am distinguished from you and others, yet on the other hand, I am integrated with you. If I would not be distinguished, then it would not make sense to talk about "me" as something separate or different. If I was not integrated and connected with others, then I would encounter no limit or border to my being, meaning I would not form an entity. In the same way, knowledge must be distinguished from its object, and at the same time connected to it. Knowledge must always decontextualize and contextualize.

The meaning and utility of the decontextualizing aspect can be easily grasped now. Symbolic, decontextualized representations are forms by which the mind is extended, allowing cognition to be more extensive and efficient. For instance, mathematics is rather unconstrained by contexts, "2" can refer to two apples, two people, etc. In this way, mathematics can be applied to any aspect of the external world making it easy to grasp its different mutual relations. Symbolic representation also helps to make knowledge cumulative and easily transmittable between people. Writing can convey information over vast distances in space and long periods of time.

Affectivity is always at the background of knowledge, and there are different modes to it. As adapted to different situations, some are quicker and "hotter," while others are slower and "colder."[23] A fight or flight situation is quick and hot and is characterized by a suitable powerful affection that elicits and motivates quick action. A calm situation is often accompanied by a more diluted mood. Both contain their rationality. Sometimes we are more engaged with the actual situation and at other times more disengaged, sometimes we are more an actor and other times more a dreamer.[24] Mind is never completely disembodied, and the embodied mind moves in two directions, it engages and disengages, contextualizes and decontextualizes.

There is an important social aspect to decontextualization. With the help of decontextualized and disembodied norms and laws people can become emancipated from a context that may be oppressive. Take the sphere of education: if all the teaching was done by guidance and in a heavily ritualized context, the student would have to follow the teacher over a long period of time, depend heavily on them, and have little room for challenging their authority. If the relation is good, it can be inspiring and uplifting. If the teacher is tyrannical, then the life of a student is a misery. If the role of the teacher is mainly to convey symbolic and intellectual knowledge written in the textbooks, the teacher's personality counts less and students have also more opportunity to challenge them on the grounds of what is made explicit in the textbook.

Or take political and juridical sphere: a community that relies mainly on intimate relations and ritualistic behavior may be nourishing to a person, if they can flourish inside this framework. But if there are abuses and the person is unhappy, they may have less opportunity to defy the system, especially if the abuses come from powerful agents. But if there are clear and explicit laws and norms (that by definition are to a large extent decontextualized and depersonalized, since they are general), as well as explicit procedures for their application, the person may use them for their emancipation from the ills of their context. In any case, it seems inevitable that the functioning of a large society of thousands and tens of thousands of people requires explicit and decontextualized laws and norms. On the other hand, each society must also foster contextual intimate relations between its members.

2.14 Meaning of Disembodiment

Symbols, rules, representations, measures, and similar disembodied or decontextualized devices are all means to offload our cognitive work to the environment, and they are also very helpful in managing a big society, as we will see in the case of Mohists and Legalists. But it would not do to take them directly as a paradigm for understanding cognition. They may be helpful in investigating some aspects of cognition (and of course, it makes life easier when we offload some of the cognition to the environment), but they cannot explain it directly.

Of course, the very fact that we are able to create and use symbols, rules, etc. means that they express some capacity that we possess. Indeed, we might say that in the final account they are grounded in our very self-transcending nature itself, i.e., in the fact that we never "are what we are" (using Sartre's expression) and that our force or energy always takes us further, into the future. In this sense, a person has a faculty to distance her from herself. If she would wholly coincide with herself, being in-herself, it would mean that she would be a mere thing; and rigorously speaking, even not a thing, because already in matter there is this force or energy of self-differentiation, albeit not so articulate as in humans. Every being is spread over a certain (even if very restrained) space and time, so that it "contracts" space and time and hence creates a spatiotemporal difference (both inside itself, by tending forward, and outside itself, by maintaining its difference from other entities). Every entity is constituted by a process of differentiation and integration by which it does not coincide with itself, but is integrated with itself over internal and external differences (it "harmonizes but does not make identical," 和而不同, discussed in 7.8). This gives every entity a "distance" from itself.

More immediately, the self-distancing capacity of humans is based on language and tools. All beings move from the interpenetrating singularities to the "forms" that are clearly distinguishable and juxtaposed, one next to another (either in physical or symbolic space). Humans with their cultural artifacts have taken the form-side further, to a clearest state of juxtaposition up to the maximum where abstract entities like 0 and 1 are one next to another (or the broken and continuous lines of yin and yang). Of course, for them to have some meaning in the real world, they must still be integrated and made to interpenetrate in some way with other entities, and they must be grounded in some embodied experience, but the superpower that gave humans an edge over other beings on Earth was the ability to exploit the distances (by language and tools), overdetermine the biological sphere culturally, and create advanced forms of juxtaposition (explicit language, norms, rules, tools).

On the other hand, there always remains the task to reintegrate them, to make them interpenetrate, so as to understand their meaning. Otherwise, those tools might not be of help, but may harm their users, as we are becoming ever more aware in the era of technological waste that has been an inevitable by-product of those tools—not to speak about the potentially hazardous direct influences of technology.

2.15 Conclusion

In this chapter we presented a series of notions related to ET. First, we listed some tenets against which the embodiment movement reacts: an understanding of knowledge as disembodied, cognitive processes squeezed between input (perception) and output (behavior), cognition as representative and computational, mind limited to the brain, emotions as external to knowledge, etc.

We then spelled out some ideas of embodiment: that knowledge is inherently embodied, embedded, enacted, extended, and affective (the 4EA). Our body fashions the way we understand the world and ourselves and knowledge is always embedded in a natural, cultural, social context. It is essentially not for contemplation but for guiding activity, and it extends outside the brain and bodily limits to tools, other persons, and features of the surrounding. All knowledge has an affective background and it is due to felt bodily needs and its vulnerability that we make distinctions in the world, create meaning, and decide to act.

To the five common topics of the ET (embodiment, embeddedness, enactment, extendedness, affectivity), we added further aspects, some of which are more and some less common in ET literature. It is often shown in ET that knowledge is essentially emergent, and not prescribed by a built-in code. Affectivity implies a self-relation or (proto-)consciousness, as a feeling manifests an interested self-relation and motivates it into action. And this self-interested activity brings the subject into contact with others. Self-relation is always already an other-relation, in relation to others that have their own perspective. We also introduced the topics of implicitness that are characteristic of embodied knowledge, and guidance by example as a way of conveying implicit embodied knowledge, which is different from a more disembodied, textbook-style learning.

In the final section, we came back to the list of disembodied tenets. They manifest a decontextualizing tendency of knowledge, which must be taken together with the contextualizing, embodied tendency. Against the background of embodiment, their meaning and value become clear: they can help to make the knowledge more uniform, efficient, objective.

3

Background

Ideas developed in recent decades in the West inside the Embodiment Theory paradigm have been the mainstream of the Chinese philosophical tradition for most of its history. In this chapter we are going first to explore some conditions—why did a contextualizing tendency prevail in China and a decontextualizing tendency dominate ancient Greece?[1] In later subsections we are going to look closer at one of the most important determinants in the Chinese background, the rituals.

3.1 Greek Sociopolitical Background

One factor that drove early Greek philosophers toward decontextualization was that they were mediators of scientific and technological knowledge hailing from nearby regions, Egypt and Mesopotamia.[2] Although these early scientific endeavors were very different from contemporary science, they favored a tendency toward abstract, mediated, and decontextualized knowledge. When searching for naturalistic explanations of the rainbow or earthquake, for example, the quality of said explanation was judged by its generalizability, its universal validity, and its ability to connect and explain other phenomena of the world.

It must now be asked, where did this emphasis on naturalistic explanation come from, and why did these kinds of theories have such a philosophical relevance to ancient Greeks? One important factor was the social and political makeup of Greece. First, the basic political entity of the Greek world was the city-state, i.e., a relatively small unit. Especially in the democratic city-states, the heart of political life was in big gatherings of citizens[3] at the agora to decide political matters, and in the court of law to decide legal matters.[4] It was feasible because the citizens were not too numerous and they were sufficiently concentrated in the city. At the same time, they were numerous enough to require more formal procedures than are necessary in a very small community. The status of a citizen, his success in politics and law, depended on his rhetorical capacities; he had to be able to make himself explicit and to manifest linguistic dexterity. This fostered a highly competitive and disputational social environment.

As Geoffrey Lloyd shows (Lloyd and Sivin 2002), the development of fundamental concepts and ideals of philosophical argument were influenced by the combative attitudes and requirements of Greek sociopolitical life. When philosophers initiated a "naturalistic" discourse about the world, it enabled them to set themselves up as new and distinct kinds of inquirers: "They invented the concept of nature to serve distinct polemical purposes—to define their sphere of competence as new-style investigators and to underline the superiority of naturalistic views to the traditional beliefs of poets, wise men, and religious leaders" (Lloyd and Sivin 2002: 241). By "naturalizing" phenomena, they ceased to simply repeat a myth and instead created a disputable logos. By doing this, philosophers could promote themselves by proposing their unique model of the world that they considered best and most adequate. Competing thinkers would offer their own accounts, and there was no central authority to establish orthodoxy.

The livelihood of teachers and philosophers in Greece mostly depended on fees from students[5] and contributions from members and donors (Lloyd and Sivin 2002: 107). Some, like Plato, were from a rich family, while others came from the middle and lower classes, even among the slaves (like Epictetus the Stoic, from the Roman period). To ensure their livelihood, philosophers had to be distinct from other teachers and schools, and explicit in their specific account of different topics. Hardly any idea was proposed, against which an exactly opposite idea was not set up (is world continuous or discrete, free or deterministic, etc.?).

Philosophers also had to be persuasive. In a philosophical context it was felt that simple rhetorical devices appealing to moods and sentiments of the audience were insufficient. Affective persuasion may have worked in political and legal settings but was too flimsy a foundation upon which to build the prestige of a philosophical school. Methods were devised to make philosophical thought less controversial, including things like syllogistics, where certain propositions can be automatically deduced, or axiomatic proofs, where a large number of truths can be inferred from a small number of axioms that cannot be demonstrated but can be proposed as self-evident. The most famous example of formalizing thought is the *Elements* of Euclid.[6] The driving force behind the development of these techniques of rigorous demonstration was not only a scientific spirit striving to express itself but the requirements of competition, the need to make one's position as unassailable as possible, and the need to outdo competitors in open debate to maintain one's livelihood.

It is interesting to note that the title of Euclid's book, *Elements*, is the same word that was used in the analysis of the basic constituents of the world, the elements (*stoicheia*), and indeed, the first attested uses of the word are in mathematical contexts. The analysis of the world in terms of four elements would be a kind of "axiomatic" analysis of the world. The four elements have, on the one hand, an intuitive ground (earth, water, air, fire), but on the other hand they can be used as abstract terms, as "axioms," from which the great multiplicity of the sensuous world can be deduced. It should be noted that when Empedocles (*c.* 494–*c.* 434 BC) first proposed the four terms, he did not use the word "element," but rather "root," *rhizoma*, and he proposed two forces, love and strife, that developed and combined these "roots." For Empedocles, the four terms were not yet "axiomatic" material building blocks, as Aristotle interpreted them, taking them to be examples of the "material cause." They probably rather referred to types of dynamic or principles of interaction. That would make Empedocles' theory more similar to the Chinese notion of the five phases (*wuxing* 五行) than to the elements in Aristotle's system, understood in terms of material causes and contrasted to formal and other causes. Some thinkers, like the Atomists, went even deeper and more abstract in this axiomatic thinking, postulating the existence of invisible and indivisible atoms from which everything else is made of (Lloyd and Sivin 2002: 142–6).

It certainly is not true that Greek philosophers would have been immersed purely in theoretical research, alien to the practical requirements of the life.[7] For ancient Greek and Hellenistic philosophers, philosophy was a way of life (see Hadot 1995), a spiritual practice, a self-cultivation. Even seemingly most theoretical conceptions had ethical relevance. For example, the Epicurians were atomists and believed in a deterministic physical world. The birth of all things is determined by the movements and interactions of different kinds of atoms in the void and their chance encounters. All things, including humans, perish when those atoms disperse. This deterministic and materialistic theoretical physics (atoms were purely theoretical constructs) was meant to reinforce a state of mind of peace and to foster a liberation of fears and worries: since everything is determined, you do not need to be worried about the future. It is sufficient to be content with simple natural desires and to discard a lust for luxury that would cause unnecessary troubles. Also, the fact that gods do not intervene in the workings of the natural world means that you do not have to fear supernatural punishment. Furthermore, since you vanish at death, there is no need to be afraid of death, because until you are, there is no death, and when there is death, you are no more. For Epicureans, the ideas of theoretical physics were closely tied to an embodied being in the world and ethical self-cultivation. All the schools draw consequences into the ethical: Stoics, Platonists, Aristotelians, Skeptics, Cynics.

It is not that the practice of philosophy in Greece was somehow disembodied or decontextualized. On the contrary, we should say that the very fact that the mainstream of Greek philosophy pursued decontextualized knowledge was a result of adapting to their socioeconomic situation and context: the need to be explicit and argumentative, and to compete with other schools suited to the sociopolitical realities of the Greek city-states. In any case, the very real disembodiment and decontextualization of much of their theoretical endeavor had consequences into the ethical. Philosophy itself was a form of self-cultivation.[8]

Western Europe experienced a long and radical rupture toward the end of Antiquity, during which most of those embodied practices were lost, profoundly transformed, or reframed. So, in later times, when ancient philosophical texts were read, most of their original context, together with their embodied motivation, had been lost. Only texts with their disembodied emphasis remained. Small influences in the early stages of a civilization have enormous influence on the following stages. In Greece, decontextualizing tendency prevailed, and this gave shape to the whole Western tradition, and it influences our worldview and conceptual system to this day. Disembodied account of knowledge is one part of this tradition.

3.2 Chinese Sociopolitical Background

Ancient China saw society and politics develop very differently. There was little room for public discussion and disagreement. The main political unit was a large territorial state ruled by a monarch, and the general stream of Chinese philosophy took such a system for granted. For their employment, philosophers depended mostly on positions in court given by the ruler, who wanted some practical advice from them in the fields of economy, warfare, and public administration. Their presence also simply enhanced his prestige, alongside musicians, dancers, entertainers, etc.

In this context, rhetoric was certainly important, but it was not to convince the masses, only the ruler. The discourse was much more personalized and there was less need for explicit argumentation and appeals to objectified knowledge. Indeed, too much explicitness may have been dangerous, as the whims of the ruler could easily lead to a scholar's dismissal or even execution. This discouraged scholars from being too explicit or too *openly* competitive (by which you could create dangerous enemies in the court). As Confucius says, "Of what use is 'eloquence'? If you go about responding to everyone with a clever tongue you will often incur resentment" (*Analects* 5.5, Slingerland 2003a: 41).

Chinese intellectuals had a more immediate influence on politics by direct advice to the ruler, by memorials to the throne, or by being employed in administrative positions. This may have been a factor that kept intellectual pursuits more down to earth and also circumspect. On the contrary, Greek philosophers had far less influence on their politics: in democratic city-states they had to compete with a large number of peers and fellow citizens; in monarchic cities the rulers rarely cared about philosopher's advice (and Plato nearly lost his life while attempting that in Syracuse). This means that they had "greater freedom to engage in abstract speculation" (Lloyd and Sivin 2002: 243). Hence, politically it was allowable for Greek intellectuals to propose all kinds of theoretical alternatives (since there was little "danger" for them to influence politics), and the intellectual concurrence even required an aggressive intellectual innovation, in order to make oneself a name and to distinguish from others. The Chinese intellectuals had to be much more cautious, since alternative theories were easily seen as critiques of the current political power, and they easily faced harsh punishments, from exile to mutilation and death (Lloyd and Sivin 2002: 243–5).

The Chinese philosophers, especially in eras of strong central imperial government, largely depended on a centralized power structure and were hence discouraged to propose radical innovations and breaks with the tradition. They therefore did philosophy in a more integrative, contextualized fashion ("to warm up the old and understand the new" 溫故而知新, *Analects* 2.11). Chinese philosophers received their accreditation if their ideas stem from ancient sages, classics, and other respectable sources, especially if these ideas are in harmony with the old. Ancient Chinese philosophers did not strive to disrupt or radically differ from other thinkers of their time—they wanted to show not so much that the other party was wrong but that it was only *partially* true, that it is in fact not *comprehensive* enough. In Greece, on the other hand, in their competition with other schools the philosophers had every incentive to propose radically different ideas (or present an old idea as a new one), in order to catch attention and show their intellectual dexterity, and also to bluntly denounce competing ideas as being false.

It should be noted that in pre-imperial China, instances of direct confrontation could be seen. Most notably, the Mohists launched a frontal attack against the *ru*'s or Confucians (see Chapter 5). Some philosophers not employed in administrative roles, and who depended on their inherited wealth and/or teaching, or who, in some cases, even were peasants produced some examples of confrontation—for example, Wang Chong's 王充 (27–100) "Critical Essays" (*Lunheng* 論衡) or Wang Fuzhi's 王夫之 (1619–92) writings.

It is not the case that the Chinese were less prone to dispute and disagreement, or less able to decontextualize than the Greeks; there was even a school of "disputers" (*bianzhe* 辯者), also called the "school of names" (*mingjia* 名家).[9] But certain sociopolitical factors favored a stronger tendency toward contextualization in knowledge: most notably the fact that they lived in large, agricultural monarchic states and mostly depended for their livelihood on the ruler. Counter-currents of decontextualization were in the later Chinese tradition quite unanimously disparaged.

3.3 Ritual Background

There is one cultural factor in the Chinese tradition that is especially important in relation to the Embodiment Theory, namely the rituals.[10] Although the ritualistic setting was sometimes challenged, especially by Mohists and Legalists, and for a time it seemed to be an underdog, it eventually managed to become the mainstream (the landmark event is often put at 136 BC, when the Han emperor set up the study of five Confucian classics in the imperial Academy, turning Confucianism into state orthodoxy), and in the process it also incorporated important elements, ideas, and intellectual tools from those two schools. In the rest of this chapter, I want first to outline the ritualistic background of the Chinese tradition and then argue that the contextualizing and embodied ideas developed in China emerge naturally from a ritualistic setting, for which purpose I shall bring additional examples from two very different cultures.

Philosophical thought in China was born in the midst of important changes in the society. The Zhou dynasty in the eleventh century BC formed a feudalistic system where the king gave fiefs to the highest ranks of his followers, who in turn had their own subordinates. By the end of the ninth century BC a formal system was established where each rank of nobility used a certain number of bronze ritual tripods, was allowed a funeral chamber of certain dimensions, and was permitted to hold certain rituals with a prescribed number of dancers and musicians (see Pines 2000: 5). The legitimacy of their rule was proved and displayed through those very rituals and paraphernalia. In the course of time the upper levels of nobles tended to lose their power to lower levels: first the Zhou king to its immediate subordinates, the local dukes; then those dukes to their ministerial grand powers, and by Confucius' time the high nobility to the lower strata of nobility, the *shi* 士. This usurpation of power was accompanied by the usurpation of ritual prerogatives.

But paradoxically, while the Zhou political system, enmeshed in rituals, degenerated, interest in rituals, on the contrary, was enhanced (Pines 2000). During the Western Zhou (1046–771 BC), the word *li* 禮 was seldom used, and then only in the concrete sense of sacrifice rituals and the required behavior in them. When the old Zhou ritual system disintegrated, a more general idea of *li* was distinguished from the concrete ceremonies that had become obsolete. The new people in power had to legitimize themselves, and to achieve it, they extracted a more general sense of *li*, so that it started to refer to the whole way of government: it is not sufficient to perform the ceremonies, but *li* involves also *good* government in terms of the welfare and strength of the state, its people and the ruler. It was useful for the new category of people in power on the one hand to divert attention from the particular ceremonies and ritual systems (according to which they were usurpers), but on the other hand to maintain rituals for their own profit as maintaining the social distinctions and hierarchies in the new, modified form where they were at the top (Pines 2000: 20). The competence in rituals helped to distinguish the ruling class in general, and it could also function as a way to social ascension: if there was a certain established set of rituals, by learning them you could promote yourself socially. So, there was already a generalization of rituals, *li*, taking place due to historical reasons.

But the philosophical thinking in the strict sense starts when rituals were also made a vehicle of self-cultivation. The most important figure in this process is undoubtedly Confucius (551–479 BC). With him, rituals, music, and dance became the core of self-cultivation process. Robert Eno (1990) has come out with the interesting claim that while early Confucianism has often been viewed as basically a political theory and political activism (even if often thwarted), in the beginning it was an apolitical movement: Confucius' fellowship was mainly a self-study group under his leadership, and later a conglomerate of such fellowships under different *ruist*[11] masters.[12] According to Confucius, an exemplary person or *junzi* 君子 should participate in government if the *dao* 道 or the Way rules in the country, and if not, then retire. But he put so high preconditions for participation in government that in practical terms, Eno argues, it equaled to rejecting office. The political rhetoric (that a *ru* claimed he could make a state prosperous, if given the opportunity) might actually legitimize and justify their attitude that otherwise could have seemed antisocial and ethically doubtful (in the context of the Chinese ancestor cult one of the most important obligations of a man was to set up a family and continue the lineage). Furthermore, due to the high requirements for entering office the claimed abilities of the *ru* could never be put to test in real life (and possibly be falsified).

> Rather than being a political movement whose essential message lay in political doctrine and whose followers were groomed to enter the governments of the times, Ruism was in its early days a cult directed toward self-improvement in which political doctrines played a legitimizing role. The instrumental function of these political doctrines was to rationalize and encourage abstinence from non-Ruist government in favor of participation in the activities of the Ruist community. Political idealism both explained a Ruist withdrawal into cult studies, and justified it in the eyes of society. Rather than appearing eccentric and selfish, Ruists could portray themselves in terms of the Warring States values of righteousness, courage, and honesty. (Eno 1990: 45)

According to Eno, the early Confucians might have seemed rather eccentric to their contemporaries: a community of followers dressed in archaic clothes, speaking in an archaizing manner, performing complex rituals, and playing old music. But they turned ritual into a vehicle of self-cultivation, where the whole of one's life was permeated with ritual that gave intrinsic gratification and joy. Whether self-cultivation was the only goal of the early Confucians, as Eno claims, or not is not as important for our purposes here as the fact that it certainly was an essential part of Confucius' teachings and that ritual behavior was subject to reflective development in his school.

Historically it is very important also that in these groups certain key elements of the tradition were preserved: rituals, music, archery; and also that these groups were involved in preserving and compiling a growing compendium of classical texts: by Confucius' time the *Odes* were already a well-constituted canon; he also refers to the *Documents* (although the reference is not so clear) and to the *Changes* (which became a respectable part of the canon only very late); the *Rites* and *Spring and Autumn Annals* were added later. In this way the Confucians were in control of the basic education, we could say. They were also needed as ritual specialists in sacrifice and mourning rituals, so that even though until the Han times (206 BC–220 AD) they were not involved in the high-level political life, as keepers of the tradition (who turned it also to a vehicle for self-cultivation) they imbued more and more the middle layers of political life.

When Yuri Pines detects a disappearance or marginalization of the concept of *li* 禮 in learned contexts (it plays only secondary role even in Mencius *c.* 372–289 BC), it is perfectly in harmony with Eno's account of early ruists as self-cultivation groups who rather performed than conceptualized it. And then, with Xunzi or perhaps somewhat earlier, *li* started to be generalized—it seems, from "bottom up," so that it was invested with a very general and even cosmic role. Perhaps Xunzi was prompted to this due to Mohist challenge to rituals (although Mozi himself rather discarded the concept than directly attacked it). We shall come back to these topics later.

3.4 Rituals as Contextualizing

Rituals move toward contextualization. It is not obvious. Rituals imply a certain repetition in time, space, bodily movements, and speech acts; and those repeated elements do not seem to arise from a particular context, but are external and extraneous to it, and indeed, seem to be agents of decontextualization.[13] There are markers that delimit the sacred sphere from the profane (see Eliade 1961), but for the people involved, from their phenomenological viewpoint, those repeating elements of the ritual *create* context, and that in this way, they are contextual and contextualizing—they integrate into ritual space, into the sacred. Broadly speaking, we can say that the rituals contextualize the cultural sphere of the people involved. Through ritual, people reenact, recreate, and reinforce mutual bonds, bonds to their ancestors, and to the forces, spirits, and deities of the nature. The decontextualizing effect of the ritual by which they enact a sacred and ritual time-space has the effect of contextualizing and integrating the minds and bodies of the people involved. It contextualizes and integrates people with wider natural surroundings, as well as with the ancestors who subsist in a more interpenetrating, sublime, or refined state in the same world with living humans. As we are going to see in later chapters, this connection to a larger context can improve philosophical knowledge. But a completely different kind of knowledge is produced when the ritual sphere as a whole is discarded or devalued and a new type of discourse is established, like the *logos* of the Greek philosophers or the *fa* 法, objective models or rules, of the Mohists.

It may seem that a ritualistic background condemns one to obeying the existing power structure and following traditional forms of thought. But there is another way to emancipate from the rituals—not by discarding them but by following them! It happens when ritual becomes a form of self-cultivation. Indeed, in every living ritual practice this aspect is always present. You become free from the rituals when you fully embody them. Then, they stop to be a burden and start to lighten the existence. And although they are to a great extent implicit and not verbalized, they need not remain mute. It is possible to find strategies how to explain or express them.

That ritual is a crucial factor in the development of the mainstream Chinese tradition becomes more plausible if we take a look at other traditions that lack many determinants specific to Chinese culture but that have a common focus on aspects of ritual. To show how ritual can foster similar ideas in different political, cultural, and religious contexts, let us take two examples from two very different places: the Kurankos in Sierra Leone, as described by Michael Jackson, and Hasidics of Eastern Europe, as interpreted by Martin Buber and Rabbi Kalonymus Kalmish Shapira. These cases will show that the contextualizing tendency in accounting for knowledge is far from being anomalous, rare, or strange, and it is likely that ritual plays an important role in it. You can produce and improve philosophical knowledge by becoming *more* involved in a ritual.

3.5 Kurankos

What is the relation of rituals and knowledge? In Jackson's (1983)[14] interpretation the initiation rituals directly instill moral and general ideas into those involved: "patterns of body use engender mental images and instill moral qualities" (336), and the form of these ideas is determined by those patterns of body use. In this way "we are able to enter the domain of words and symbols by the back door, so to speak, and show that what the Kuranko themselves say about initiation can be correlated at every turn with what is done with the body" (336). Jackson gives several examples:

1) Facial impassivity while enduring pain is correlated with the control of emotion.
2) Taboos on calling for food or referring to food at the initiation lodge inculcate the value of moderation.
3) The interdiction on the neophytes speaking out of turn, moving or crying out during the operations is directly connected to the virtues of keeping secrets, promises and oaths, and of forbearance and circumspection.[15]

4) The "importance placed on listening to elders during the period of sequestration in the bush is correlated with the virtue of respecting elders" (and respect for elders is vital for all traditional societies, as they are repositories of living knowledge).
5) The sleepless night at the smoke-filled initiation house just before the return from the bush "is a way of instilling in them the virtues of withstanding hardship and being alert."
6) Enforced confinement at the initiation lodge "is connected to the value placed on self-restraint and self-containment."
7) Keenness of smell developed during the initiation "is correlated with the quality of discrimination" and "control of the eyes is connected with sexual proprieties" (one should not see certain objects associated with the other sex).
8) "The donning of new clothes suggests in the initiate's mind the assumption of a new status, while the women's imitations of men are sometimes explained similarly as a way women take on 'male' virtues of fortitude and bravery which they feel they sorely lack."

In this way, Jackson argues the actions of the body are the foundation for what is thought and said. This permits a "personal realization of social values, an immediate grasp of general precepts as sensible truths." The participants "proceed through bodily awareness to verbal skills and ethical views" and "bodily self-mastery is thus everywhere the basis for social and intellectual mastery." In this "kinaesthetic learning," knowledge is imparted directly, so that "the Kuranko do not need to formulate the meaning of the rite in terms of verbal elaborations or moral concepts" (337). We see here the role of implicit knowledge that has an important place in the embodied knowledge.

Metaphors used to describe this learning are related to bodily and practical activity:

> Thus, initiation is said to be a process of taming (unruly emotions and bodies), of moulding (clay), of making dry or cool (as in cooking, smoking and curing), of ripening (as of grain and fruit), of strengthening (the heart), hardening or straightening (the body), of getting "new sense" (*hankili kura*). (337)

These metaphors are not mere figures of speech, for they disclose real connections between personal maturity and the ability to provide food and support for others. A person has reached maturity "when inner thoughts are consistent with spoken words and external actions" (337).

Jackson stresses two important aspects of ritual action (also discussed in the next chapter on Confucius): overdetermination and levity. First, the overdetermination, ambivalence, and semantic richness of ritual action stand in contrast to verbal expression that remains poor and partial.

> It is because actions speak louder and more ambiguously than words that they are more likely to lead us to common truths; not semantic truths, established by others at other times, but experiential truths which seem to issue from within our own Being when we break the momentum of the discursive mind or throw ourselves into some collective activity in which we each find our own meaning yet sustain the impression of having a common cause and giving common consent. (339)

Ritual action thus guarantees the anchoring of some socially and individually central ideas in our bodily, experiential knowledge. Verbal communication runs the risk of remaining abstract, detached, and without immediate relevance. In ritual action, on the other hand, one immediately feels a richness of meanings. The overdetermination of ritualistically shaped behavior helps to renew knowledge. I can always give new verbal interpretations of the ritual, without the danger of exhausting its meaning or being stuck to one established way of verbalizing it.

Second, the fact that the techniques of the body transport us "into a world where boundaries are blurred and experience transformed" means the formation of a common body. Dance and music are paradigmatic examples of this kind of behavior. They nullify divisions which dominate everyday life (also in the "Treatise of Music" *Yueji* 樂記 music integrates and "harmonizes"; see Chapter 7). "Kuranko say that music and dance are 'sweet'; they loosen and lighten, by contrast with normal behavior which is contractual, binding, and constrained"; they "promote a sense of levity and openness in both body and mind, and make possible an empathic understanding of others, a fellow-feeling, which verbal and cognitive forms ordinarily inhibit" (338). This community in ritual action and music is "often experienced bodily before it is apprehended in the mind"; we immediately grasp other's intentions in our own subjectivity; we create a fellow-feeling (338). We will be able, if pressed, to extract general ideas from the ritual behavior, but we have performed and instantiated these ideas already before a reflective or explicit understanding of them. We produce those ideas "bottom up" rather than deduce a concrete behavior from an abstract principle in a "top down" fashion.

In this brief sketch about Kurankos, we notice various themes that were also important in the Chinese philosophical tradition: the priority given to action over discursive knowledge, the value of implicit knowledge and overdetermined expression, the importance of "ease" and joy, self-cultivation through ritual action, and the belief that rituals are crucial in guaranteeing social cohesion. The Kuranko example helps us to see how ritual may elicit similar ideas in different cultures.

3.6 Hasidic Tradition

Similar ideas on ritual and knowledge spring forth from other ritualistic contexts. Hasidism is a Jewish spiritual movement, founded by Israel ben Eliezer (c. 1700–1760), also known as the Baal Shem Tov (בעל שם טוב) or Besht (בשט), who lived in what is today Western Ukraine, and at the time was the Polish kingdom. It is said that Hasidism is not so much about studying Torah but embodying it:

> "What is the sense of their speaking Torah? Man should act in such a way that all his behaviour is a Torah, and he himself is a Torah." And at another place it is said, "The aim of the wise man is to make himself into a perfect teaching, and all his acts bodies of instruction; and where it is not vouchsafed him to attain to this, his aim is to be a transmission of the teaching and a commentary on it, and to spread the teaching by each of his movements." (Buber 1948: 73–4)

From this follows the "guidance by example" we discussed in 2.11:

> Again and again, it says in the Hasidic writings that one should learn "from every limb of the tzaddik," and he refers as well to the Ḥasidic teaching that "a person shall act that all his conduct shall be a Torah and himself a Torah."¹⁶ Later in the same book, Buber presents the following teaching from Rabbi Leib, son of Sarah: "I did not go to the Maggid in order to hear Torah from him, but to see how he unlaces his felt shoes and laces them up again"—and Buber called this teaching "Thora sagen und Thora sein" (Saying Torah and Being Torah). (Shonkoff 2017: 139)

A Hasidic master, Rabbi Kalonymus Kalmish Shapira gives an example of how knowledge is embodied and enacted, discussing "a Talmudic passage (Berakhot 55a) where Bezalel, the chief builder of the desert Tabernacle, corrects Moses' instructions regarding the building of the Tabernacle" (Jacobson-Maisels 2016: 193). According to Shapira, Bezalel the carpenter, has more knowledge than Moses, the architect, reversing the Aristotelian assumption that theoretical knowledge is above the practical and thus the architect is above the carpenter (cf. below, 8.2):

> It is his shadowed individual nature, which is precisely the same as his embodied nature, which allows him [i.e. Bezalel—M.O.] to receive this additional revelation, inaccessible to Moses. It is his actual performance of the action, the carpenter rather than the architect, that gives him a kind of detailed knowledge that Moses lacks. […] While the architect, the theorist, looks at the plans, a reductive structure that can never include all the details, the carpenter, the one who acts, must hold a range of tacit details in his body-mind for each and every action he performs and relate directly to the concrete details of the situation. (Jacobson-Maisels 2016: 195)
>
> It is precisely the aspect of the body and concrete action that enables certain kinds of knowledge, understanding, and vision that would otherwise be impossible. (Jacobson-Maisels 2016: 194)

The carpenter has an embodied tacit knowledge that one has to gain by experience (cf. below, in 8.2, the example of wheelwright in the *Zhuangzi*).

Ritual practice can become embedded in everyday life:

> To highlight this foundation of Ḥasidic spirituality, Buber employed the term "sacrament," and it is significant for our purposes that he defined sacrament precisely as the "binding of meaning to the body" (*Bindung des Sinns an den Leib*). This concept dissolves dichotomies of religious truth and corporeal activity. Moreover, Buber sensed that Ḥasidic sacraments are not limited to the particular rituals of Halakhah. "To the question what (in the sacramental sense) is important, the answer was given: 'What one is engaged in at the moment.'" Hence, Buber's description of Ḥasidic piety as one of "pansacramentalism" and "sacramental existence." Every action is potentially sacramental; every moment and place can harbor the binding of divine meaning to bodily life. (Shonkoff 2017: 137–8)

This embodied knowledge is implicit (Jacobson-Maisels 2016: 190–1). To describe different levels of the unfolding of this implicit knowledge, Shapira uses a Hasidic distinction between inspiration (*hashra'ah* השראה) and reward (*sakhar* שכר): "while the aspect of hashra'ah is a kind of knowledge that is beyond the comprehension of an Israelite and rests upon him, *sakhar* is a kind of knowledge that is integrated into the very self and bones of the person" (Jacobson-Maisels 2016: 191). This would introduce a further distinction in the contextualized personal knowledge. It is interesting to note how ideas are unfolded from the embodied ritual practice.

> Inspiration, a knowledge beyond understanding, cannot be grasped intellectually, but it can be felt in the body. Not only can it be felt and experienced, but the felt-sense of the inspiration does not have to remain beyond the person and

inaccessible. [...] [F]rom this felt-sense that which was inaccessible (*hashra'ah*) and inexpressible can be integrated and known (*sakhar*). It is just that it can only be integrated and known through bodily feeling and not through the intellect. (Jacobson-Maisels 2016: 191)

It is the embodied and integrated knowledge that allows an "individual (*pratit* פרטית) revelation" (Jacobson-Maisels 2016: 194) and that is why Bezalel knows more than Moses: Moses has a monistic undistinguished direct revelation, where he can distinguish little, like looking directly into the Sun, whereas Bezalel, precisely thanks to his "shadowed" individual nature has a more nuanced and detailed understanding, expressed in his capacity to produce marvellous works of art (Jacobson-Maisels 2016: 195).

It has even been claimed that Hasidism was not based on doctrine (Shonkoff 2017: 136).[17] Its meaning is embedded in the everyday life and emerges in concrete situations and encounters, especially with other people. Buber, who in his own thinking stresses the dialogue, the "I-Thou" relationship, lays a special emphasis on the emergent character of meaning in Hasidism and Hasidic encounters.[18] Shonkoff analyzes some subtle means by which Buber in his translations of Hasidic stories strengthens the embodied and emergent character of the meaning: concrete presence, face-to-face situation etc. (Shonkoff 2017: 151-2), to emphasize "a wholly embodied theological instruction" (Shonkoff 2017: 154).

3.7 Ritual Knowledge

In the light of the above examples of Kurankos and Hasidism we may agree with Kevin Schilbrack that rituals are a form of thinking and that they imply an ontology or "metaphysics":

> Ritual knowledge is metaphysical, then, to the extent that the ritualists inquire into the way things are in general or under all circumstances. Rituals provide a structured corporeal engagement with some particular aspect of human life, such as health, dreams, song, house building, dance, childbirth, voice, or eating. Insofar as a ritual induces one to pursue metaphysical knowledge, however, it offers an invitation to understand these particular aspects of life as emblematic of the nature of human experience or things more broadly. (Schilbrack 2004: 141)

We saw how Kurankos view parts of their rituals as emblematic of general moral values. Schilbrack stresses that a ritual does not try to change the world, but rather the ritualists seek to transform themselves through the ritual (Schilbrack 2004).

This is very clear in the case of Kuranko initiation rituals, the goal of which is to inculcate certain virtues in the participant. This accords also with the self-cultivation ideals of the Confucians through the rites.

Although rituals vary in different cultures, they are not altogether arbitrary and there is an emergent truth in them: "ritualizing is a process embedded in and emergent from interactions between people and their environments" (Schilbrack 2004: 145). We discussed in the previous chapter that space and time are not homogeneous for us, but we always make axiological distinctions there, according to the perspectives of our activity. The same applies on the collective level: every society articulates its environment in a certain way. These articulations cannot be completely arbitrary but are based on the articulations and capacities of human bodies and interactions, as well as the articulations and capacities of other things, beings, and environments. The effective distinctions made by a society emerge historically in the process of ongoing interactions. And although rituals may be goal-oriented (like securing a good catch or a good weather), they have a strong reflexive component that modulates our subjective and intersubjective being:

> Rather than harboring the forces of the "natural world," so to speak, as techniques of fire building might be said to do, rituals are body techniques which harbor the powers and potentialities of both our own subjectivity, as an embodied way of being-in-the-world, and those of the social world. (Crossley 2004: 46)
>
> Rituals are subjective and intersubjective technologies which, qua physical actions, tap into the deeper corporeal basis of our (inter)subjective lives, effecting desired transformations. (Crossley 2004: 49)

Rituals are overdetermined, as we saw also in the case of Kurankos and Hasidism; they express more than can be explicitly said. And this is exactly an important role of the ritual:

> [P]art of the value of the ritual, qua body technique, is its capacity to "condense" meaning and circumvent verbal negotiation. The meanings of the handshake, the funeral rite, the wedding ceremony, etc., are multiple and complex. Indeed, in certain respects they are too extensive, complex, and subtle to be spelled out. … By way of ritual, however, we can seal them without having to spell them out. The ritual brings them to pass. Furthermore, because the ritual typically circumvents negotiation we can seal them in largely non-negotiable terms, drawing upon a power of society or the social group which is prior to and deeper than our capacity for rational negotiation and agreement. (Crossley 2004: 39–40)

The examples we brought of Kurankos and Hasidism show that an embodied account of knowledge and being seem naturally to stem from a ritual setting.

It seems quite natural, since rituals by definition involve bodily actions in a certain context. In the above subsections I tried to show how the Chinese tradition was born from a ritualistic background, and in the following chapters I try to show how it reflectively developed its consequences for thought (Confucianism and also Daoism) or how it stimulated opposition (Mohism and Legalism). A ritualistic background could explain the similarities between the mainstream embodied understanding of knowledge in Confucianism and the two examples of Kurankos and Hasidism as shown above (and also the similarities of both of them with the contemporary Embodiment Theory).

Although the Jewish philosophy has over two thousand years orbited in the field of influence of the Greek philosophical tradition, it has maintained, like the traditional Chinese philosophy, strong connection with ritualism.[19] This may warrant further research along the ET lines, for example, around the theme of existential embeddedness in a social world and interactions with "Thou's." While the Chinese tradition has, in this respect, focused on the "natural" relations (the "five relations" of ruler-subject, father-son, husband-wife, elder brother-younger brother and friends), several proponents of the Jewish tradition have laid a special emphasis on the stranger. Steven Kepnes, while discussing the philosophy of Hermann Cohen (1842–1918), says:

> Cohen suggests that religious love begins with love for the stranger. And he argues that this is the key to our understanding of human love of God and God's love for humans. … The meaning of God's love is his compassion for the stranger. And as we imitate God, and come to love the stranger, the one who is different and seemingly beyond us, we come to love God who is the very definition of difference and that which transcends us. (Kepnes 234)

Through the rituals, the hardships of Egyptian enslavement of early Jews are remembered, and this fosters a compassion for other human beings, even if (or especially if) they are poor, unattractive, and oppressed. This would point to another direction in the development of ritualistic embodied knowledge, that is different from the Chinese way.

3.8 Conclusion

In this chapter we investigated the background for the contextualizing and embodying tendency in the mainstream Chinese philosophical tradition. It should be emphasized that the talk is about tendencies and dominant streams.

It is not that a tradition would exclude one or another way of thinking, but in the course of an ongoing process of relating to the historical heritage, it is inevitable that some strains become more emphasized than others. Just as when water is poured on an even ground, it will find small differences in the terrain that initially may be tiny, but may give an initial direction to the stream; and when more and more water goes preferentially in a certain direction, it will carve an ever-deepening waterway. Of course, human tradition is not so unidirectional, but a similar carving out of preferred topics and ways of arguing takes place. Someone asks a question, others start to reply, and the topic is set, and ways of discussing take shape. It will be more difficult to raise completely new topics later. Inevitably they must relate to what came earlier, and in this way are shaped by it.

We brought out some political and sociological factors comparatively for ancient Greece and ancient China. In Greece, in a democratic city-state, questions concerning the community were discussed in public meetings of the citizens, and lawsuits were equally decided in public disputes. Also, the philosophers did not depend on the patronage of a ruler, but they gathered a group of followers that represented the basis for the financial support of the teaching and its continuation. For this, the thinkers had to be as distinct as possible from others, bringing forward radically new ideas, attacking directly their opponents, disputing and competing with them. The competitive polis-state setting of Greece favored a decontextualizing tendency in intellectual endeavors and the development of argumentation and logic, a technique of speech, which would depend as little as possible on the contingencies of a situation and would make it as general and unassailable as possible, in any situation.

In China, the political life was centered on rulers, and there was little room for public debate. In order to gain the support of the ruler, and at the same time not to enrage or shock him, or make dangerous enemies in the court, more indirect speech was encouraged, avoiding direct confrontation and engaging in a discourse that preferred to situate itself in the context of the existing tradition (presenting oneself as a continuator of an old tradition) and of the current intellectual situation (not presenting one's position as true and others' as false, but rather claiming that one's ideas were the most comprehensive, and other's more limited and partial, so that one would include the merits of others, but they would not include some of your merits).

We then discussed the role of the ritual as a dominant factor in the Chinese tradition and what historical and political factors guaranteed its continuation. It could have been expected that with the demise of the Zhou political power, its ritual system would have also collapsed, but it did not happen. The usurpers found it more useful to turn the ritualistic setting to their own profit rather than to discard it; they rather reinterpreted the rituals, distancing them from particular historical forms, and giving them a more general meaning: rituals must accord with good management of the state.

We also speculated how rituals mean a contextualization of thought, even if they may seem a decontextualizing factor: a ritual involves a certain repetition of actions and formulas that do not arise from the context but are often anachronistic and quite alien to it. We showed that this very alienation sets up a ritual context and that it reinforces and integrates the community in their mutual relations and in their relations with ancestors and the forces of nature.

In order to show the contextualizing power of ritual, two traditions very different from China, Kurankos and Hasidics, were seen to have also formulated contextualizing and embodied ideas about ritualistic practices that are similar to those discussed in the section of the embodiment theory and to those that we are going to see below in the Chinese tradition. We argued that it is a form of condensed knowledge that has its generality, which is different from the explicit and abstract generality of a decontextualized knowledge.

In the following we shall turn directly to the Chinese philosophical tradition: first in the embodied knowledge of Confucius, then to two challenges that moved toward decontextualization: Mohist and Legalists. Then, we will come back to the embodied account of knowledge to explore two developments of it, in the *Record of Music* and in the *Zhuangzi*.

4

Embodied Foundations: Confucius 孔子

In this section, we shall focus on Confucius' *Analects* from the point of view of the Embodiment Theory.[1]

4.1 Embodied

With the help of the embodiment theory, we can make sense of parts of the *Analects* that seem of little philosophical interest to a Western reader. Book 10, for example, "is often skipped over in embarrassment by Western scholars" (Jones 2008: 121). "Largely concentrated in book 10 of the *Analects*, the passages concerning Confucius' everyday style are perhaps some of the most puzzling in the text" (Olberding 2007: 360). Book 10 of the *Analects* has traditionally been understood as describing Confucius' behavior, although originally it was probably a ritual manual that was interpolated into the *Analects* (Van Norden 2002: 16) and attributed to Confucius.[2] Since Confucius represents the paragon of an exemplary person, it does not make much difference whether the person described in that book refers to the historical Confucius or simply a general understanding of a noble person.[3]

Confucius' embodied knowledge can be best detected from his countenance:

When he saw someone fasting or mourning, he invariably assumed a changed expression, even if they were an intimate acquaintance.
When he saw someone wearing a ritual cap or a blind person, he would invariably display a respectful countenance, even if they were of low birth.
When riding past someone dressed in funeral garb, he would bow down and grasp the crossbar of his carriage. He would do so even if the mourner was a lowly peddler.
When presented food with full ritual propriety, he would invariably change expression and rise from his seat.

He would also change expression upon hearing a sudden clap of thunder or observing a fierce wind. (10.25; 108–9, translation modified)⁴

見齊衰者, 雖狎, 必變。見冕者與瞽者, 雖褻, 必以貌。凶服者式之。式負版者。有盛饌, 必變色而作。迅雷風烈, 必變。⁵

The term translated here as "expression" is *se* 色. It also means "color" (this is the dominant meaning in modern Chinese) and refers here first of all to the hue of the face, and by extension, the countenance, the expression of the face, and of the whole body (cf. Wong 2014: 176, 183). Certain attitudes and principles transpired in his facial expression and perhaps even in the hue of the face. It is a common physiological reaction that our face acquires different patterns of color (red when one is angry or happy or blushes with shame), has different hue when healthy and sick or tired, etc. The facial expressions and hue are difficult to control:

> Zixia asked about filial piety. The Master said, "It is the demeanor that is difficult. If there is work to be done, disciples shoulder the burden, and when wine and food are served, elders are given precedence, but surely filial piety consists of more than this." (2.8; 10)
>
> 子夏問孝。子曰:「色難。有事弟子服其勞, 有酒食先生饌, 曾是以為孝乎?」

Again, the word translated as "demeanor" is "(facial) color," *se* 色. It is not enough just to perform the correct ritual actions, shoulder the burden, and give elders precedence, but it must be accompanied by correct inner attitude, expressed on the face and in bodily demeanor. A long process of self-cultivation internalizes ritual values so that one completely embodies them, even up to the subtle expressions on one's face.

Shigehisa Kuriyama, in his magnificent book *The Expressiveness of the Body and the Divergence of the Greek and Chinese Medicine*, dwells at length on *se* 色 (1999: 153–92): while for the Greeks skin was an impediment for the eye to see the inner organs, in Chinese medicine the skin was an important tool of diagnosis, since it expresses what happens on the interior, and from the *se* 色 it is possible to detect the start of an illness, even before it becomes visible in morphological structures.

We all have certain intuitions about other people's moods and health from their face and demeanor, but it is not always easy to pinpoint what gave us a cue that the other is dissatisfied, tired, or ill. In Chinese medicine there were efforts to systematize this knowledge and force it into the system of five colors, which can be correlated to the five phases' analysis of other phenomena (sounds, viscera, etc.). Yet, this knowledge remains highly contextual and requires long habituation and training. Greek medical practitioners also certainly paid attention to facial hue, but they did not develop a comparable body of knowledge from it.[6]

4.2 The Singular and the Intensive

What strikes us in *Analects* 10.25 is that it does not describe what Confucius' countenance and demeanor were like, but it says that it "changed" (*bian* 變) or "changed color" (*bian se* 變色).[7] The text does not describe things and properties, and only mentions that there was a change, without even taking the trouble of precisely stating what kind of change it was.

Above, in Section 2.12, I tried to show how the disembodied account is situated only on the level of the actual and the juxtaposed, while the embodied account straddles different levels of actualization and interpenetration. For this passage of 10.25 it is not so important to characterize the end result and the actual forms that result from a situation but rather to mark out the singular points of the situation. Confucius is said to "change" at certain moments; he lays out singularities in a topological space of human behavior. The precise change of properties and the stasis or dynamics of things are not so important. Rather, it is important where important changes should happen. For example, when you encounter a mourner, when food is offered in a ritual manner, or when notable events happen in the natural world, such as lightning or a gust of wind.

Confucius sometimes laments about the changes in ritual forms: when the shape of some ritual vessel changes (6.25) or when local nobility usurps certain rituals that used to be a prerogative of the king (3.1). Yet the emphasis on singularities of good behavior accommodates a change in actual forms, provided that the distribution of singularities remains the same (the same meaning is achieved with a new configuration). For example, Confucius approves of a new custom where lambs are no longer killed (but only ritual preparations are made, 3.17), or when a silken cap replaced a linen one (9.3). But when the change expresses a different singularity, Confucius denounces the change, for example, when people had started to bow after ascending the stairs to the ruler, and not downstairs as in the old times (9.3): the custom articulates relations between the ruler and the subject, and the new custom implies a diminished deference.[8]

> The Master said, "When we say, 'the rites, the rites,' are we speaking merely of jade and silk? When we say, 'music, music,' are we speaking merely of bells and drums?" (17.11; 205)
> 子曰:「禮云禮云, 玉帛云乎哉?樂云樂云, 鐘鼓云乎哉?」

From this passage we can see that actualized forms ("jade and silk," "bells and drums," or the vehicles of rituals and music) can actually impede understanding of the true meaning of rituals, that is, the distribution of its singular points that imply several aspects of human relations and determine the meaning of the ritual.

4.3 Embedded

Confucius expresses correct behavior in a specific context, so that his behavior is inherently embedded in it. In the following passages note again the reference to the countenance or color, and how Confucius' behavior changes according to the situation:

> When called on by his lord to receive a guest, his countenance would become alert and serious, and he would hasten his steps. When he saluted those in attendance beside him—extending his clasped hands to the left or right, as their position required—his robes remained perfectly arrayed, both front and back. Hastening forward, he moved smoothly, as though gliding upon wings. Once the guest had left, he would always return to report, "The guest is no longer looking back." (10.3; 99)
> 君召使擯, 色勃如也, 足躩如也。揖所與立, 左右手。衣前後, 襜如也。趨進, 翼如也。賓退, 必復命曰:「賓不顧矣。」

> When entering the gate of his Duke, he would draw himself in, as if the gate were not large enough to admit him. He would not come to a halt at the center of the doorway and when walking would not tread upon the threshold. When passing by his appointed place, his countenance would become alert and serious, he would hasten his steps, his words falling to a whisper as if he could barely get them out. When he ascended to the Duke's dais with the hem of his gown gathered in his hands, he would draw himself in, slowing his breath to the point that it seemed as if he were not breathing at all. Upon leaving the Duke's dais, his expression would relax as he descended the top stair, and he would seem at ease. On reaching the bottom of the stairs, he would hasten forward smoothly, as though gliding upon wings. When returning to his own place, he would resume his attitude of cautious respect. (10.4; 99)

入公門, 鞠躬如也, 如不容。立不中門, 行不履閾。過位, 色勃如也, 足躩如也, 其言似不足者。攝齊升堂, 鞠躬如也, 屏氣似不息者。出, 降一等, 逞顏色, 怡怡如也。沒階趨進, 翼如也。復其位, 踧踖如也。

Alert and serious, his expression would be like someone about to go into battle, and he would walk with shortened steps as though each movement were carefully scripted. (10.5; 100)

勃如戰色, 足蹜蹜, 如有循。

These passages show Confucius' speech, behavior, and even physiological reactions change adequately according to the situation (cf. also 7.9, where he does not eat his full, when a mourner is present).[9] His actions have attained such a grace, smoothness, and ease that he "seems to glide upon wings," *yi ru ye* 翼如也 (10.3 and 10.4). His steps, countenance, breathing, and his entire demeanor change according to context. On official occasions he is serious, barely breaths, and hastens his steps; at home he is relaxed.

Confucius' actions can be interpreted in a prosaic sense, as in Slingerland's explanation: "Most prosaically, one does not stand in the middle of the doorway as a courtesy to others, to avoid impeding their movement, and one does not tread upon thresholds to avoid dirtying them, which would in turn dirty the flowing robes of others" (Slingerland 2003a: 99). But thresholds have a further significance for many different cultures, symbolizing a separator between the outer and the inner, and connected to special customs and taboos;[10] in China, important mansions have especially high and wide thresholds to clearly distinguish the interior from the exterior.

The same book of the *Analects* describes Confucius' (or the exemplary person's) way of dressing, eating, sleeping, sitting, riding a carriage, etc. This shows that all his behavior is ritualized, up to the details of his everyday life (and even unconscious behavior—sleeping, dreaming, cf. 7.5; 65). It is indeed an *ars contextualis*, as Hall and Ames (1998a) put it. His behavior changes according to context and expresses relevant aspects of it (threshold, robe, pace, etc.). Confucius' behavior is embedded in a context, yet he also creates a context with his behavior and embeds others into it.

Especially in the West, people are prone to overestimate the autonomy of the individual and their command over their behavior. It has been shown by various experiments how our behavior can be widely changed by minor details of our surroundings. A pen gifted by a company to doctors strongly influences their choices, even if the doctor themself denies it: "participants who found dimes in the return slots of public payphones were fourteen times more likely to help a passerby gather a dropped stack of papers than those who had not" (see Sarkissian

2010: 2). This means, in turn, that minute signals that we ourselves emit—and that we cannot refrain from emitting—may have a large impact on other people's perception of ourselves and on their behavior, and on how the interpersonal situation unfolds (Sarkissian 2010: 7; cf. Sarkissian 2017). Our posture, tone of voice, facial expression, clothes we wear, etc. influence the situation.

It is possible to rephrase the above descriptions of Confucius' behavior in a disembodied fashion or to understand those descriptions as disembodied rules. It is also possible to stipulate that if you go to the ruler, you should bow below the stairs; if you meet a mourner, you should look serious; in an official situation, you should walk with small steps, etc. But it would be difficult to codify each situation in this way. And more importantly, the main focus is not on these forms themselves but on the intensive system from which those forms arise, the marking out of what are important, sensitive points of social interaction. Confucius' highest values—humaneness (*ren* 仁), appropriateness (*yi* 義), the way (*dao* 道), ritual (*li* 禮), etc.—refer to a virtual distribution of those singularities, and they are not tied to actual definitions that would have a determined form and fixed, "metrical" relations. Specific actual forms simply aid one to access the virtual singularities. A formulation in terms of laws and rules with a more rigid and metric structure would betray all that.

There is another important aspect of embeddedness, namely *temporal* embeddedness. What is most important is the timeliness of knowledge and behavior. This topic appears at the very beginning of the *Analects*: "To learn and then have occasion to practice what you have learned—is this not satisfying?" (學而時習之, 不亦說乎, 1:1; 1). Knowledge in itself is not sufficient; it is at least as important to know when and how to apply it. This thread appears also in the final passage of book 10, where Confucius says: "This pheasant upon the mountain bridge—how timely it is!" (山梁雌雉, 時哉! 時哉!, 10.27; 109–10). This phrase may seem to say little, but the timeliness that Confucius mentions has been traditionally understood as describing his own behavior—Confucius is a "timely sage." In the embodiment theory it is stressed how the agent is embedded in a context, and this context should not be understood only in spatial terms but also in temporal terms. An action always takes place at a certain time, with certain temporal modulations (e.g., the swiftness or relaxation of Confucius' steps), and at a certain age of the agent:

> My master only spoke when the time was right, and so people never grew impatient listening to him. (14.13; 159)[11]
> 夫子時然後言, 人不厭其言

To speak when it is not yet time to speak—this is called being rash. To not speak when it is time to speak—this is called being secretive. To speak without taking into account the countenance of one's lord—this is called being blind. (16.6; 195)

言未及之而言謂之躁, 言及之而不言謂之隱, 未見顏色而言謂之瞽。

Confucius said, "The gentleman guards against three things: when he is young, and his blood and vital essence are still unstable, he guards against the temptation of female beauty; when he reaches his prime, and his blood and *qi* have become unyielding, he guards against being contentious; when he reaches old age, and his blood and *qi* have begun to decline, he guards against being acquisitive." (16.7; 195, tr. mod.)

孔子曰:「君子有三戒: 少之時, 血氣未定, 戒之在色; 及其壯也, 血氣方剛, 戒之在鬭; 及其老也, 血氣既衰, 戒之在得。」

This means that for Confucius, there cannot be a completely context-independent set of principles that one could apply anytime anywhere.[12] Or to put it differently, the most universal principles necessarily have to be enacted according to the age, time, and context that modify them. The same action can be right or not right, depending on the conditions. For example, killing another person is surely a crime, but doing it in self-defense may be justified in our legal system.

4.4 Flexible

Flexibility is an inevitable part of timely and adaptive embodied and embedded behavior (see Valmisa 2021). A smooth and graceful action is an action that is able to change and adapt itself in real-time feedback from the environment.[13] We can see this in our daily lives. For example, when I walk around, my feet and body spontaneously adapt to the conditions of the terrain (slippery, rocky, steep ascent or descent, etc.). Another example, when I write with a pencil I automatically adapt to the specific pen and paper I have at hand (its thickness, degree of pressure needed, quality of the paper, smoothness of the table, etc.). Flexibility as sensitivity to context is highly valued by the Confucians:

The Master was entirely free of four faults: arbitrariness, inflexibility, rigidity, and selfishness. (9.4; 87)

子絕四: 毋意, 毋必, 毋固, 毋我。

The Master said, "The gentleman is true, but not rigidly trustworthy." (15.37; 188)

子曰:「君子貞而不諒。」

On one occasion, two students ask Confucius the same question, but he gives two different answers to them. A third student overheard both exchanges and asked for the reason. Confucius replies:

> The Master said, "Ran Qiu is overly cautious, and so I wished to urge him on. Zilu, on the other hand, is too impetuous, and so I sought to hold him back." (11.22; 120)
> 子曰:「求也退, 故進之; 由也兼人, 故退之。」

A good teacher can adapt their message according to their listeners:[14] a cautious person should be encouraged and an impetuous person restrained. Both have different obstacles to overcome; recall the example of two infants (above, 2.7), one of whom had to slow down and the other to be more energetic (Thelen and Smith 1996: 247–78). A good teacher can help students with their specific problems.

The goal of embodied self-cultivation is to include as many variables of the situation as possible, and to make them interpenetrate each other, so that one is able to react adequately to each of them, and that it does not take any time, since there is no need to process an external rule or principle, but the particular situation already tends toward a certain solution. Interaction with a cautious person creates a certain field of tensions, and interaction with an impetuous person creates a different configuration of tensions, and each elicits a different behavior from the teacher. We saw above that Confucius pays attention to minute details of his behavior and demeanor, and it goes hand in hand with a similar acute attention to the nuances other's behavior and tendencies.

Confucian self-cultivation extends flexibility to complex situations of social behavior. Experientially, such adaptivity is clear and easy, but computationally, due to the real-time feedback and the nonlinearity that arises from it, it is extremely complex.[15] This is why machines, while excelling in things we find difficult (computing), tend to be clumsy in things we find easy (smooth movement).

4.5 Enacted

Confucius makes it clear that true knowledge is enacted, that it expresses itself in corresponding action. Knowledge is meant to enlighten action and action reveals the level of knowledge:

The Master said, "I can talk all day long with Yan Hui without him once disagreeing with me. In this way, he seems a bit stupid. And yet when we retire and I observe his private behavior, I see that it is in fact worthy to serve as an illustration of what I have taught. Hui is not stupid at all" (2.9; 11).

子曰：「吾與回言終日，不違如愚。退而省其私，亦足以發。回也，不愚。」

The Master said, "Look at the means a man employs, observe the basis from which he acts, and discover where it is that he feels at ease. Where can he hide? Where can he hide?" (2.10; 11).

子曰：「視其所以，觀其所由，察其所安。人焉廋哉? 人焉廋哉?」

Someone who is accomplished is upright in his native substance and fond of rightness. He examines other people's words and observes their demeanor, and always takes the interests of his inferiors into account when considering something. (12.20; 135)

夫達也者，質直而好義，察言而觀色，慮以下人。

The Master replied, "I observed him sitting in the presence of adults, and also walking alongside his elders. He is not looking to improve himself, but is just after quick success." (14.44; 173)

子曰：「吾見其居於位也，見其與先生並行也。非求益者也，欲速成者也。」

Knowledge is understood to be expressed in embodied action, and there is no hint to some sandwich model where cognition lays squeezed between perceptual input and behavioral output (see above, 2.1. and 2.4). Little is said about epistemology in the *Analects* (an epistemology is outlined in a later text of roughly Confucian lineage, *Record of Music*, that we discuss below, in Chapter 7), and in terms of the *Analects* one might say that epistemology and ethics are really not two distinct and independent areas of philosophical investigation. Both reactions and actions of a person give us an idea of their singularities, at what points do they change, and what is important for them. From this, one can understand whether they are an exemplary, "noble" person (*junzi* 君子), or a common, "small person" (*xiao ren* 小人). A small or petty person is after profit,[16] revealing a crude distribution of singularities of their life. An exemplary person, on the other hand, has a more refined and nuanced configuration of singularities and their behavior is more complex.

Confucius' teaching is not conveyed only through words. Therefore his behavior is described in such detail, and that may be the reason why the general prescriptions of a former ritual manual were attributed to a concrete person, Confucius. His teaching is conveyed also by his behavior, by the way he walks, breaths, eats, and sleeps (remember how Hasidic students went to see how the master ties his shoelaces, see 3.6 above). The effort of self-cultivation does not simply concern an ability to master and expound certain ideas but to embody and enact them; "it is the demeanor that is difficult" (*se nan* 色難, in Section 4.1. above).

Ritual action is overdetermined in relation to linguistic expression; there is always more in it, more implicit meaning than can be put into words. Or, what is the same, ritual action can be expressed in words in different ways and it is important to grasp that embodied ground where they come from. One should "observe the basis from which he acts" (*guan qi suo you* 觀其所由), and this basis cannot be hidden. Words, speaking, and language are important aspects of expression, but they are also suspect, as they are produced much more easily and cheaply than behavior:

> The Master said, "People in ancient times were not eager to speak, because they would be ashamed if their actions did not measure up to their words." (4.22; 36)
> 子曰:「古者言之不出,恥躬之不逮也。」

The foundation of Confucius' thought is the practice of rites, which is a set of choreographed movements, songs, and utterances, making it intrinsically embodied and enacted.

4.6 Extended

One aspect of the embeddedness and contextuality of knowledge is that it is *extended* (Aizawa 2014). It opposes the conception of knowledge as essentially inextensive operation with symbols. Extendedness should not be understood in the sense of juxtaposition, but in the sense of extending over certain juxtaposed parts of the world: not only the brain and not only the inside of the skin, but also the wider environment.

For a Confucian, appropriate usage of musical instruments, ritual clothes, vessels, books, bows, and arrows is crucial for knowledge and meaning-making.[17] Let us repeat a citation brought above (4.3):

> When he saluted those in attendance beside him—extending his clasped hands to the left or right, as their position required—his robes remained perfectly arrayed, both front and back. (10.3; Slingerland 2003a: 99)
> 揖所與立,左右手。衣前後,襜如也。

The fact that he did not mess his robe in saluting others shows that he controlled his body and did not overdo his physical movements, which in turn expresses his capacity for restraint and sense of measure.

It is not so that the robe would be a simple external prop for Confucius' knowledge that could be expressed in some other medium, like the linguistic sign "tree" that is made arbitrarily to denote the concept of tree. Of course, Confucius ritual knowledge is expressed in all kinds of different situations and with the help of different human and non-human collaborators; it is a certain *style*. But if this style did not include Confucius' relations to robes, it would be a different style, a different knowledge.

Furthermore, it is not so that Confucius would simply exploit the robe in an external and disinterested fashion. He is well versed in the qualities of the material and the design of the robe, he is familiar with its affordances, how it behaves in relation to certain movements that have a certain velocity, strength, angle, etc. The robe is agentive, an active participant in the process of knowledge. Confucius turns wearing his robe into an art, or even more than art, since the ritual is an important part of the cosmological and religious structure of the world.

In other passages, the kind of robes he wore on different occasions is specified: at court, at home, while mourning, during certain ceremonies, during fasting, while sleeping, etc. Each of these occasions could warrant different requirements for design, color, combination, ornaments (see 10.6, 7, 14, 19, see Slingerland 2003: 100–2, 105, 107). Additionally, when he encountered people with certain attire say, for mourning or courtly rituals, his countenance and behaviors changed accordingly (10.25). Not only did he convey messages himself, but he also interacted appropriately with meanings inscribed in the clothing of other people. We can see clothes as agents of meaning and knowledge, both in their physical affordances and their symbolic overcoding.

In another example Confucius uses a zither to convey a particular meaning:

> Ru Bei [sent a messenger expressing his] wish to have an audience with Confucius, but Confucius declined, saying that he was ill. As soon as the messenger went out the door, however, Confucius picked up his zither and sang, making sure that the messenger could hear him. (17.20; 208)
> 孺悲欲見孔子，孔子辭以疾。將命者出戶，取瑟而歌，使之聞之。

Confucius did not say directly that he did not want to receive Ru Bei or his messenger, but expressed it by playing his zither, ostentatiously showing that he was not ill. That he used a zither may add further connotations, since the zither was the instrument of an educated and well-bred person. Hence, part of this overdetermined meaning may have been that Ru Bei should cultivate himself. With the zither, Confucius extends his expressive body.

Another example of a passage discussing the usage of a particular ritual object references the jade tablet:

> When grasping the official jade tablet, he would draw himself in, as if he could not bear its weight. Sometimes he held it high against his forehead as if saluting, while at other times he held it low at his waist as if offering a gift. (10.5; 100)
> 執圭, 鞠躬如也, 如不勝。上如揖, 下如授。

The jade tablet helped to structure ritual behavior. It was given by the ruler as a token to an envoy to a foreign country. Confucius seems to bend under its weight, as if he could not bear it or as if he was overpowered (*sheng* 勝).[18] The tablet is not heavy, but by acting as if it was heavy, Confucius draws attention to the metaphoric *gravity* of the situation and of his responsibilities. In the second phrase, we see how the tablet helps to distinguish different phases of the rituals and hence to articulate the ritual meaning. For example, in the introductory phase, it embodies the authority of the envoy's ruler: it is held high, focusing on the origin of the envoy's authority while leaving his person on the background. Then the tablet is lowered and the envoy himself starts to act, as a representative of his ruler. Historically, such an interpretation may not be accurate, but it is easy to understand how this kind of meanings could be inscribed in the ritual, with the help of ritual utensils.

To conclude from the three examples—robe, zither, jade tablet—we can see how Confucius is well familiar with the material affordances of these objects and uses them aptly, so that there is no clear distinction between material and metaphoric meanings: he knows how the robe behaves with certain bodily movements and how to express the notion of restraint or appropriateness with it. He also knows how, with sounds, you can communicate something to a person whom you don't see, by implying a notion of *refinement* or "culture" in the very choice of the medium for making sounds, that is, the zither of a refined person. Third, he knows how one can play with the perceived weight of the jade tablet, giving one's performance more *weight*. The meaning in all these cases is realized in the interplay between Confucius' bodily behaviors and certain material objects, with their affordances and cultural significations.

In these examples, the ritual vessels infuse deeper, more intensive, layers of meaning in human life, and a more nuanced engagement in the situation. Confucius' aims may not have aligned with those in their then contemporary surroundings by insisting on ancient rituals, music, and speech (cf. Eno 1990). Yet, their dominant aim was not to blindly parrot existing cultural forms,[19] but to refine oneself. This refinement should reach a point where these forms become natural, as for example, in Confucius' famous saying that at the age of seventy he had finally attained a stage where he could "follow my heart's desires without overstepping the rules of propriety" 七十而從心所欲, 不踰矩 (2.4; Slingerland 2003: 9, translation modified). It is again an *ars contextualis*. This "contextual art" changes according to the context and expresses relevant aspects of it, such as the folds of the robe, the sounds of the zither, and the weight of the jade tablet. Confucius' behavior is embedded in a context, but he also *creates* a context—an all-englobing ritualism—with his behavior, and embeds others into it.

It is interesting to note that in the Western embodiment descriptions very often technical devices are used as examples of extended knowledge (e.g., hammer in the analysis of the "things at hand" by Heidegger 1996: 94–7), rather than music instruments or ritual utensils. The fact that the pool of prototypical examples of extending and displaying knowledge in Confucianism was not technical, but ritual, may be one of the contributing factors that gave the Chinese philosophical tradition an embodied fundament. While the purpose of the technical aspect is to achieve a certain goal that can usually be defined and delimited quite clearly, the aim of ritual behavior is more global and comprehensive: self-cultivation, with the improvement of society, and better harmony with the natural environment. In this framework, there is less motivation to make a clear distinction between humans, as the only rational agents able to maintain and improve technology, against "others," both living beings and inanimate beings. Other participants in ritual behavior can be seen on a more equal basis. Also, it is less compelling to localize cognition in the mind or in the brain of a human agent. A robe, zither and jade tablet are not mere useful "tools" like a hammer; they have more active and important roles in ritual meaning-making, and their use is more indirect and diffuse.

4.7 Other-relation

One of the most important operations of knowledge involves other human beings. It requires the displacement of one's viewpoint and the adoption of other's viewpoint. Confucianism has his own formulation of the "golden rule" (sometimes, in this negative formulation it is called "silver rule"):

Do not impose upon others what you yourself do not desire. (12.2 and 15.24; 126 and 183)

己所不欲，勿施於人。

It is interesting to note that in the first appearance of this maxim, it is presented in the context of a dialogue:

Zigong said, "What I do not wish others to do unto me, I also wish not to do unto others."
The Master said, "Ah, Zigong! That is something quite beyond you." (5.12; 44)
子貢曰：「我不欲人之加諸我也，吾亦欲無加諸人。」子曰：「賜也，非爾所及也。」

If by appearing earlier in the *Analects* we take this citation to be chronologically earlier (cf. Van Norden 2002), then we may detect a formulation of decontextualized laws during the editing process of the *Analects*. The passage from 5.12 concerns just Zigong, but the passages in 12.2 and 15.24 are phrased as a general rule (although a special one, as we shall see soon). In any case, the golden rule is a prerequisite for becoming humane, *ren* 仁. It is both descriptive and prescriptive: on the one hand, humans have a proclivity to empathize with others (as Mencius later explains with his thought experiment that we spontaneously want to help a child who is about to fall into a well, Mencius 2A6). On the other hand, during our lifetime we should expand and develop this capacity. It potentiates self-awareness: I am aware of others being aware of me.[20]

Even if the golden rule is phrased as a general rule, its operation is different from abstract rules of the disembodied kind of knowledge. Its content is empty, because it does not specify what exactly you have to do or not to do, in relation to the other.[21] No concrete action can be established a priori according to the golden rule; it depends on the context as to what you should do. It is not just about decontextualization (distancing from one's perspective and formulation of a general rule) but it also requires a recontextualization (regrounding in another's perspective). Here, the self-relation cannot be fully developed without an other-relation, experiencing others as sources of their own experiential life. Therefore, self-cultivation is not simply an extension of one's subjectivity, but also a displacement into other subjectivities, making the self relationally and contextually constituted (cf. Lai 2006a: 52[22]; Lai 2007; Valmisa 2021).

A subject is decentered in their relations with others, and recontextualized in each of those relations (Thompson 2017). This constitutes humaneness, *ren* 仁, that is arguably the most important Confucian notion (see Lai 2014; Wong 2014: 177–86 for some introduction). It is traditionally etymologized according to the two parts of the character: "human" and "two," a relation between two persons. It forms a "profoundly relational person" (Hall and Ames 1987: 115): the self has little "irreducible core" and is constituted by its different relations, most importantly with relatives, but also with other people and even with plants, animals, stones, and other participants of the environment. Those relations always work in both directions, toward the self and toward the other, and both are, to an extent, always active.

Thomas Kasulis (2002) has called it "intimate" subjectivity that is formed at the intersection of different relations: with other people, but also with other beings, things, environments, and ideas. The configuration of these relations is in each case unique, but this uniqueness is not determined by any definition, essence, or nature. Kasulis distinguishes intimate subjectivity from what he calls "integral" subjectivity, where there is a core of a subject, a personal identity. Here, relations to others come second: first there is a person, and then they enter into relations with different things and environments.

A useful exemplification of this distinction is the difference of chess and *weiqi/go*: in chess, although the strength of each piece is influenced by other pieces, every piece has its own characteristics (how it can move, how it can capture) and it occupies its own field on the chessboard: its domain or property. In *weiqi/go*, a piece has no unique value in itself, and its role is determined by its relations to other pieces and by the patterns it enters into. Symbolically, *weiqi/go* pieces do not occupy squares, but are placed at the intersection of lines (see Deleuze and Guattari 1987: 352–3).

Confucian self-cultivation involves cultivating one's relations. A humane or authoritative person (*ren* 仁) "is one who not only extends his sphere of concern to embrace and serve the interests of his community, but who literally extends himself to take in this community" (Hall and Ames 1987: 122). A small or petty person searches only his own advantage and profit, but a humane or authoritative person takes into consideration others.

This Confucian extension of subjectivity is rather different from Mohist and Legalist extension of subjectivity, which we are going to discuss in the next two chapters. Both of those cases start from a radical decontextualization and strive to construct a new civic morality, one that is different from the contextual and intimate Confucian morality (see below, 5.3 and 6.6). The Confucian recontextualization of selfhood in mostly human relations is in turn different from Daoist reterritorialization of selfhood to a broader set of relations with nonhuman things and events (see below, 8.5); the Daoists ground the self finally in the groundless Dao or the overall transformation of all things (8.7).

4.8 Emotive

In the Confucian framework, emotions are not inherently impediments to knowledge; the aim of self-cultivation is not to rid oneself from emotions but to refine and deepen them. A ritual without emotions is dead, without any real meaning and value. Our being-in-the-world and being-with-others are laden with emotive valences. Some of our strongest emotions are related to fellow human beings, for example, between parents and children, husband and wife, friends, etc. This is what happened after the death of one of Confucius' special relations, his favorite student:

> When Yan Hui passed away, the Master cried for him excessively. The disciples reproved him, saying, "Master, surely you are showing excessive grief!" The Master replied, "Am I showing excessive grief? Well, for whom would I show excessive grief, if not for this man?" (11.10; 114)
> 顏淵死，子哭之慟。從者曰：「子慟矣。」曰：「有慟乎? 非夫人之為慟而誰為！」

Two things are important here. First, Confucius behaves in this way not just in any situation but in this special case, and his teaching to other students is to show how important teacher-student relation is. And second, Confucius does not seek to inhibit himself at the death of his favorite student; that is, he is a sensitive human being who is emotionally affected by this intimate human relation. Feelings come first and ritual comes later (see 3.8; 20).

Emotional engagement is an important prerequisite for rites:

> The Master said, "A man who is not humane—what has he to do with ritual? A man who is not humane—what has he to do with music?" (3.3; 17, translation modified)
> 子曰：「人而不仁，如禮何? 人而不仁，如樂何?」

For the rituals and music to have meaning, one must be a humane person who is able to take the viewpoint of other persons and can share an emotional connection with them. It is better to *not* overdo the external intricacies of a ritual, and in the case of mourning rituals, it is perfectly legitimate to overdo the emotions:

> Lin Fang asked about the roots of ritual. The Master exclaimed, "What a noble question! When it comes to ritual, it is better to be spare than extravagant. When it comes to mourning, it is better to be excessively sorrowful than fastidious." (3.4; 18)

林放問禮之本。子曰：「大哉問! 禮, 與其奢也, 寧儉; 喪, 與其易也, 寧戚。」

Emotions are a basic aspect of life and with the help of rituals one can refine them, thus improving the whole human personality. The goal is not to become detached and impartial, but a humane person is engaged and axiologically oriented: only he is "capable to like and dislike others" (4.3, cf. Virág 2014: 206). Still, an exemplary person is free from certain negative emotions:

> Sima Niu asked about the gentleman. The Master replied, "The gentleman is free of anxiety and fear." "'Free of anxiety and fear'—is that all there is to being a gentleman?" "If you can look inside yourself and find no faults, what cause is there for anxiety or fear?" (12.4; 126)
> 司馬牛問君子。子曰：「君子不憂不懼。」曰：「不憂不懼, 斯謂之君子已乎?」子曰：「內省不疚, 夫何憂何懼?」

These negative emotions of anxiety and fear are not so much discarded by a conscious effort, but rather disappear by themselves when the personality is refined (cf. below, 4.11).

4.9 Implicit

Contextuality of knowledge leads to specific linguistic practices. On the one hand, with words and sentences we can distance from the immediate situation (to plan, to remember, to imagine). On the other hand, this very distancing capacity of language runs the risk of not suiting into the context. Sometimes, it is better to give hints and suggestions than to give too many general explanations, letting the person concerned work out their own understanding based on the particular context.

> The Master said, "I will not open the door for a mind that is not already striving to understand, nor will I provide words to a tongue that is not already struggling to speak. If I hold up one corner of a problem, and the student cannot come back to me with the other three, I will not attempt to instruct him again." (7.8; 66)
> 子曰：「不憤不啟不悱不發舉一隅不以三隅反則不復也。」

The main aim of studying is to attain, on the basis of some actual configuration, its virtual articulation, and on the basis of extensive parts, its intensive tendencies. The teacher gives one "corner," one aspect, and the student has to provide the other, related aspects or "corners." In another fragment, Confucius approvingly says:

> Zigong, you are precisely the kind of person with whom one can begin to discuss the Odes. Informed as to what has gone before, you know what is to come. (1.15; 7)
>
> 賜也始可與言詩已矣! 告諸往而知來者。

As we have also seen above (4.3, 4.6), embodied knowledge is inherently overdetermined and the linguistic strategies that conform to this knowledge must also be greatly implicit, in an intentional attempt to imply in an utterance more than is explicitly said. An attempt to directly phrase an idea would remain inherently partial and poor.

This kind of implicit way of talking was also common in Zhou dynasty diplomacy and high-society interaction, where one could confer coded messages by citing some poem from the *Odes*. In the context of self-cultivation, implicit speech has not only this kind of utilitarian value but becomes a way of self-refinement: the aim is to proffer utterances that fit the situation. This kind of teaching was later taken to the extreme in the encounter dialogues of *chan* Buddhist tradition, where a certain way of (spontaneous, cryptic) speaking and behaving was deemed to express enlightenment. Confucius' acts and words were also taken to express the right Way or *dao*, a certain broader way of existence that one had to unfold for oneself from the cues given.

4.10 Emergent

Contextual and embodied knowledge is essentially emergent. It does not contain universal ideas that are given beforehand but arises in specific contexts between specific interacting agents. We considered the *Analects* 11.22 where Confucius gave different advice to different students according to the situation. This shows that Confucius did not have ready precepts, but that the knowledge of right action emerged out of the specific situation, taking into account the character of the given student. Another example is the following:

> The Master said, "Do I possess wisdom? No, I do not. [For example, recently] a common fellow asked a question of me, and I came up completely empty. But I discussed the problem with him from beginning to end until we finally got to the bottom of it." (9.8; 89)
>
> 子曰:「吾有知乎哉? 無知也。有鄙夫問於我空空如也我叩其兩端而竭焉。」

This is also a model to follow: one should encounter a situation with as few presuppositions as possible, being as "empty" as possible, and so let the articulations of the situation emerge by themselves. The problem with pregiven knowledge is that it makes you "full," so you are not able to see the situation impartially but take some arbitrary familiar aspects of it and bend the whole situation according to some preexisting matrix. Instead, if one is "empty," then one does not impose a ready-made framework on the situation and is able to attend to the nuances of that particular situation and respond adequately.

Even "good" inner dispositions are not the best, because they tend to bias one's understanding of a situation that is always variable and changing (see Seok 2013: 151). Instead, when the mind is empty, then "Like still water, the mind reflects the world without imposing its own dispositions, desires, or expectations. That is, by not holding unto anything, the mind can invite the world to illuminate and guide its understanding of the Way" (Seok 2013: 152). Experimental psychology shows that the influence of situation is overwhelming on our behavior and that it is much more crucial than the force of character. Indeed, the usefulness of the notion of character types or traits has been seriously questioned (Doris 2002).

4.11 Ease and Joy

The thorough ritualization of life should not be understood to mean that Confucius was rigidly formal all the time (against this, cf. above in 4.8, his reaction to Yan Hui's death). We also see that he switched between appropriate effort in official occasions and relaxation in other times (cf. "In his leisure moments, the Master was composed and yet fully at ease," 子之燕居申申如也夭夭如也, 7.4; 65), and that he eventually achieved an ease also in those official occasions. In the words of Confucius' student You Ruo:

> When it comes to the practice of ritual, it is harmonious ease that is to be valued. It is precisely such harmony that makes the Way of the Former Kings so beautiful. If you merely stick rigidly to ritual in all matters, great and small, there will remain that which you cannot accomplish. Yet if you know enough to value harmonious ease but try to attain it without being regulated by the rites, this will not work either. (1.12; 5)
> 禮之用和為貴。先王之道斯為美小大由之。有所不行知和而和不以禮節之亦不可行也。

Ritual practice is necessary, but not sufficient, and one should strive to achieve a "harmonious ease" (he 和).

Affectivity was shown to be an important part of ET (cf. above, 2.6), and it plays an important part also in Confucianism. Based on the work of a leading scholar of Chinese philosophy and Confucianism Kwong-loi Shun 信廣來 (2017), we can distinguish between different kinds of joy and sorrow.

First, there is *xi* 喜 that is transient and depends on external influences. *Xi* 喜 forms a word pair with "anger," *nu* 怒: "*xi* is triggered by things going in accordance with one's wishes, by contrast to *nu*, which is triggered by things going against one's wishes" (Shun 2017: 136, referring to Zhuangzi). Hence, *xi* would be a first form of joy, a passive joy that ensues from a pleasant encounter with some external factor, and *nu* is a passive sorrow resulting from an unpleasant encounter.

Then there is a second kind of joy, that is, *le* 樂.[23] This is an active affect that results from an integration of factors inside the mind, as well as an integration with external factors, so that one would form a "common notion" with them and would understand how their influence exerts. Shun relates *le* with the "harmony/blending" *he* 和. According to Shun, *he* refers to a state of mind where different elements blend together in a mutually supporting and reinforcing manner. These elements or aspects remain differentiated, and they are integrated through that difference itself (in contrast to a homogeneous indistinct mass; cf. below 7.8) (Shun 2017: 139). This gives "joy" a stability and peacefulness.

There is also a certain kind of sorrow and worry related to the *le*—not as a contradiction to the active, integral joy but as an expression of it. This sorrow would not destroy peace of the mind (as says Wang Yangming, cited in Shun 2017: 144), and this worry comes from the intention to pursue integration or harmonization inside the mind and with other beings. (We will treat a similar topic from a slightly different angle below, in 8.7.)

Furthermore, Kwong-loi Shun claims that we should distinguish a third kind of joy, which he calls "idealized state of *le*." It contains a reflective aspect that need not be actualized and may remain latent, but which guarantees one's continuing active stance toward their state of self-cultivation:

> [T]he basis of one's *le* is not just one actually following the Way, but also endorsing it as the direction of one's life. In this sense, the idealized state of *le* is grounded in a certain reflective stance, namely, one's awareness that one is following the Way and one's affirmation of such an orientation. This does not mean that one consciously reflects on one's way of life while in a state of *le*; it means only that, if one were to reflect on it, one would have affirmed the direction of one's life. (Shun 2017: 143)

This "third" kind of joy is usually not thematically made conscious, but it can be. While a "second" kind of joy (like being immersed in a music) precludes worries and sorrows, because one is so immersed that one forgets about them, the third kind of joy endorses the Way and can persist through rightful sorrows (like the loss of a parent), and is accompanied by a "worry" not to drop off *the Way*. The worries that are forgotten in the second kind of joy are related to personal goods, material conditions of life, and appreciation of others (Shun 2017: 145). The worry that one does not forget in the third kind of joy is related to self-cultivation itself, to the maintenance of *he* 和 as the difference and integration of the different aspects of the mind, and difference and integration of oneself and others. The most famous quotation in this respect is 2.4:

> The Master said, "At fifteen, I set my mind upon learning; at thirty, I took my place in society; at forty, I became free of doubts; at fifty, I understood Heaven's Mandate; at sixty, my ear was attuned; and at seventy, I could follow my heart's desires without overstepping the bounds of propriety." (2.4; 9)
> 子曰：　「吾十有五而志于學三十而立四十而不惑五十而知天命六十而耳順七十而從心所欲不踰矩。」

Here Confucius in his old age is finally able to "forget" about the ritual, so that even when he follows his heart's desires, he does not overstep propriety.

This higher joy is directly related to the ability to live out one's years:

> Min Ziqian was attending the Master, standing at his side in a straight and correct manner; [also attending were] Zilu, looking bold and uncompromising, and Ran Qiu and Zigong, both of whom appeared happy and at ease. The Master was pleased, but remarked, "Someone like Zilu will not get to live out his years." (11.13; 115)
> 閔子侍側誾誾如也；子路行行如也；冉有、子貢侃侃如也。子樂。「若由也不得其死然。」

As we mentioned in the case of emotions in general, and also in the case of joy, emotional self-cultivation does not imply suppressing it but rather regulating it:

> Confucius said, "Beneficial types of joy number three, as do harmful types of joy. Taking joy in regulating yourself through the rites and music, in commending the excellence of others, or in possessing many worthy friends—these are the beneficial types of joy. Taking joy in arrogant behavior, idle amusements, or decadent licentiousness—these are the harmful types of joys." (16.5; 194)
> 孔子曰：　「益者三樂，損者三樂。樂節禮樂，樂道人之善，樂多賢友，益矣。樂驕樂，樂佚遊，樂宴樂，損矣。」

An exemplary person harmonizes and blends different elements of the mind and body, and in this process certain pleasures are naturally discarded—those that touch us only partially and superficially.

This leads to a *wuwei* 無為 situation, to effortless action (for discussion on this topic, see Slingerland 2003b; Sarkissian 2010; Wong 2014: 186–90):

> The Master said, "One who rules through the power of Virtue is analogous to the Pole Star: it simply remains in its place and receives the homage of the myriad lesser stars." (2.1; 8)
> 子曰:「為政以德譬如北辰居其所而眾星共之。」

> The Master said, "How majestic! Shun and Yu possessed the entire world and yet had no need to actively manage (*yu* 與) it." (8.18; 84)
> 子曰:「巍巍乎! 舜禹之有天下也而不與焉。」

> The Master said, "Is Shun not an example of someone who ruled by means of *wu-wei*? What did he do? He made himself reverent and took his proper [ritual] position facing south, that is all." (15.5; 175)
> 子曰:「無為而治者其舜也與? 夫何為哉恭己正南面而已矣。」

Mihalyi Csikszentmihalyi's (2014) notion of "flow" may be related to this kind of effortless action. But while he speaks about the feeling of flow in the specific case of an athletic or musical performance, here the feeling arises from life as a whole, most of one's actions being adequate to the context. And as David Wong (2014) argues, this mode of being need not be in contradiction or tension with the supposedly quite arduous process of self-cultivation.

4.12 Self-cultivation

Michael Polanyi (1962) distinguishes between explicit and tacit knowledge, and embodied knowledge is very much about the second. Explicit knowledge can be specified in detail and transmitted over big spatiotemporal gaps, and its understanding can be nearly instantaneous (e.g., if I learn the fact that 1+1=2 or that Zhu Xi 朱熹 was born on October 18, 1130). Embodied knowledge, on the other hand, is to a large extent tacit, as it cannot be adequately specified, and its teaching involves personal example and a process of experience that cannot be shortened at will (see above, 2.10 "Implicitness" and 2.11 "Guidance by example").

Much of Confucius' educational program is precisely about how to convey tacit, implicit, embodied knowledge, and Confucius' personal example was extremely important (see Wong 2014: 175–7). This kind of apprenticeship for students involves personal development and self-cultivation. Ritual, for Confucius, is by itself self-cultivation:

> The Master said, "If you are respectful but lack ritual you will become exasperating; if you are careful but lack ritual you will become timid; if you are courageous but lack ritual you will become unruly; and if you are upright but lack ritual you will become inflexible." (8.2; 78)
> 子曰：「恭而無禮則勞慎而無禮則葸勇而無禮則亂直而無禮則絞。」

The ritual decides whether a characteristic trait (carefulness, courage, respect, uprightness) becomes a weakness or strength. The ritual has an integrating and modulating effect on different aspects of an individual's character. A weakness is something that is separated from the rest of the personality, community, and nature; it is a solidified part of the person. Music and rituals soften and integrate those hard and dispersing aspects. They refine the character as a whole, develop its different aspects, and prevent it from remaining one-sided.[24] This self-cultivation entails both effort and noneffort:

> The Master said, "When native substance overwhelms cultural refinement, the result is a crude rustic. When cultural refinement overwhelms native substance, the result is a foppish pedant. Only when culture and native substance are perfectly mixed and balanced do you have a gentleman." (6.18; 59)
> 子曰：「質勝文則野文勝質則史。文質彬彬然後君子。」

Self-cultivation is not only a conscious striving but it engages the person as a whole, including unconscious strivings. The hopeful outcome is not to artificially create a new character but to cultivate and refine one's natural character. As in Mencius' famous simile: one should not force one's nature like plucking the seedlings in order to "help them grow" (2A2), but rather take care of one's nature and gradually cultivate it, so that it may naturally grow and become more nuanced.

Ritual is a kind of ascesis:

> Yan Hui asked about humaneness. The Master said, "Restraining yourself and returning to the rites constitutes humaneness. If for one day you managed to restrain yourself and return to the rites, in this way you could lead the entire world back to humaneness. The key to achieving humaneness lies within yourself—how could it come from others?" Yan Hui asked, "May I inquire as

to the specifics?" The Master said, "Do not look unless it is in accordance with ritual; do not listen unless it is in accordance with ritual; do not speak unless it is in accordance with ritual; do not move unless it is in accordance with ritual." Yan Hui replied, "Although I am not quick to understand, I ask permission to devote myself to this teaching." (12.1; 125, translation modified)

顏淵問仁。子曰：「克己復禮為仁。一日克己復禮天下歸仁焉。為仁由己而由人乎哉?」顏淵曰：「請問其目。」子曰：「非禮勿視非禮勿聽非禮勿言非禮勿動。」顏淵曰：「回雖不敏請事斯語矣。」

Zizhang asked about getting by in the world. The Master replied, "In your speech, be dutiful and trustworthy, and in your conduct be sincere and respectful. (15.6; 176) […] When you stand, let these thoughts appear before you; when you ride in your carriage, let them appear, leaning on the carriage bar beside you. Only then will you get by in the world." Zizhang then wrote these words on the end of his sash. (15.6; 176 and Eno 2015: 83)

子張問行。子曰：「言忠信行篤敬[…] 立則見其參於前也; 在輿則見其倚於衡也。夫然後行。」子張書諸紳。

Ritual becomes a constant means of self-monitoring, a vehicle for self-development, and also a high ideal. Graceful and meticulous performing of the rites is meant to develop a feeling of flow that one should try to maintain in every life-situation. By perfecting the rites in the narrow sense, Confucius' followers refine their psychosomatic capacities and learn to become "empty," eventually extending this attitude to all of existence. The feeling of ease and joy it is meant to bring must be immediately rewarding, not to mention its generally positive effects on one's social interactions.

4.13 Conclusion

In this section, we have mapped the main topics of ET described in Chapter 2 on to Confucius' *Analects*. In this way it is possible to make sense of parts of the text that otherwise seem without philosophical interest. Interpreted in the light of ET, they draw an image and example of an accomplished person or a sage whose knowledge is embodied, contextual, and enacted. The *Analects* presents interesting examples of ET and also some important nuances. As it was shown in 4.1, this way of presenting takes some load off from particular ritual forms, and emphasizes rather the distribution of "singularities," i.e., of what is important and what is not important. This makes Confucius' tradition adaptive and flexible: it is possible to change certain cultural and ritual forms, while retaining the distribution of singularities, the main value-centers.

This kind of knowledge is emergent; i.e., it is not governed by disembodied and general rules, but arises from the interplay of different participants of the situation. Other people are the most important factors. It gives rise to a relational self (which Thomas Kasulis 2002 distinguishes from an "integral," autonomous self).

In case of extended knowledge, we pointed out the role of ritual implements and how they participate in meaning-making. In the Western context, technical tools are more often brought as an example of extended knowledge. The words and metaphors we use are not innocent, and one may wonder whether ritual implements would present the account of extended knowledge in a somewhat different light.

We also discussed in some detail the importance of emotions, especially joy, based on Kwong-loi Shun's (2017) account of joy in the *Analects*. We distinguished between three kinds of joy. (1) A passive joy (*xi* 喜) that ensues from an encounter with a pleasant thing or event. Its counterpart is a passive anger (*nu* 怒) that is elicited by an encounter with an unpleasant thing or event. (2) A joy (*le* 樂) of a second kind is more stable and active than the previous, passive joy. One is immersed in it (for instance, while listening to music or speaking to a friend) and forgets about all worries and sorrows. (3) A joy (*le* 樂) of a third kind includes a potentiality of reflection and can be expressed by a rightful sorrow while mourning a parent or a justified worry about whether one stays tuned with the Way.

This kind of embodied understanding of cognition and behavior became, in the long run, the basis of the mainstream Chinese philosophy. But there were also important counter-currents that instead strove toward disembodied rules. In the next two chapters we shall discuss two of those currents, first Mohism, and then Legalism (on the example of Han Feizi).

5

Mohist Disembodied Reaction: Mozi 墨子

5.1 Introduction

During the Warring States period (475–221 BC) there emerged different schools proposing a disembodied and decontextualized account of knowledge and advocating for a reliance on general, objective, and explicit rules. The most prominent movements were Mohists, Legalists, and the Disputers (or the School of Names). In this and the next chapter I shall discuss the first two.[1]

Historically, these movements follow from the transition from a Zhou aristocratic and ritualistic feudal society to a Warring States centralized, bureaucratic legal society. The Zhou dynasty was based on the ruler, or "Heaven's son" (*tianzi* 天子), who gave fiefs to his relatives and allies and who retained a religious and ritual supremacy: only he could perform rites to Heaven (the supreme deity) and he conferred ritual distinctions (e.g., tripods) to his subordinates. Throughout the Zhou dynasty, the supreme rulers grew ever weaker economically and militarily, whereas local leaders became stronger and stronger, eventually usurping the ruler's privileges until he became a mere figurehead.[2] During the Warring States period, not only was the power of the king usurped by local vassals but the power of those local leaders was eventually usurped by ministers from powerful high aristocracy, and in turn the power of those new usurpers was usurped by lower strata of nobility (cf. above, 3.3). A centralized state was a way out of this fragmentation, instability, and turmoil.

Major changes that occurred during the fall of the Zhou dynasty were also due to economic reasons: iron was introduced, which made the fabrication of tools and weapons easier; agricultural productivity grew, which meant that population grew; and aristocratic armies were replaced by popular mass conscription armies. Maintaining and supplying those huge armies in turn placed a heavy burden on the economy and logistics of the country, pushing for centralization and requiring also new intellectual tools of management. Warring

States scholars were very conscious of the fact that waging a war was not just a military endeavor, but also economic and administrative. Organizing and providing for a big army poses high requirements on the administrative capacity of a state. To conscript soldiers, provide them with weapons, clothing, transport, and food: this all required good economy and good organization. The incessant wars and military requirements turned the states of the Warring States period into totalitarian war machines where society and economy were subjugated to maintaining armies. This further strengthened the idea of the necessity of unity, strong leadership, and a hierarchical society, as these are necessary for military strength and organization. The most successful of those states was Qin, who finally unified China in 221 BC.

New intellectual movements of the Warring States period advocated a set of values contrary to typical Confucian values: disembodied (vs. embodied), abstract (vs. embedded), theoretical (vs. enacted), ready-made (vs. emergent), cold (vs. emotive), third-person (vs. first and second person), ideal (vs. extended), explicit (vs. implicit), quantitative (vs. intensive), detached (vs. engaged). We shall see aspects of this trend in the following sections, as well as in the next chapter.

This new set of ideas was adapted to new social and political environment that required a more predictable and meritocratic administration, for which more objective intellectual tools were warranted. In anticipation we can say that in the long run a synthesis was made with the new disembodied ideas and methods, and the more moralistic and personal embodied philosophy, that also had to reform itself due to the attacks from the "disembodied" camp, especially the Mohists and Legalists.

In this chapter, we will look deeper into the Mohist ideas, and in the next chapter, those of the Legalists. The Mohists get their name from Mozi 墨子 (c. 470–390 BC) and the eponymous book *Mozi*, which includes both Mozi's ideas and those of his followers. It is probable that Mozi was originally a carpenter, and his followers came mostly from similar social classes: craftsmen, merchants, and soldiers (see Fraser 2020a, §1). This social background seems to have strongly influenced the content of their thought (see Fraser 2020b), so that they were less interested in the rituals and music of the higher classes, and leaned toward technical matters, from which they obtained metaphors for decontextualized knowledge, as we will see later. Also, they were eager to promote meritocracy based on objective criteria, in contrast to the birthright of nobility. Mohist thought is consequentialist and utilitarian, and this gave them an edge in open discussions with their adversaries. They could present clear and palpable arguments. For example, they could argue that doing music is wasteful in many ways and it has bad outcomes, whereas their opponents had to rely on weaker and more vague notions, for example, that it does have indirect good influence on social cohesion and personal morals (indeed, that they had to justify themselves and start reasoning is greatly thanks to Mohists).

The social background of the Mohists and the historical dynamics certainly played a role in that the Mohists strived to develop a decontextualized mode of knowledge. They tried to find disembodied, explicit, and clearly observable criteria for personal and social action: *fa* 法 "norm, model, law," *li* 利 "profit, usefulness," *guiju* 規矩 "compass and square, rule," *quan* 權 "balance, weigh," etc., as well as methodological and explicit ways of proving one's point: *bian* 辯 "argue," *shuo* 說 "explain," etc.³ Let us look at this more closely.

5.2 Disembodied Standards

One of the Mohist's central tenets is the necessity of introducing universal standards or criteria.⁴ Mozi likes to use comparisons from handicraft, especially with carpenter's tools (it is possible that he himself had an experience in this, like Socrates in stonemasonry):

> Master Mo Zi said: "Those who work in the world cannot do so without standards and rules. No-one has ever been able to accomplish anything without standards and rules. Even those officers who are generals and ministers all have standards. Even the hundred craftsmen in doing their work all have standards too. The hundred craftsmen make what is square with a square, make what is round with compasses, establish what is straight with ink line, determine the horizontal with a water level, and the vertical with a plumb line. Whether skilled or unskilled, craftsmen all take these five things as standards. Skilled craftsmen are able to comply with these standards whilst unskilled craftsmen, even if they are unable to comply with them, will still surpass themselves if they follow them in their work. Thus the hundred craftsmen all have standards with which to measure their work." (MZ 1.4 "On Standards and Rules" 法儀, Johnston 2010: 24–5, translation modified)
>
> 子墨子曰：「天下從事者，不可以無法儀，無法儀而其事能成者無有也。雖至士之為將相者，皆有法，雖至百工從事者，亦皆有法。百工為方以矩，為圓以規，直以繩，［衡以水，］正以縣。無巧工、不巧工，皆以此五者為法。巧者能中之，不巧者雖不能中，放依以從事，猶逾己。故百工從事，皆有法所度。」⁵

In order to achieve good results in any activity, for Mozi and his followers, we have to rely on external and uniform standards and rules, just as carpenters use square, compass, ink lines, water levels, and plumb lines. The use of these tools does require a modicum of dexterity, but with their help even a beginner can surpass a master carpenter if the latter is deprived of those tools. According to this metaphor, knowledge does maintain some contextuality (different tools are to be used, whether you measure a square or a circle, determine a horizontal or vertical plane), but it is radically reduced to only a handful of discrete and clearly distinguished types: by hand, you may draw whatever line you like, but tools prescribe a certain type of line: straight, rectangular, circular, horizontal, vertical, and perhaps some others. Knowledge becomes a knowledge of these types (what kinds there are of them, where to use them). Cognition is decontextualized and "deterritorialized"; it relies on an external standard that is more distanced from the immediate context or "territory." Not only, for example, hand, drawing tool, and wood but hand, drawing tool, L-square, and wood. The L-square guides the hand, hand relies on it, it does not need to be very keen on the surface and muscular modifications, but it can simply apply force from a certain angle, and rely on the L-square for the exact direction.

Yet it is interesting to note that the tools as standards mentioned by Mozi are not ready-made intellectual *forms*. They are not like platonic ideas, for example (those duplicates in mind of the physical things), but they rather give the *genetic* or generative principles of a form, i.e., directions how to obtain it.[6] In this respect, consider two different definitions of a circle: the static one, "a circle is a set of points in a plane that are at an equal distance from a given point, the center," and a genetic one, "a circle is traced out by a point that moves so that its distance from a given, fixed point is constant." Although the contingencies of the agent and circumstances become less urgent with tools-standards (nearly anyone can use an L-square), there remains the logical time of constructing the geometrical form with the indicated tool ("take a compass and draw a circle"), so that it is not so completely detached from the context and the "sensible world" as a platonic idea. It is not simply just there, and it has not to be simply recalled, but it has to be constructed, there is some intrinsic construction necessary in those standards.

The tools-as-standards are also useful for verification:

> Now a wheelwright takes hold of his compasses in order to measure whether things in the world are round or not, saying: "What accords with my compasses is called round and what does not accord with my compasses is called not round." In this way the roundness or non-roundness of all things can be ascertained and

known. Why is this so? It is because the standard for roundness is clear. (MZ 7.2, "Will of Heaven 2" 天志中, Johnston 2010: 259, translation slightly modified)

今夫輪人操其規，將以量度天下之圜與不圜也，曰：中吾規者謂之圜，不中吾規者謂之不圜。是以圜與不圜，皆可得而知也。此其故何？ 則圜法明也。

As we see, compasses and squares are not only external standards or tools to create circular and square shapes but also criteria or tools to judge the circularity and squareness of existing shapes. They are both tools of construction *and* verification. And just as a compass constructs a circle progressively, when we use it for verification, this process is progressive as well: we have to follow the borders of an existing form with the compass and see whether there are significant discrepancies toward the interior or exterior. These construction and evaluation processes also admit quantification; they are measurements (in effect, in both citations the word for "measure," *du* 度 is used). Tools help show *how much* a shape deviates from the required circular or rectangular form, or horizontal or vertical position. Therefore, Mohist standards can be quantified more easily than platonic ideas, which remain more qualitative.

Although the Later Mohists—and most probably already Mozi himself—were interested in technical and scientific matters (several chapters were dedicated to military defense techniques; the Mohist "Canons"[7] define time, space, point, etc.), the main application of those standards in the *Mozi* is social, through a reference to "Heaven's will" (*tianzhi* 天志) or "Heaven's intention" (*tianzhiyi* 天之意). Our previous citation is followed by this argumentation:

> Thus Master Mo Zi's having Heaven's intention is [for this]: Above to estimate the conduct of government by the kings, dukes and great officers of the world, and below to measure the world's ten thousand people, taking their writings as expressing what they are saying.
>
> 故子墨子之有天之意也，上將以度天下之王公大人之為刑政也，下將以量天下之萬民為文學出言談也。

If their conduct, speech, and government agree with Heaven's intention, they can be deemed good; otherwise they are bad. Following Heaven's intention is the "standard of appropriateness" (*yi zhi fa* 義之法) and the basis of humaneness.

Heaven's intention or will is a standard for social and individual action in the same way as a tool gives standards in carpenter's working process. Heaven's intention or will is conceived as a similar decontextualized tool as a compass. It gives a standard to construct and evaluate conduct, speech, and government. Things are valued as good if they accord with Heaven's intention of will, and bad if they do not.

5.3 Extension of Subjectivity: All-Inclusive Care

What is Heaven's intention or will?

> Heaven is broad and unselfish in its actions, and is generous in its bestowing without considering itself virtuous. Its radiance is enduring and does not decay. Therefore, the sage kings took it as the standard. […] This being so, what does Heaven desire, what does Heaven abhor? Undoubtedly what Heaven desires is that there be mutual love and mutual benefit among people. What it does not desire is that there be mutual hatred and mutual harm among people. How do we know that Heaven desires mutual love and mutual benefit among people and does not desire mutual hatred and mutual harm among people? Because it is universal in loving them and universal in benefiting them. How do we know that Heaven is universal in loving them and universal in benefiting them? Because it is universal in possessing them and universal in feeding them. (MZ 1.4, "On Standards and Rules" 法儀, Johnston 2010: 27)
>
> 天之行廣而無私，其施厚而不德，其明久而不衰，故聖王法之。[…] 然而天何欲何惡者也？天必欲人之相愛相利，而不欲人之相惡相賊也。奚以知天之欲人之相愛相利，而不欲人之相惡相賊也？以其兼而愛之，兼而利之也。奚以知天兼而愛之，兼而利之也？以其兼而有之，兼而食之也。

Heaven itself universally loves and benefits people. And it wants people to do the same. The ethical goal of such a conception is, of course, to promote human solidarity and mutual empathy, especially toward those more vulnerable (old, young, weak, ill, etc.). It is interesting to compare this Mohist principle of all-encompassing love or care (*jian'ai* 兼愛) with Confucian Golden Rule (see above, in 4.7) that also promotes empathy. The Confucian Golden Rule is empty in its form; it just gives the mechanism how to empathize with others but does not prescribe what to do in each situation or what principle to follow—the content must emerge from the context and real-time interactions and guidelines formed according to the requirements of the situation. The Mohist principle or standard, on the other hand, does have a positive content and prescriptive function, as determined by the "benefit" or "usefulness" (*li* 利). To love all-encompassingly is to want to benefit. There are some particular cases (most notably, robbers) where the benefit of the whole of the society might weigh up the benefit of the individual (Mozi favors their punishment and even execution), but in most cases the Mohists conceive social and individual benefit to go hand in hand. This general utilitarian principle is Mohists' core idea and with its help they argue against offensive warfare (Chs. 17–19), luxury (Chs. 20–5 and 32–4), fatalism

(Chs. 35–7), and for the promotion of belief in ghosts (Chs. 29–31). The principle of benefit or usefulness as a formal rule is to a large extent decontextualized, disembedded: if you start from the idea that people in general strive to live, enjoy, and avoid death and suffering, then offensive warfare can be denounced a priori. And luxury can be decried for the same reason: if some people consume too many resources, others would be deprived.[8]

From Confucian viewpoint, the Mohist standard of utility is too blunt a tool. First, what counts as benefit depends very much on the context. Different people in different contexts need different things. The "benefit" of an overly eager and an overly passive student is different: you need to hold back one and stimulate the other. Second, there are different kinds of benefit or utility: if a person in need receives material support but is left without emotional support, the person may still not be happy. Humans do not live "by bread alone." Therefore, Confucians were more willing to allocate resources on some refined aspects of the culture like music and rituals that supposedly give a "higher," more diffuse, and refined benefit; or rather, they would like to eschew the notion of "benefit" altogether, since it has strong materialistic connotations, and rather emphasize more mutualistic interactions where it may not be easy to tell apart who benefits whom and what is exactly their benefit (notably, think of parent-child relation).

Again, Mohists can show that this forgoing of objective criteria easily leads to all kinds of abuse by the powerful, and that the distinction of levels of utility easily leads to an overemphasis on some refined aspects of culture: the privileged few enjoy refined music and dance performances with super-expensive sets of bronze bells, while a great part of the population may be starving.

5.4 Meritocracy

Mozi held an idea of society as hierarchical (see the "Identification with the Superior" chapters, *Mozi* 11–13), and his meritocratic views serve the goal to disembody and decontextualize human skills. First, the institution of this kind of society is based on a myth somewhat similar to Thomas Hobbes' account of the end of natural state and the establishment of social contract.

> In ancient times, when Heaven first gave rise to people, there were not yet leaders of government and each person was his own master. If each person was his own master, then for one person there was one principle, for ten people ten principles, for a hundred people a hundred principles, for a thousand people a thousand principles and so on up to the point where the great number of people could

not be counted. At this time, then, what were termed principles also could not be counted. This meant that everyone affirmed their own principles and denied the principles of others, with the result that what was weighty was contentious and what was trivial was [also] contentious.⁹ (MZ 3.3 "Identification with the Superior III" 上同下, Johnston 2010: 119)

> 古者，天之始生民，未有正長也，百姓為人。若茍百姓為人，是一人一義，十人十義，百人百義，千人千義，逮至人之眾不可勝計也，則其所謂義者，亦不可勝計。此皆是其義，而非人之義，是以厚者有鬥，而薄者有爭。

The main problem with the ancient times, according to Mozi, was namely the plurality of standards or principles (*yi* 儀/義). The problem was not directly in people's actions and behaviors toward one another but in the incompatibility of the *principles* of their actions and behavior. This created a latent enmity and disagreement. Most importantly, with such incompatibility, society could not reach its full potential, as material and intellectual resources were left unused:

> [E]ach person took his own principle to be right and the principles of others to be wrong, so there was mutual disagreement. Within, amongst fathers and sons, and older and younger brothers, there was resentment and enmity since all were quite disparate in their minds and were unable to reach mutual accord. As a result, any surplus strength was set aside and not used in mutual toil, excellent doctrines were kept secret and not used in mutual teaching, and surplus materials rotted and decayed and were not used for mutual distribution. The disorder of the world was comparable to that amongst birds and beasts. (MZ 3.2 "Identification with the Superior II" 上同中, Johnston 2010: 99)
>
> 以人是其義，而非人之義，故相交非也。內之父子兄弟作怨讎，皆有離散之心，不能相和合。至乎舍餘力不以相勞，隱匿良道不以相教，腐臭餘財不以相分，天下之亂也，至如禽獸然。

To end this situation, the most capable was selected as ruler:

> This resulted in the world's desire to unify the principles of the world, so there was the selection of one who was worthy, and he was established as the Son of Heaven. (MZ 3.3 "Identification with the Superior III" 上同下, Johnston 2010: 119)
>
> 是故天下之欲同一天下之義也，是故選擇賢者，立為天子。

And the emperor or "Heaven's son" in turn chose the next worthy persons as his aids, and these in turn selected capable men to aid them, all the way down to local administration. In turn, this mythological description of the beginning of monarchy and hierarchy served as a prescriptive account of how things should be in the present society. Historically, this account can be seen as a reflection of the contemporary change from an earlier aristocratic and decentralized society to a more bureaucratized and centralized state that evolved during the Warring States period.[10] Although the Mohist description gives the impression of a rather oppressive totalitarian state,[11] this idea had important emancipative potential. In a Mohist kind of system, it is specifically the measurable efficiency of an individual's performance in benefiting the state that was important. It was not the whole of the character that mattered but only the part of the person that was relevant to the task. This kind of measurement of particular skills would not be possible in a completely consistent contextualism because, first, one would always have to evaluate the whole person and, second, there would be no clear control of the one who evaluates. Without clear objective standards for evaluation, the judgment will easily depend on the arbitrary decision of the person in power. Of course, a complete contextualism never exists and there are always some more or less externalized standards (ritual norms, common agreement, etc.).

But for a Mohist ruler there would be clear and objective standards to be respected. They are given by the Heaven itself that is the ultimate superior and to whom the ruler or "Heaven's son" (*tianzi* 天子) is responsible.[12] The Mohists' intention was *also* to subject the ruler to clear and objective standards (this idea was developed by the Legalists, as we shall see in the next chapter). In principle, this system allowed greater social mobility, as developing certain skills allowed for the possibility of social ascension. The whole of society in this way depended less on the personal characteristics of the individual who filled the office, and more on the description of the tasks of her office and the evaluation of her performance according to it.

5.5 Explicitness

The Mohist quest for explicit rules led to spectacular development that was codified in the so-called Neo-Mohist Canons (*Mozi*, books 40–5), written probably between late fourth and mid-third century BC. In this late development of Mohism, explicit definitions and explanations are given for some key terms of Mohism and redefinitions of some Confucian ones. Take the following redefinition of the Confucian appropriateness *yi* 義:[13]

> C: To be *yi* (righteous/dutiful/moral) is to benefit.
> E: In intent, he takes the whole world as his field; in ability, he is able to benefit it. He is not necessarily employed.
> (A 8, Graham 1976: 271)
> 義, 利也。
> 義: 志以天下為芬, 而能能利之, 不必用。

Compare it with the following statement from Confucius' *Analects*:

> The Master said, "The exemplary person understands rightness, whereas the petty person understands profit." (Slingerland 2003: 35, tr. mod.)
> 子曰:「君子喻於義, 小人喻於利。」

We can notice immediately that the Mohist definition opposes the Confucian one: Confucius banishes the notion of profit from appropriateness, but the Mohists define the latter through benefit (and due to the difference of value, the translation of the same term, *li* 利, in the two cases is different: either profit or benefit). Also, the Mohist definition is more abstract, treating the defined terms in themselves, while the Confucian presentation goes through the persons that embody those terms (an exemplary and a petty person). The Mohists give a straightforward definition (of the type "A is B"), while Confucius conveys his message through a parallel sentence ("A is *x*; B is *y*"), where from wider context or cultural knowledge, we should understand A as opposed to B and, in a parallel fashion *x* to *y*.

Let us add two more examples of Mohist definitions, those for the key Mohist notions of benefit and standard:

> C: *Li* (benefit) is what one is pleased to get.
> E: If you are pleased to get this one, this is the beneficial one, and the harmful one is not this one.
> (A26, Graham 1976: 282)
> 利, 所得而喜也。
> 利: 得是而喜, 則是利也。其害也, 非是也。
> C: The *fa* (standard) is that in being like which something is so.
> E: The idea, the compasses, a circle, all three may serve as standard.
> (A 70, Graham 1976: 316)
> 法, 所若而然也。
> 法: 意、規、員三也, 俱可以為法。

Quite unusually for early Chinese philosophy, the neo-Mohists present a list of definitions (of which the above examples should give some idea). Those definitions tend to be less embodied and less contextualized. To put it in another way, Mohist definitions tend to be more conceptual and universal. The meaning in those definitions depends less on the person who pronounces them or on the context where they are uttered: compare the above definitions to the description of Confucius' purported behavior, described in book 10 of the *Analects*, which we discussed above. The question for Mohists is not to imitate Mo Di's behavior and manner of speech, or if so, then the goal is to be as *detached* from one's person, from one's egoistic desires and preferences as possible, to be as universalistic as possible.

The Mohist definitions carry more of their own semantic content in themselves and in this sense they are more "full." As a single statement, they lose in *significance* (a more implicit statement, by Confucius, for instance, can have nearly infinite significance), but taken collectively they win in *signification*, creating a net of concepts with explicit meanings. They also win in autonomy, exactly because they are more distanced from particular contexts. Due to this, they are more easily manageable and more quickly learned (and do not need so much "guidance by example," cf. above, 2.11 and 4.12). On the Confucian hand, to understand the meaning of the notion of appropriateness, it is necessary to cultivate oneself for years. On the Mohist hand, it is possible, in principle, to understand the meaning of the Mohist definition of appropriateness more or less instantly. Whether something is appropriate or not should be evident from the application of the standard of usefulness, and while this application may need some training, it is much easier, since it relies more on palpable, explicit criteria. For example, in principle, you could verify whether the calorie intake of the population did rise after some appropriate policy was implemented, and measure, by how much.

One of the characteristics of an embodied knowledge is that the processes involved in its development cannot be easily compressed and need to be played out in their whole duration. A disembodied knowledge, in contrast, is more easily compressed in temporal duration, so that big amounts of knowledge can be acquired in a relatively small amount of time. You master the multiplication table much quicker than the true meaning of filial piety or appropriateness. This compression is a necessity if some specialized and uniform technical knowledge is to be transmitted.

It is both an advantage and a disadvantage in transmitting knowledge that disembodied knowledge is not closely related to the person emitting it. Insofar as a math teacher teaches math well, it is of little importance if they gamble or smoke in their leisure time. In the case of a knowledge that is as highly embodied as that of Confucius, those personal characteristics are extremely important. Perhaps it is not a coincidence that we know relatively much about Confucius, but very little about Mozi (who is closer to us in time). While there may be external reasons for it (lack of interest by the elites or even suppression), it is also motivated by Mozi's teaching itself: because he intended to profess a general and universal teaching, his particular life events were not so important (while in Confucianism, on the contrary, general ritual manuals may have been turned into accounts of Confucius' person).

Generally speaking, the merit of decontextualization in education is that both the teacher and the student are to a certain extent emancipated from each other and from particular contexts, so that more information can be passed on and teacher exerts less mind control over the students. Multiplication tables speak for themselves. One need not obey the teachers as such, but accept the truths they convey. The disadvantage is that the significance of that information decreases, it tends to remain "external," and it doesn't concern the person "deep inside."[14] Every pedagogical system involves both aspects, and so must have done Mohist and Confucian systems, but inherently they tend toward divergent strategies.

Together with defining terms, the Mohists tried to order argumentation or disputation (see Fraser 2015a):

> C: *Bian* (disputation) is contending over claims which are the converse of each other. Winning in disputation is fitting the fact.
> E: One calling it an "ox" and the other "non-ox" is "contending over claims which are the converse of each other". Such being the case they do not both fit the fact; and if they do not both fit, necessarily one of them does not fit. Not like fitting "dog".
> (A74, Graham 1976: 318)
> 辯，爭彼也。辯勝，當也。(經上)
> 辯: 或謂之牛，或謂之非牛，是爭彼也。是不俱當。不俱當，必或不當，不若當犬。
> (經說上)
>
> C. To say that there is no winner in disputation necessarily does not fit the fact. Explained by: disputation.
> E. The things that something is called are either the same or different. In a case where they are the same, one man calling it a "whelp" and the other man a "dog", or where they are different one calling it an "ox" and the other a "horse", and neither winning, is failure to engage in disputation. In "disputation", one says it is this and the other that it is not, and the one who fits the fact is the winner. (B 35, Graham 1976: 402–3)

謂辯無勝, 必不當。說在辯。(經說下)
謂:「所謂非同也, 則異也。同則或謂之狗, 其或謂之犬也; 異則或謂之牛, 牛或謂之馬也。俱無勝。」是不辯也。辯也者, 或謂之是, 或謂之非, 當者勝也。

The crux of a discussion is driven to the most clear-cut situation possible, i.e., determining which one of the contradictory claims fits the fact. A disputation in the strict Mohist sense is only when there are contradictory claims of the type: A or not-A, so that one of the claims necessarily has to be "this" or true (*shi* 是) and the other one "not-this" or false (*fei* 非). In a disputation, one says it is this and the other that it is not, and "necessarily one of them does not fit" (A 74, Graham 1976: 318). We can discuss whether *x* is an ox or not-ox, but not whether *x* is an ox or a horse (because it might be neither of the two).

The requisite of mutually exclusive claims makes the discussion as explicit as possible: first, a clear opposition of two converse claims, and then, an equally clear outcome where one of the claims fits and the other does not. While more embodied-type discussion allows lots of different degrees of persuasiveness and lots of different possible positions, here in the disembodied-type discussion the situation of continuous degrees of truthfulness (the "analog" mode) is replaced by a situation with discrete options for truth and falsity (the "digital" mode: indeed, just two, like in the modern computers, 0 or 1).

The Later Mohists also gave attention to methodology and consider the forms of reasoning and discussion:

> "Analogy" (*pi*): "Bringing up other things and using them to clarify it."
> "Parallelizing" (*mou*): "Comparing expressions and jointly proceeding."
> "Pulling" (*yuan*): "Saying, 'You are so, how is it that I alone cannot be so?'"
> "Pushing" (*tui*): "On the grounds that what they don't accept is the same as what they do accept, propose it." (cf. Graham 1976: 483; Robins 2010: 250; NO 11, Fraser 2015a, section 7.2)
> 辟也者, 舉他物而以明之也。
> 侔也者, 比辭而俱行也。
> 援也者, 曰「子然, 我奚獨不可以然也?」
> 推也者, 以其所不取之同於其所取者, 予之也。

As Chris Fraser argues, it does not lead to a formal logic of a priori reasoning like in the Aristotelian syllogisms. The Mohist logic is all about analogical reasoning, and in fact the four forms are brought out mainly as possible sources of confusion and bad reasoning that arise from merely formal similarities, disregarding the actual content of the terms involved. It is interesting to note that while the Mohists go far into disembodying and decontextualizing their thought, they refuse to go into a completely mechanical form of reasoning that would be (at least in appearance) wholly independent of any context and persons, like the syllogisms.[15]

5.6 Conclusion

In the *Mozi* we see that theories of disembodied and decontextualized knowledge were present in China. One of their main motives was the emancipating potential of this kind of knowledge: as it is made explicit and disembodied, no one could appeal in discussion to some implicit contextual knowledge but had to *explain* themselves. It was perhaps also related to the sociological background of the two main figures: Confucius was a descendant of nobility (albeit impoverished); Mo Di was a member of an emergent class of craftsmen and specialists. As we tried to show above, Mozi developed a theory of knowledge much in contrast to Confucius' embodied account. Knowledge should have explicit and objective criteria, disembodied from the person who proffers them, not implicit in the action but separated from it, belonging to an autonomous realm of knowledge. Emotions have no place in this kind of argumentation, for which the Mohists devised certain rules and methods.

Mohist ideas were eventually used to construct a totalitarian Legalist state apparatus that unified China in 221 BC. This relation to the harsh Legalist state government earned both Mohism and Legalism a bad reputation in the subsequent Chinese tradition, but without Mohist emancipatory and universalizing impetus perhaps Chinese philosophy would not have acquired the autonomy and diversity it developed over the centuries. And of course, Mohist ideas directly or indirectly influenced the whole Chinese tradition. Their disembodied account of knowledge did not prevail, but parts of it were incorporated into other schools.

6

Legalist Disembodied Reaction: Han Feizi 韓非子

6.1 Introduction

Another movement toward disembodied knowledge was what has been grouped under the term "legalism" (*fajia* 法家).

Several strains of statecraft theories were grouped under this label, but the term acquired bad currency after the harsh reign of Qin dynasty (221–206 BC) that unified China in 221 BC and that had used Legalist ideas. Actually, some of its early proponents may have had emancipatory ideas and worked against the powerful. Such was reputedly Deng Xi 鄧析 (*c.* 545–501 BC), who is said to have helped people to defend their case in court for a modest remuneration: a coat for a big case and jacket and trousers for a small one. People "learnt litigation" (*xue song* 學訟) from him[1] (*Lüshi chun qiu* 18.4[2]).

Deng Xi is also said to have written a code of law on bamboo strips. This "Bamboo Law" has not survived, but the very material on which it was written is telling. Formerly certain decrees were cast in bronze, inscribed on the ding-cauldrons. This is obviously very costly and sets limits both on the length of the text and on the ease of issuing and changing it. Bamboo texts, on the other hand, were common and cheap; they could be produced, copied, corrected, and edited easily. It did not have official status in Deng's lifetime but was adopted later. In any case it means that he did consider it important for the society to have an explicit code of law that was easily accessible. This code of law could be used by people against the whims of the powerful. But representatives of the establishment saw disembodied rules to be morally and socially dangerous: a reference to an objective code of law could encourage common people to overstep their prescribed position and thus sow disorder.

That is exactly the opposite of what the Legalists themselves thought to be the case. To Legalists, a ruler must put forth and adhere to explicit laws and norms. The ruler should not rely on Confucian humaneness and righteousness, because if he, out of compassion, is lenient and cancels a punishment or if he, out of sudden rage, makes an unlawful punishment, he would create exceptions to the implementation of laws, which would jeopardize his whole system of government. To Legalists, it is precisely morality that creates disorder, i.e., if morality is allowed to overrule the established laws. Also, the ruler cannot just rely on the words of his subordinates but must receive reports about the economy and society (objective book-keeping is inevitable in a large society), as well as rate the performance of his ministers objectively, comparing the task that they have taken upon themselves with the outcome of their activity.

The following treatment of Legalism is based mainly on the works of Han Feizi 韓非子 (*c.* 280–*c.* 233 BC), who synthesized various strands of Legalist thought.

6.2 Laws (*fa* 法)

One of the key targets of Legalist criticism are exactly the supposed embodied virtues required for ruler and civil servants by the Confucians. A society has to be ruled by laws, norms, rules, or models (that all translate the word *fa* 法) that do not rely on embodiment but constitute a legal and administrative system that underpins society. Han Feizi says:[3]

> Moreover, Yao and Shun[4] as well as Jie and Zhou[5] appear once in a thousand generations; whereas the opposite types of men are born shoulder to shoulder and on the heels of one another. As a matter of fact, most rulers in the world form a continuous line of average men. It is for the average rulers that I speak about *shi* [propensity, authority, position]. The average rulers neither come up to the worthiness of Yao and Shun nor reach down to the wickedness of Jie and Zhou. If they uphold the law and make use of their august position, order obtains; if they discard the law and desert their august position, chaos prevails. Now suppose you discard the position and act contrary to the law and wait for Yao and Shun to appear and suppose order obtains after the arrival of Yao and Shun, then order will obtain in one out of one thousand generations of continuous chaos. Suppose you uphold the law and make use of the august position and wait for Jie and Zhou to appear and suppose chaos prevails after the arrival of Jie and Zhou, then chaos will prevail in one out of one thousand generations of continuous order. To be sure, one generation of chaos out of one thousand generations of order and one generation of order out of one thousand generations of chaos are as different from each other as steed-riders driving in

opposite directions are far apart from each other. (Ch. 40, 2: 204–5)

且夫堯、舜、桀、紂千世而一出，是比肩隨踵而生也。世之治者不絕於中，吾所以為言勢者，中也。中者，上不及堯、舜，而下亦不為桀、紂。抱法處勢則治，背法去勢則亂。今廢勢背法而待堯、舜，堯、舜至乃治，是千世亂而一治也。抱法處勢而待桀、紂，桀、紂至乃亂，是千世治而一亂也。且夫治千而亂一，與治一而亂千也，是猶乘驥、駬而分馳也，相去亦遠矣。

Han Fei concedes here that an extraordinarily virtuous person may perhaps obtain good results in government and an extremely wicked person may ruin it. But extremes are rare and so only seldom does one have so virtuous or wicked rulers. But an average person with the help of law maintains his position and creates order, whereas without them he will lose his position and chaos will ensue. So even supposing that a very wicked person may manage to ruin a good state mechanism, and a very virtuous person may be able to rule the state without laws, the result will still be chaos in 999 cases out of 1000. But with the help of laws, there will be order in just as many cases. So, the main focus in designing a state system should not be on the character of the person who rules but on the system itself.

In fact, Han Feizi is making a concession here, for he believes that even Yao and Shun could not govern, at least in the time of Han Feizi (when states had become very large and complex), without explicit laws, so that without laws there would actually be chaos in 1000 cases out of 1000:

> Indeed, when you abandon the tools of stretching and bending and give up the scales of weights and measures, then though you try to make Xi Zhong construct a carriage, he would not be able to finish even a single wheel. Similarly, without the promise of reward and the threat of penalty, and casting the position out of use and giving up the law, then even if Yao and Shun preached from door to door and explained to everybody the gospel of political order, they could not even govern three families. Verily, that *shi* [propensity, authority, position] is worth employing, is evident. To say that it is necessary to depend upon worthiness is not true. (Ch. 40, 2: 206)

夫棄隱栝之法，去度量之數，使奚仲為車，不能成一輪。無慶賞之勸，刑罰之威，釋勢委法，堯、舜戶說而人辯之，不能治三家。夫勢之足用亦明矣，而曰必待賢則亦不然矣。

Thus legal standard and personal inclination are in conflict. Without any fixed standard, however, even ten Yellow Emperors would not be able to rule. (Ch. 49, Liao 1939: 285).

法、趣、上、下，四相反也，而無所定，雖有十黃帝，不能治也。

The question Han Feizi wants to tackle is clear—in case of a mediocre monarch, how may we avoid chaos? Han Feizi's answer—rule by law (if not rule *of* law). There must be a set of explicit rules and laws, and the ruler must enforce them. This requires a centralized state under a ruler's full authority who is able to enforce the laws for every subject. Han Feizi does not design explicit institutions (e.g., a written constitution, independent courts) to check the ruler. There is no authority above or next to the ruler. But then what guards against the absolute monarch indulging in all of their desires and committing any crime they want? Han Feizi's system is designed to absorb some irregularities by the rulers, but if they become really wicked as Jie or Zhou, the system will break up and they will lose power and perhaps even their life due to rebellion, invasion, or plotting. Han Feizi does not expect lawful behavior from the internal high moral standards of the ruler, but the ruler is forced to lawful behavior by an external force, by the constraints of the state system itself. They must prescribe and enforce explicit laws, and also abide by these laws themselves; they must also heed to Han Feizi's recommendations for wielding power (*erbing* 二柄 or the two handles of rewards and punishments, *wuwei* 無爲 or refraining from activity, etc.). Otherwise, they will lose power. If wicked rulers do not correct themselves, the system itself will correct them. Of course, this correction will be violent, and this is a shortcoming in Han Feizi's system: that he does not foresee a regular, lawful, and peaceful transfer of power in case of an inadequate ruler.

With explicit standards and laws, even a mediocre ruler should be able to govern successfully:

> Therefore, the ruler, even though not worthy, becomes the master of the worthies; and, even though not wise, becomes the corrector of the wise men. (Ch. 5, 1: 32)
> 是故不賢而為賢者師, 不智而為智者正。

It is because they do not have to rely on their own limited perceptual and intellectual capacities, but they will make other people perceive, think, and act for them:

> Certainly for this reason, though the lord of men neither teaches the officials with his own mouth nor finds the culprits and ruffians with his own eyes, yet the state is always orderly. The lord of men does not have to possess such eyes as those of Li Lou in order to be bright, nor does he have to possess such ears as those of Musician Kuang in order to be acute. If he does not trust to measures but relies on his eyes alone for his brightness, then what he sees will be little. For it is not the technique to avoid delusion. If he does not count on his august position but relies on his own ears alone for his acuteness, then what he hears

will be little enough. For it is not the way to avoid deception. The intelligent sovereign would make All-under-Heaven inevitably see and hear on his behalf. Therefore, though his person is confined in the innermost court, his brightness illumines everything within the four seas. (Ch. 14, 1: 121–2)

夫是以人主雖不口教百官，不目索姦衺，而國已治矣。人主者，非目若离婁乃為明也，非耳若師曠乃為聰也。目必不任其數，而待目以為明，所見者少矣，非不弊之術也。耳必不(固)〔因〕其勢，而待耳以為聰，所聞者寡矣，非不欺之道也。明主者，使天下不得不為己視，天下不得不為己聽。故身在深宮之中而明照四海之內。

If the rulers make others work for them, then nobody will be able to deceive. In this way the position of the ruler is dissociated from the person who fills it. It is the "earthworm riding the clouds" (see Ch. 40). The ruler should use objective measures or "numbers" (*shu* 數) and the power of the position (*shi* 勢). With numbers and measures, the ruler is able to avoid delusion (*bi* 弊) about the reality and the state of affairs; and with the correct use of the position, they are able to avoid deception (*qi* 欺) by cunning ministers. This would enable any person, even a mediocre one with limited acuteness and intellect, to give orders and rule successfully—as long as he remains faithful to the system itself (abiding by the law, wielding the handles of power, avoiding preferences). In fact, Han Feizi argues that the ruler should refrain from micromanagement.

> If the ruler has to exert any special skill of his own, it means that affairs are not going right. If he is conceited and fond of displaying his ability, he will be deceived by the inferiors. (Ch. 8, 1: 53)
> 上有所長,事乃不方。矜而好能,下之所欺

If the ruler starts to manage affairs too closely, he will inevitably show his special skills and preferences. But in this way he has acquired a definite form and the sycophants can start to make use of this knowledge, trying to please the ruler from a particular angle, pretending to exhibit the same preferences (cf. below, 6.5).

We cannot wait for 999 generations for a benevolent ruler, and similarly the ruler cannot depend on only exceptional officials. Most of them are inevitably average men:

> Now there are not more than ten truly merciful and faithful men in this country, whereas there are hundreds of official posts. So, if only merciful and faithful men are selected for public service, the candidates will not be sufficient for filling all the official posts. (Ch 49, 2: 289)
> 今貞信之士不盈於十，而境內之官以百數，必任貞信之士，則人不足官。

By disentangling the positions of the ruler and officials from the persons filling it, Han Feizi and other Legalists are "disembodying" the political system, in view of stabilizing the system and emancipating the members of society from the arbitrary decisions of powerholders, both for the good and for the bad. The system should work by itself, and also correct itself. Better than to hope for a benevolent ruler is to design a system where the personal characteristics of the powerholder do not count at all.

6.3 General and Explicit

The rules and laws of the Legalists are not embedded in a context but, on the contrary, are general, public, and easy to understand:

> When laws and prohibitions are clear and manifest, all officials will be in good order. (Ch. 46, 2: 240)
> 法禁明著,則官治
>
> In administrating ordinary civil cases, not to use standards that ordinary men and women plainly understand, but to long for those theories which even the wisest do not comprehend; that certainly is the negation of government. (Ch. 49, 2: 288, translation modified)
> 民間之事,夫婦所明知者不用,而慕上知之論,則其於治反矣。

Laws and rules are also abstracted from specific situations; they are not tied to an enactment in a concrete situation. This allows them to be applied to different cases and also future, unforeseeable cases. Laws do not emerge from a particular situation but are stipulated for all situations. Laws and rules must also be known beforehand for people to be able to abide by them.

A law should be known to and apply to everyone, regardless of social or state position (although, as said, there was no institution to control the ruler, and they were controlled by the logic of the system itself).

> The law does not fawn on the noble; the string does not yield to the crooked. Whatever the law applies to, the wise cannot reject nor can the brave defy. Punishment for fault never skips ministers, reward for good never misses commoners. (Ch. 6, 1: 45)
> 法不阿貴, 繩不撓曲。法之所加, 智者弗能辭, 勇者弗敢爭。刑過不避大臣,賞善不遺匹夫。
>
> When reward and punishment are never unjust, the people will attend to public duties. (Ch. 46, 2: 240)
> 賞罰不阿, 則民用。

Therefore, the intelligent sovereign makes the law select men and makes no arbitrary promotion himself. He makes the law measure merits and makes no arbitrary regulation himself. (Ch. 6, 1: 40)
故明主使法擇人，不自舉也；使法量功，不自度也。

The laws must also be explicit and easy to understand. This is contrary to Confucian implicit morality, which is full of ritualistic speech, metaphors, and allusions to classic texts. It is interesting to see how Han Feizi employs a metaphor used by Confucius about the three missing corners (in the *Analects* 7.8, see above 4.9), but in exactly the opposite sense. Han Feizi says:

> Once compasses and squares are established and one angle is made right, the other three angles will come out one after another. (Ch. 8, 1: 57)
> 規矩既設，三隅乃列。

While for Confucius it was about the ability to understand the implicated and being able to unfold from it, for Han Feizi it is about the ability to use explicit tools and rules how to deduce from one explicit thing (one corner) to other explicit things (three missing corners). Han Feizi does not move between different levels of implication and explication, of folded and unfolded knowledge. For him, the knowledge stays on the level of the unfolded and actual. If you are in possession of the context-independent rule, you can deduce the remaining angles. It is much closer to the geometrical procedure and much less metaphorical than Confucius' simile.

Again, with the help of correct rules and tools, an average person can attain perfect results (as we saw already above, in case of Mozi):

> Without the severity of the whip and the facility of the bridle, even Zaofu could not drive the horse; without the rule of the compasses and squares and the tip of the inked string, even Wang Er could not draw squares and circles; and without the position of authority and power and the law of reward and punishment, even Yao and Shun could not keep the state in order. Now that rulers of the present age thoughtlessly discard heavy punishment and severe censure and practise love and favour, to realize the achievement of the Hegemonic Ruler is also hopeless. (Ch. 14, 1: 128)
> 無棰策之威，銜橛之備，雖造父不能以服馬；無規矩之法，繩墨之端，雖王爾不能以成方圓；無威嚴之勢，賞罰之法，雖堯、舜不能以為治。今世主皆輕釋重罰嚴誅，行愛惠，而欲霸王之功，亦不可幾也。

A Confucian-type embodied learning of rituals takes a considerable amount of time and effort, requires gifted persons, and needs some preliminary openness of mind. Just before the citation about divining the three corners from one, Confucius says:

I will not open the door for a mind that is not already striving to understand, nor will I provide words to a tongue that is not already struggling to speak. (7.8, Slingerland 2003a: 66)

不憤不啟，不悱不發

Still, the outcome remains ambiguous and cannot be concretely evaluated. Confucians have models to emulate like Yao, Shun, or Duke of Zhou, but they are not objective, and it takes intensive personal interpretation to understand how exactly to imitate them. In the case of a penal code, it is much easier and more straightforward to deduce appropriate lawful action. Of course, some interpretative work in the application of laws does remain and it cannot be cancelled to such an extent as the Legalists wanted or pretended it to be—that the punishments and rewards would somehow automatically follow from a deed. The lawmaker may have some moral ideas when they design a particular system of laws and regulations, in order to promote a certain kind of morality in the society, but this need not bother the individual, for whom abiding by the law is sufficient, without any moral considerations.

6.4 Generality of Basic Preferences

Not only are the laws themselves general but there are also general conditions of their application. Han Feizi bases his political philosophy on the fact that people like profit and fame, and dislike harm and shame. On these two principles are the most basic tools for directing a society based, the so-called "two handles"—rewards and punishments:

> To choose safety and profit and leave danger and trouble, this is human nature. (Ch. 14, 1: 118)
> 夫安利者就之,危害者去之,此人之情也。
> Ministers are afraid of censure and punishment but fond of encouragement and reward. (Ch. 7, 1: 46)
> 為人臣者畏誅罰而利慶賞
> Knowing this well, the intelligent sovereign simply establishes the system of advantages and disadvantages. (Ch. 14, 1: 121)
> 明主知之,故設利害之道以示天下而已矣。
> Generally speaking, the order of All-under-Heaven must accord with human feelings. Human feelings have likes and dislikes, wherefore reward and punishment can be applied. If reward and punishment are applicable, prohibitions and orders will prevail and the course of government will be

accomplished. As the ruler has the handles in his grip and thereby upholds his august position, what is ordered works and what is prohibited stops. The handles are regulators of life and death; the position is the means of overcoming the masses. (Ch. 48, 2: 258)

凡治天下，必因人情。人情者有好惡，故賞罰可用；賞罰可用，則禁令可立，而治道具矣。君執柄以處勢，故令行禁止。柄者，殺生之制也；勢者，勝眾之資也。

Whoever exerts his strength and risks his life, will be able to accomplish merits and attain rank and bounty. (Ch. 46, 2: 240)

使士民明焉，盡力致死，則功伐可立而爵祿可致

There are two things to be noted. First, social system should capture human natural desires: a system where people are only made to do things they dislike cannot endure. On the other hand, Han Feizi thinks that if people are allowed to do only things they like, this system also will bring chaos like a spoiled child without the stern direction of father. There have to be incentives and checks, rewards and punishments. With these two handles the ruler can maintain his position of power or "august position" (*shi* 勢), which helps him to avoid being deceived by the ministers (see above, 6.2). In this way, people can be made to do hard things. Ordinarily people would not like the hardships of tilling the soil and exposing oneself to danger in war, but if they are given the incentives of material profit from selling their products and symbolic fame from feats in war, then they are more willing to do it. This effect is reinforced if there are harsh punishments for deserting the army, or fines for not producing,

> Indeed, tillage requires physical force, and is toil. But the people who perform it say, "Through it we can become wealthy." Again, warfare, as a matter of fact, involves risks. But the people who wage it say, "Through it we can become noble." (Ch. 49, 2: 290)
>
> 夫耕之用力也勞，而民為之者，曰：可得以富也。戰之〔為〕事也危，而民為之者，曰：可得以貴也.

It is through these two handles—reward and punishment—that the Legalist system becomes embodied in a generally predictable way. In this way, the system is not only externally imposed but internally endorsed for personal motives of striving for reward and avoiding punishment.

At the same time all this is impersonal and works quite universally: everyone has likes and dislikes, and although the preferences may be different, with material and symbolic profit it is possible to induce action in most people, and with fear of punishment (material, physical, and symbolic harm), it is possible to deter from action most people. Therefore, while a subjectivity is presupposed in this system (people themselves spontaneously strive for certain things and avoid other things), this is englobed in an objective general framework; the first-person outlook is integrated into a third-person state machinery.

6.5 Staying Cool

Han Feizi makes a strong case that rulers should not let their personal preferences and emotions interfere with governance (contrary to the emotional engagement of Confucian setting that applies also to the relation between the superior and inferior: loyal feelings from the part of the subject and benevolence from the ruler), and in this sense has to stay cool, even actively suppress emotional responses. If a ruler's subjects can see his likes or dislikes, what pleases or displeases him, then the ministers can act accordingly and thus encroach the ruler's position and ultimately usurp the throne. This is one of Han Feizi's leitmotivs (a good analysis can be found in Jullien 2004b). For example, take the following passage:

> Because the king of Yue admired valor, many of his subjects looked on death lightly. Because King Ling of Chu liked slim waists, his state was full of people starving themselves. Because Duke Huan of Qi was jealous and loved his ladies in waiting, Shudiao castrated himself in order to be put in charge of the harem; because Duke Huan was fond of unusual food, Yiya steamed his son's head and served it to him. Because Zikuai of Yan admired worthy men, his minister Zizhi made it clear that he would not accept the throne were it offered to him.
>
> Thus if the ruler reveals what he dislikes, his ministers will be careful to disguise their motives; if he shows what he likes, his ministers will feign abilities they do not have. In short, if he lets his desires be known, his ministers will know what attitude to assume in order to hide their true characters. (Ch. 7, Eno 2010: 7–8)
>
> 故越王好勇，而民多輕死；楚靈王好細腰，而國中多餓人；齊桓公妒而好內，故豎刁自宮以治內，桓公好味，易牙蒸其子首而進之；燕子噲好賢，故子之明不受國。
>
> 故君見惡則群臣匿端，君見好則群臣誣能。人主欲見，則群臣之情態得其資矣。

This is the first step in usurpation: if the ruler shows his preferences, the subjects will know how to conform themselves accordingly. If he likes courage, then the minister tries to perform courageous feats; if he likes asceticism, the minister fasts, etc. By doing what the ruler likes, the minister endears himself to him, so that the latter becomes complacent, endows special favors to the minister, lets the minister to issue orders or even gives his throne to the minister (as happened to the ruler of the state of Yan, with disastrous results):

> Hence Zizhi, by playing the part of a worthy, was able to seize the throne from his sovereign. Shudiao and Yiya, by catering to the ruler's desires, were able to encroach upon his authority. In the end, Zikuai died in the chaos that ensued, and Duke Huan was left unburied for so long that maggots came crawling out beneath the door of his coffin chamber. What were the causes? These are examples of calamity that comes when a ruler reveals his true feelings to his ministers. Ministers do not necessarily feel true love for their ruler; they serve him only in the hope of substantial gain. (Ch. 7, Eno 2010: 8)
> 故子之託於賢以奪其君者也，豎刁、易牙因君之欲以侵其君者也，其卒子噲以亂死，桓公蟲流出戶而不葬。此其故何也？人君以情借臣之患也。人臣之情非必能愛其君也，為重利之故也。

Since the root cause of those disasters was the fact that the ruler showed his likes and dislikes, Han Feizi repeatedly insists that the rulers should hide them:

> Do away with likes, do away with hates, and the ministers will reveal their unadorned characters. (Ch. 7, Eno 2010: 8)
> 去好去惡，群臣見素。
> So, discard both like and hate and make your empty mind the abode of Dao. (Ch. 8, 1: 57)
> 故去喜去惡，虛心以為道舍。
> Hence the saying: "The ruler must not reveal his wants. For, if he reveals his wants, the ministers will polish their manners accordingly. The ruler must not reveal his views. For, if he reveals his views, the ministers will display their hues differently." (Ch. 5, 1: 31)
> 故曰：君無見其所欲，君見其所欲，臣自將雕琢；君無見其意，君見其意，臣將自表異。

The ruler must remain "empty,"[6] an enigma like Lacanian psychoanalyst. Only then will Lacan's patient show her true character or the minister in Legalist state show his "unadorned character" (*su* 素). The latter term is close to an important concept from the *Laozi* (whom Han Feizi extensively commented upon), the "uncarved" (*pu* 樸):[7] the old masters were "uncarved" (§15), one should "return to the uncarved" (*fugue yu pu* 復歸於樸, §25), one suppresses the desires with the uncarved (§37), and finally, the Dao itself is "uncarved" (§32). In *Laozi* the "simple" and "uncarved" refers to a state of virtuality prior to differentiations into actualized forms, and it is also a form of self-cultivation. Han Feizi brings it into a political context of government: if the ruler is empty and uncarved, he will induce a similar state in his subjects; but the latter must propose policies, and so inevitably they must go out of the uncarved state and show their authentic intentions and tendencies, carving out their uncarved state, once they do or say something. And then the ruler has the upper hand, since he knows the subjects, but the subjects will not know the ruler.

Staying cool and hiding likes and dislikes require a considerable amount of self-restraint from the ruler. If they do not have this self-control, Han Feizi warns, they will be in great danger. The position of the ruler is inherently a precarious one, as it is the summit of the political order and, according to Han Feizi, everyone strives to arrive at that position themselves. Han Feizi makes no illusion about the intentions of ministers: they by nature strive to replace the ruler, and if they have not done it yet, it is simply because their power base is still not sufficient. The ruler must remain constantly vigilant to prevent ministers from encroaching or usurping.

6.6 Decontextualized Civic Morality

While Han Feizi may seem to promote amoral Realpolitik, what he is trying to do is actually establish a new, civic morality based on the rule by law (or even rule of law), and not on traditional kinship and family-based allegiances (see Winston 2005). This new morality is less contextualized, relying on more objective norms:

> In consequence, as long as laws do not fail to function, the body of officials will practise neither villainy nor deception. (Ch. 49, 2: 289)
> 故法不敗，而群官無姦詐矣。

Han Feizi explicitly says that the rule of extremely immoral rulers like Jie or Zhou is unstable, and he wants to devise a legal system that tolerates a moderate amount of ineptness by the ruler. Han Feizi is realistic also in the sense that he does not require the ruler to possess exceptional intellectual capabilities. On the contrary, such intelligence may hamper the ruler if he meddles too much in the everyday business of government. The ruler should listen to different proposals and accounts and then let the minister proceed with his cross-verified proposal. In case the minister does not fulfill his task (either underperforming *or* overperforming), he is punished, like in the following famous story:

> Once Marquis Zhao of Han got drunk and fell asleep. The Keeper of the Hat, seeing that the duke was cold, laid a robe over him. When the marquis awoke,

he was pleased and asked his attendants, "Who covered me with a robe?" His attendants replied, "The Keeper of the Hat." The marquis thereupon punished both the Keeper of the Hat and the Keeper of the Robe. He punished the Keeper of the Robe for failing to do his duty, and the Keeper of the Hat for overstepping his office. It was not that he did not dislike the cold, but he considered the harm of one official encroaching upon the duties of another to be a greater danger than cold. (Ch. 7, Eno 2010: 14–15)

昔者韓昭侯醉而寢，典冠者見君之寒也，故加衣於君之上，覺寢而說，問左右曰：「誰加衣者？」左右對曰：「典冠。」君因兼罪典衣與典冠。其罪典衣，以為失其事也；其罪典冠，以為越其職也。非不惡寒也，以為侵官之害甚於寒。

The rationale behind such an extreme response is that the maintenance of the general order is of supreme importance, overshadowing personal preferences or considerations. Also, an overperforming official may become proud, unruly, pretentious, and in this way encroach the ruler's authority.

Han Feizi often stresses, contrary to Confucians (cf. Sarkissian 2014: 106), that there is *no personal affectionate relation* between the ruler and his subjects. He cannot rely on their goodwill but has to use the two handles of reward and punishment, so that they "inevitably" do him good.

> From such a viewpoint, I can see that the sage in governing the state pursues the policy of making the people inevitably do him good but never relies on their doing him good with love. For to rely on the people's doing him good with love is dangerous, but to rely on their inevitability to do him good is safe. (Ch. 14, 1: 121)
>
> 從是觀之，則聖人之治國也，固有使人不得不愛我之道，而不恃人之以愛為我也。恃人之以愛〔為〕我者危矣，恃吾不可不為者安矣。

Now the relationship between superior and inferior involves no affection of father and son, if anyone wishes to rule the inferiors by practising righteousness, the relationship will certainly have cracks. Besides, parents in relation to children, when males are born, congratulate each other, and, when females are born, lessen the care of them. Equally coming out from the bosoms and lapels of the parents, why should boys receive congratulations while girls are ill-treated? Because parents consider their future conveniences and calculate their permanent benefits. Thus, even parents in relation to children use the calculating mind in treating them, how much more should those who have no affection of parent and child? (Ch. 46, 2: 239)

今上下之接，無子父之澤，而欲以行義禁下，則交必有郄矣。且父母之於子也，產男則相賀，產女則殺之。此俱出父母之懷衽，然男子受賀，女子殺之者，慮其後便，計之長利也。故父母之於子也，猶用計算之心以相待也，而況無父子之澤乎?

Han Feizi mercilessly lays bare the soft underbelly of Confucian morality: they pretend to disdain calculating attitude in human relationships, but in their behavior, they exhibit a strong preference for boys over girls. If people are calculating even in their most intimate relations, then for even a greater reason it is justified to believe that they will do the same in other social relations.

This does not necessarily mean that there is no affection in the civic life. But the question is, how to use the two handles so that people would be emotionally involved in the common good? In Han Feizi's opinion, this involves countering family and community affections. One should report to the authorities a relative or community member who has committed a crime. Confucius was obviously responding to proto-Legalist ideas in the following dialogue from the *Analects*:

> The Duke of She said to Confucius, "Among my people there is one we call 'Upright Gong.' When his father stole a sheep, he reported him to the authorities." Confucius replied, "Among my people, those who we consider 'upright' are different from this: fathers cover up for their sons, and sons cover up for their fathers. 'Uprightness' is to be found in this." (13.18; Slingerland 2003a: 148)
>
> 葉公語孔子曰：「吾黨有直躬者，其父攘羊，而子證之。」孔子曰：「吾黨之直者異於是。父為子隱，子為父隱，直在其中矣。」

For Confucius, family ties are stronger than obligations to the state, and piety is found between family members before it is found between ruler and subject. But Han Feizi replies:

> Of old, there was in the Chu State a man named Zhigong. Once his father stole a sheep, wherefore he reported to the authorities. Thereupon the prefect said, "Put him to death", as he thought the man was loyal to the ruler but undutiful to his father. So that man was tried and executed. From this it can be seen that the honest subject of the ruler was an outrageous son of his father. [...] Naturally, following the punishment of the honest man by the prefect, no other culprit in Chu was ever reported to the authorities. (Ch. 49, 2: 285–6)
>
> 楚之有直躬，其父竊羊，而謁之吏。令君曰：「殺之!」以為直於君而曲於父，報而罪之。以是觀之，夫君之直臣，父之暴子也。[...] 故令尹誅而楚姦不上聞

The ruler cannot proclaim Confucian benevolence because it would undermine the stability of his rule. Civic obligations come before familial ones. It should be noted that it is also part of our criminal code that to hide a criminal, even a relative or neighbor, is a criminal offence. Confucians would prefer to leave it to the family and community to decide how to deal with the criminal. From things like lynching and mob justice, we know that this is not always even in the interest of the culprit, let alone civil order. In any case, administering a large bureaucratic state required a new civic morality, based on general, disembodied, and decontextualized rules.

6.7 Objectivity, Quantity

Broadly speaking, the Legalist account does not rely on a first-person and personal description but on objective, third-person view. There should be objective criteria for evaluation of behavior (laws, norms, job descriptions, task definitions, etc.) and the ruler should also collect quantitative data about the society and economy. Han Feizi says:

> Indeed, the most enlightened method of governing a state is to trust measures and not men. For this reason, the state with methods is never mistaken if it does not trust the empty fame of men. If the land within the boundary is always in order it is because measures are employed. If any falling state lets foreign soldiers walk all over its territory and can neither resist nor prevent them, it is because that state trusts men and uses no measures. Men may jeopardize their own country, but measures can invade others' countries. Therefore, the tactful state spurns words and trusts laws. (Ch. 55, 2: 332 translation modified)
> 夫治法之至明者，任數不任人。是以有術之國，不用譽則毋適，境內必治，任數也。亡國使兵公行乎其地，而弗能圉禁者，任人而無數也。自攻者人也，攻人者數也。 故有術之國，去言而任法。

Whereas Chinese traditionalists did not go so far as Jewish traditionalists who depict David's census (see 2 Samuel 24) as being blasphemous, they still certainly considered quantitative methods in government as something of secondary importance. In Han Feizi's system, on the other hand, the quantitative tools are essential. To wage a war in the Warring States period certainly required a lot of quantitative data and planning, in order to evaluate one's resources, the resources needed for an expedition or fortification, the concrete details of a military deployment (how many soldiers? how much food? how many carriages? etc.).

The most important sphere of using "regulations and measures" (*dushu* 度數, literally "measures and numbers")[8] is in the evaluation of officials' performance. This is the "method" (*shu* 術) of government:[9]

Indeed, men with a method, when ministering to a ruler, would enforce theories of regulations and measures to clarify the law of the sovereign and harass wicked ministers in order to glorify the sovereign and tranquillize the state. Accordingly, as soon as theories of regulations and measures are enforced, reward and punishment will infallibly become applicable. The lord of men will then earnestly illustrate the method of the sage but never have to follow the commonplaces of the world. He will decide between right and wrong according to the relation between name and fact and scrutinize words and phrases by means of comparison and verification. (Ch 14, 1: 119–20, translation modified)

夫有術者之為人臣也，得效度數之言，上明主法，下困姦臣，以尊主安國者也。 是以度數之言得效於前，則賞罰必用於後矣。人主誠明於聖人之術，而不苟於世俗之言，循名實而定是非，因參驗而審言辭。

This is the method of matching the "name" (*ming* 名) and "form" (*xing* 刑/形). In terms of ministers, it is matching the job or task description of an official and their actual performance. If an official has promised to do something, and the ruler allows such task to unfold, the official will proceed and later the ruler will verify whether the official has performed what was promised (he "compares and verifies to judge them" 參驗以審之, Ch. 14). The objectified and quantified criteria help in this process. The ruler lets "names appoint themselves to task and affairs settle themselves" (使名自命，令事自定, Ch. 8, 1: 53). The subjects toil; the ruler facilitates:

> The inferior ruler exerts his own ability; the average ruler exerts people's physical strength; and the superior ruler exerts people's wisdom. (Ch. 48, 2: 260)
> 下君盡己之能，中君盡人〔之〕力，上君盡人之智。

The ruler calls for a gathering of their officials and lets them to express their opinions and propose tasks for themselves. The decisions and tasks are then a common knowledge in this group of officials, and they can be used to control each other. Also, the decisions and tasks are written down and later compared with the results and bestows rewards and punishments accordingly.

> If tasks are successfully accomplished, the ruler harvests their fruits; if they fail, the ministers face criminal charges. (Ch. 48, 2: 260–1)
> 事成則君收其功，規敗則臣任其罪。

We see, here, how the principle of power delegation and using other people's wisdom and force (cf. above, 6.2.) is combined with objectified and decontextualized methods of government: written records of promises that can be later used to verify the results. This could emancipate the government from contextualized power relations and make it more meritocratic. People are appointed and maintain their position not by birthright but according to whether they have been able to make good proposals and to carry them out. The proposals can be thus "measured" objectively. And indeed, the Qin state was able to unify the warring states of China with such principles of government. In more stable times, however, it seems unavoidable that ordinary court intrigues to step in and meritocracy is eroded. Although Han Feizi conceived the ruler as being mysterious toward his subjects and in a sense "empty," he did not conceive of a state system where the place of a ruler would be literally empty, and divided by different branches of power, like in modern democracies (cf. Ott 2013). This one further step toward decontextualization and disembodiment would have probably been too much even for Han Feizi's innovative and exploratory intellectual endeavor.

6.8 Conclusion

In this chapter we explored another decontextualizing current of the Chinese tradition, the Legalists, whose most famous proponent was Han Feizi. Han Feizi proposed a meritocratic model of state, based on clear, explicit, and general laws and rules. This would enable any ruler, even a mediocre one, to govern a state successfully.

Han Feizi's philosophy was a synthesis of statecraft that was developed during the Warring States period that saw the rise of bigger, more centralized and militarized states. The role of traditional nobility was eroded, and the state became more bureaucratic and meritocratic. The administration of such a state and its military efforts required also objective quantified data about the society, the economy, and the army.

In addition to the general structure of the state, Han Feizi devised general principles for its functioning. One of his main concerns was how to maintain a hierarchical power structure. To avoid usurpation of power by the ministers, the ruler had to remain secretive and cool, refrain from showing emotional preferences, so as not to give ministers a leverage point with which to usurp power.

For Han Feizi, the ruler should not be overly active and should avoid micromanagement, instead letting the ministers propose policies. The ruler should then select among the proposals, have it written down, and later verify whether the minister had accomplished what had been promised. This seems to be similar to Confucius' ideal ruler who rules by "effortless action," *wuwei*

無為 and is like a Polar star, around which everything turns (cf. above, 4.11). Han Feizi's ruler also does very little and functions in a *wuwei* mode. However, Confucius' ideal ruler obtains their abilities through personal charisma and virtue (*de* 德), whereas Han Feizi's ruler obtains their abilities through good and intelligent statecraft.

Han Feizi's decontextualized and disembodied system was very far from Confucius' ideal of moral government and ruling by personal example. According to Han Feizi's realistic understanding, rule by morals would lead to chaos, as rulers are seldom extremely virtuous and capable. Han Feizi's ruler should keep calm and secretive, showing no preferences and abiding by the rules and laws. Otherwise the impersonal system would inevitably correct itself in this way that the ruler's position will be usurped by the subjects.

Another method of practical statecraft was the application of "two handles," rewards and punishments. Human motivations are certainly much richer and more nuanced, but for government purposes, these two are sufficient most of the time and for most people. We can see, how even for the purpose of embodying the Legalist state, Han Feizi proposed two very general (and hence decontextualized) methods, motivating with a promise of reward, and inhibiting with a menace of punishment.

After the exposition of disembodied and decontextualized tendencies of Mohists and Legalists, one might pose the question, why did theories focused on decontextualized learning and knowledge not become dominant in China,[10] despite its obvious usefulness in state management? One answer is that the disembodied account was, in fact, maintained and the Chinese state bureaucracy relied on methods initially worked out by Legalist thinkers and statesmen. It was simply banned from the mainstream of philosophical thought (where, for example, numbers entered mostly in relation to the *Yijing* correlational thinking, and not for some quantitative approach to nature). And this was largely due to the profound discreditation of Legalist philosophy after the rule of Qin dynasty (221–206 BC) that had used Legalist statecraft and had united China after massive warfare. That dynasty was later traditionally depicted as extremely harsh and inhumane. It is true that after unification, Qin rulers undertook massive public works that created hardships for lots of people, and that they had harassed dissident scholars. But it is also true that the extremely bad reputation of Qin dynasty is partially due to the subsequent Han propaganda. In any case, after the fall of Qin, hardly any thinker openly proclaimed to be a Legalist.

7

A Confucian Development of Embodiment: Record of Music (*Yueji* 樂記)

7.1 Mencius

Confucian responses to disembodied challenges came in many ways that reaffirmed a basically embodied understanding of humans and the world. Two of the most famous solutions were that of Mencius 孟子 (372–289 BC) and Xunzi 荀子 (c. 310–after 238 BC). To the Mencian statement that "human nature is good" (*renxingshan* 人性善), Xunzi opposed his own claim that "human nature is bad" (*renxing'e* 人性惡). They seem diametrically opposed, but from a larger perspective it is rather a question of emphasis. Both Mencius and Xunzi believed that there is a certain natural endowment in humans and that it needs to be developed. But Mencius emphasized the side of naturalness, and Xunzi that of development.

Therefore, Mencius spoke of the "four sprouts" (*siduan* 四端) of human nature:

> As for what [humans] are inherently, they can become good. As for their becoming not good, this is not the fault of their potential. (6A6; Mengzi 2008: 149)
> 乃若其情, 則可以為善矣, 乃所謂善也。若夫為不善, 非才之罪也。

Mencius goes on to claim that humans all have four basic feelings: compassion (*ceyin* 惻隱), disdain (*xiuwu* 羞惡), respect (*gongjing* 恭敬), and a sense of right and wrong (*shifei* 是非). And that if these "sprouts" are properly developed, they will become, respectively, benevolence (*ren* 仁), righteousness (*yi* 義), propriety (*li* 禮), and wisdom (*zhi* 智). The sprouts of plants require delicate care, and they cannot be forced. To illustrate this, Mencius tells the famous story of a man who tried to "help sprouts to grow" by pulling them. By doing this, he uprooted them, and destroyed his harvest. Similarly, one has to take good care of the "sprouts" of the character, and furnish the necessary conditions for human development, but one should not force too much, lest the person broke. Overall, the human development is presented by Mencius as an embodied process that is tightly embedded in a context, and the outcome should be a person who is as highly responsive to the environment and other persons as Confucius was.

> When Confucius left the state of Qi, he just scooped up the rice he was about to cook and went. When he left the sate of Lu, he said, "I'm in no hurry." This is the Way to leave the state of one's parents. When one should go quickly, he went quickly; when one should delay, he delayed; when one should stay, he stayed; when one should remain, he remained; when one should take office, he took office—such was Confucius. (5B1, Mengzi 2008: 132)
> 孔子之去齊, 接淅而行; 去魯, 曰:『遲遲吾行也。』去父母國之道也。可以速而速, 可以久而久, 可以處而處, 可以仕而仕, 孔子也。

Mencius sums it up, saying that Confucius was a "sage of timeliness" (聖之時者; Mengzi 2008). In the same context, Mencius brings the example of three other sages who behaved appropriately in situations that required radically different reaction. Also, different sages may behave differently in situations that may seem similar but are, in fact, essentially different, and if they "had exchanged places, each would have done as the other" (4B31, Mengzi 2008: 114; cf. Van Norden 2019: §2). They do not observe a fixed rule or law, but they follow the Way that requires ever new solutions in the changed environment.[1]

Confucians tended to be traditionalists, custodians of traditional rituals, music, texts. And references to persons and texts from the past were a standard part of philosophical texts (one can detect pressure of this requirement even in the core chapter of *Mozi*, so defiant of tradition, where later versions of the same chapters tend to have more references to the past and to canonical texts). Already Confucius recognized that times change, and Mencius reaffirms this conviction, but an adequate response to this cannot be encapsulated in a law. Mencius could perhaps recognize that new laws and regulations may be necessary in face of new situations, but they can never grasp the whole of the Way. A sage in her embodied responses takes into account much finer and subtle contextual nuances of the situation. A decontextualized law would be way too coarse and crude.

It is related to Mencius' repudiation of the notion of "profit" (*li* 利) that was central to Mohists. An explicit profit is only a partial expression of the situation. When we have profit in mind, we approach the situation with a narrow and biased mindset. We detach a portion of reality and hypostatize it as limited and contextually insensitive entity. At the very beginning of the *Mencius*, Mencius berates king Hui of Liang for seeking "profit": if people think in terms of profit, they start to compete with each other, that leads to strife, violence, and chaos.

A ruler who wants to make his country rich and populous views everything from this angle, and this narrow-minded approach can backfire. For instance, he builds up a huge army with good weapons, but if this army lacks motivation and loyalty by inner conviction, it can easily lose cohesion and succumb to an enemy who "on paper" is much smaller and weaker. Or the ruler may lose sight of the interpenetration of different dimensions of social wellbeing: in 1A3, the same king Hui of Liang wonders why the population of his state does not grow, although he has alleviated famine and the administration of his state works well. Mencius replies that King Hui is fond of war that interferes with agricultural activities and hence impedes population growth. Under a truly benevolent ruler there would even be no need of aggressive warfare, but other states will readily submit themselves to him.

History does not do justice to this idea, since China was united by Qin dynasty, who designed their state according to Legalist principles. But this dynasty did not last for long, and later, in Han dynasty, in second century BC, the basis of legitimacy was switched to Confucianism (although in a remarkably syncretic version of it): you may conquer a state on horseback (by sheer power), but you will not be able to sustainably rule it on horseback, as Lu Jia (陸賈, died in 170 BC) warned Liu Bang (劉邦, 256–194 BC), the founder of Han dynasty and reunifier of China.

On personal level, it is true that we always inevitably focus on certain aspects of reality at the expense of others, but according to Confucians, the goal of a refined person should be to make different aspects of reality and different considerations to bear on each other, so that each aspect or consideration would imply more of reality.

Embodied emotions play an important role here. In 1A7 there is a famous dialogue between Mencius and, again, king Hui of Liang. The king had once seen an ox that was led to be sacrificed. He could not bear the sight and ordered the ox to be replaced by a sheep. He did not dare to cancel the sacrifice altogether, but at least he commiserated with the ox. Mencius lauds king's attitude but admonishes him to extend his kindness to his own suffering people. The king has a good and responsive heart, so that he has a good starting point. Now he would have to extend his feeling.

This is quite different from Mohist's extension of the scope of care which is—at least in its philosophical explanation[2]—rather the result of a rational, and even game-theoretical calculation (see Van Norden 2019: §4). This universal care is thoroughly decontextualized. But in Mencius, particular emotional contexts are essential. One should not leave them behind or fight against them, but on the contrary, should cultivate and enlarge them. While Confucius introduced the golden rule that has the effect of making one's behavior more reflective, Mencius also has the idea of enlarging the scope of emotional engagement (especially for the ruler). Mozi's requirement of enlarging the scope of care has had its effect. Yet, differently from Mozi, in Mencius it remains contextualized, tied to particular situations like when the king had pity of the ox.

7.2 Xunzi

Xunzi, on the other hand, maintained that if you trust only the spontaneous development of a person, that person will grow crooked and become bad. Mencius could have readily agreed with that, since the sprouts do need care, but Xunzi places relatively greater emphasis on the part of conscious effort (*wei* 偽) in development. You cannot trust those natural tendencies only. You have to take an active stance in correcting and bending them: Xunzi uses the metaphor of bending a piece of wood in a mold with the help of steam. After it has dried, the wood will maintain the form of the mold. This idea is introduced at the very beginning of the book (in 1A1), so that it must have been considered a key idea for the editors of *Xunzi*.

Yet this natural endowment is still there: you cannot produce an exemplary person out of scratch; the developmental process is still based on a certain endowment of capacities.

> Inborn nature is the root and beginning, the raw material and original constitution. Conscious activity is the form and principle of order, the development and completion. If there were no inborn nature, there would be nothing for conscious exertion to improve; if there were no conscious exertion, then inborn nature could not refine itself. Only after inborn nature and conscious exertion have been conjoined is the concept of the sage perfected, and the merit of uniting the world brought to fulfilment. (19.6, Knoblock 1994: 66)
> 性者、本始材朴也; 偽者、文理隆盛也。無性則偽之無所加, 無偽則性不能自美。性偽合, 然後成聖人之名, 一天下之功於是就也。

The notion of an external mold and conscious effort may leave the impression that Xunzi introduces disembodied and decontextualized means into the education process. But when we take a closer look at what are those "molds," we will discover that these are, first of all, traditional ritual forms and classical texts. So, it is not a question of universal truths that are valid anywhere anytime, but ways of behavior inscribed in a certain culture. Xunzi is well aware of the variability of those forms in different cultures, so that they are not necessary, but historically contingent, although he deems the forms of his own culture (especially concerning mourning rituals) to be in the best harmony with the Way.

Xunzi explicitly makes rituals the cornerstone of social organization. Rituals are, as we already saw earlier, quite different from laws: rituals are contextual—they are embodied in participants, embedded in tradition, extended in ritual implements—while laws are much more decontextualized. Of course, the implementation of laws cannot do without ritual elements (gestures, garments, formulae, etc.), and, on the other hand, especially in traditional cultures, rituals had also the function of laws and norms that could be made explicit. But generally speaking, rituals are good examples of contextualizing social behavior, and laws are examples of decontextualizing tendencies of social relations.

While Mozi emphasizes the universality of care, and Legalists the generality of laws, Xunzi stresses that rituals help to maintain differences and distinctions. Mohists and Legalists also had a hierarchical vision of society, but this hierarchy was supposed to be maintained by administrative measures. Xunzi deems this not to be sufficient, since it is too external, too decontextualized. But rituals can foster internal cohesion between individuals. All the different dimensions of embodiment are involved: embodied involvement in rituals, enacted gestures and utterances, extended ritual utensils that support ritual practices, embeddedness of rituals in a traditional heritage, a sense of implied larger meaning, etc. In this way, both cohesion is obtained and distinctions are maintained. In a detailed description of a village wine ceremony (20.12; we will come back to this below, in 7.9), Xunzi describes how the main guest is treated with more attention than other guests and how guests drink wine in age order, without anyone being left out. Everyone participates, but some are deferred more. Since everyone ages, they naturally move up the ladder of deference. This is again quite different from Mohist and Legalist meritocracy (although admittedly they discussed it for public administration, not private ceremonies). It is more inclusive, since never mind your abilities, in the long run everyone will be honored (of course, supposed that they live long enough).

Sometimes Xunzi makes a finer distinction and attributes the aspect of distinction to rituals and cohesion to music:

> Music joins together what is common to all; ritual separates what is different. (20.3, Knoblock 1994: 84)
> 樂合同, 禮別異

This is a topic that is more fully developed in the *Record of Music* (*Yueji* 樂記) that we will discuss in most of the remainder of this chapter and that can be seen as an epitome of this strain of thought.

7.3 Record of Music

The *Record of Music* (*Yueji* 樂記) is included as Chapter 19 in the "Book of Rites" (*Liji* 禮記) and was most probably "compiled in Western Han by Liu De 劉德, Mao Chang 毛萇, and other Han Confucian scholars" (Liu 2014: 241), bringing together older material. The more philosophical parts have much in common with *Xunzi's* (c. 310–c. 230) chapter "On Music" *Yuelun* 樂論, sometimes citing it verbatim. In *Xunzi* the chapter on music follows immediately the chapter "On Rituals" 禮論 and precisely music and rituals are selected in *Yueji* as the foundation of politics and cosmology.

The *Record of Music* is predominantly Confucian, but it "has integrated various pre-Qin schools' thoughts on music, including Daoism, Legalism, Mohism, Yin-yang School and Miscellaneous School, into Confucian thoughts" (Liu 2014: 242, referring to Cai Zhongde). Parts of this text show a very high degree of philosophical sophistication and they help us to further develop certain topics related to the embodied knowledge. It demonstrates what an ontology may look like if it is based on an embodied understanding of knowledge. It is also a good example of what reflective, embodied knowledge can accomplish.

It is interesting to note that a lot of the disputes in ancient China between philosophers who leaned either toward contextualizing or decontextualizing knowledge were fought around music: it was central for Confucius, and Mozi dedicated a separate chapter, "Against Music," to denounce the Confucian inflation of rituals and music. The Confucian Xunzi, in turn, fought back, and took pains in his chapter on music to counter the Mohist attack and reestablish music as a central part of social life and self-cultivation. In the *Annals of Lü Buwei* (239 BC), music is even given cosmic importance: it is said to originate in the

"Great One," *Taiyi* 太一, and when the Great One has unfolded and coagulated to yield actual forms, it will make sound (Chapter "Great Music" *Da yue* 大樂[3]).

7.4 Emotions

The *Record of Music* starts with epistemological questions. Right away it is made clear that feelings and emotions are not considered something external to cognition but as the very basis of it (see above, 2.6). Take two excerpts from the beginning of the *Record of Music*:[4]

> Generally speaking, the melodies are born from the hearts of men. The movement of men's hearts is made so by [external] things. They are affected by things and move, thus they take shape in [human] sound. (1.1; Cook 1995: 24; 1.1, tr. mod.)
> 凡音之起, 由人心生也。人心之動, 物使之然也。感於物而動, 故形於聲。

> All melodies are born from the hearts of men. Emotion is stirred within and thus takes shape in sound. Sound forms patterns, and this is called melodies. (1.4; Cook 1995: 29; 1.3, tr. mod.)
> 凡音者, 生人心者也。情動於中, 故形於聲。聲成文, 謂之音。

Human nature has the capacity to be affected by the external world, and when it happens, the heart/mind starts to move, which is experienced as an emotion. Body is the vehicle through which external things affect us, or rather, it is the place itself of being affected. The heart/mind permeates our whole body; it is our embodied experience, and has both emotive and cognitive aspects. Cognition is not squeezed between bodily input and output as in the "classical sandwich" (see above 2.1, 2.4), but they are on the same level, and cognition is a modulation of those external influences—cognition is what happens when the "soundboard" of heart-mind resonates with external things.

Emotions can also disturb cognition, but not as something completely alien to it. Also, the aim of self-cultivation is not to *eliminate* or suppress the emotions but rather to *refine* them. This is what the whole *Yueji* is about. The capacity to be affected, or the internal "stillness," is called "Heaven's nature" (*tian zhi xing* 天之性). When it is indeed affected by external things and it starts to move, it is human desires[5] ("human nature's desires" *xing zhi yu* 性之欲):

> A person is born and is still—this is Heaven's nature. She is affected by [external] things and [then] moves—this is [her] nature's desires. (1.11; Cook 1995: 38; 1.7, tr. mod.)
> 人生而靜, 天之性也; 感於物而動, 性之欲也。

If initially, the heart/mind is characterized by a general openness toward things, after being affected by them, it becomes more concretely intentional, directed toward things, and this is what is called a "desire." When desire is linked to the value of their affection that is positive or harmful, the heard/mind forms "likes and dislikes":

> Things arrive and the [faculty of] knowledge apprehends [them]—only then do likes and dislikes take shape therein. (1.11; Cook 1995: 38; 1.7)
> 物至知知，然後好惡形焉。

This is natural and unavoidable. The only problem is how to change this initial apprehension, consciousness, or knowledge (*zhi* 知) into reflexive understanding. One must "come back to oneself/to one's body"[6] (*fangong* 反躬). If this does not happen, the moving of the heart/mind is haphazard and enticed toward its objects (objects of desire), so that the basic natural articulations become distorted, forgotten, veiled, or "destroyed":

> If likes and dislikes have no regulation within and the [faculty of] knowledge is enticed from without, [a person] can not return to [reflect upon] herself, and heavenly veins are destroyed. (1.11; Cook 1995: 38; 1.7; translation modified)
> 好惡無節於內，知誘於外，不能反躬，天理滅矣。

It means that the person is "transformed by things" or even that she "becomes a thing" (*renhuawu* 人化物):[7]

> Now if a person's being affected by things is without limit and the likes and dislikes of a person have no regulation, then this is [a matter of] things arriving and a person being transformed [by] things. For a person to be transformed [by] things is to destroy the heavenly veins and to extend human desires to the limit. (1.12; Cook 1995: 38; 1.7, translation modified)
> 夫物之感人無窮，而人之好惡無節，則是物至而人化物也。人化物也者，滅天理而窮人欲者也。

Given these premises, the text proposes music as one of the best ways for regulating desires. This does not change the basic fact that we receive the objects of our knowledge from the external world with our body and that it is intimately related to the emotion. Emotion is an inherent part of the gnoseological process. And precisely, if we know it and take it into account, then we can influence this process by influencing upon emotions—and music is such a powerful tool for modulating emotions.

7.5 Returning to One's Body: Individual Transformation of Emotions

Embodied and contextual accounts of knowledge give us ontologically justified, positive means of individual and collective transformation. First, let us take the individual level. In the sphere of sounds there is a gradation of refinement:

> All melodies arise in the hearts of men. Music is that which connects with [ethical] human relationships and [ontological] veins. For this reason, those who know sounds but do not know melodies—these are the birds and the beasts. Those who know melodies yet do not know music—these are the common masses. Only the superior man can know music. (1.7; Cook 1995: 33; 1.6, translation modified)
> 凡音者,生於人心者也。樂者,通倫理者也。是故知聲而不知音者,禽獸是也; 知音而不知樂者, 眾庶是也。唯君子為能知樂。

Unreflective responses to external stimulations are just sounds or voices (*sheng* 聲), and humans have this in common with animals and birds. When those sounds are arranged according to musical rules (e.g., five tones) and means (e.g., wood, metal, stone instruments), then it is called melodies (*yin* 音), performed by common folk. When it is connected to "human relationships and veins" (*lunli* 倫理), only then it may be properly called music (*yue* 樂). "To know music is to enter the interpenetrating level of rituals" (知樂則幾於禮, later in the same paragraph). The person who manages this is a superior or an exemplary person (*junzi* 君子).

The influence of music can reach to varying depth. (1) In the simplest case, it is just a reaction upon an impulse and produces sounds. (2) In a more developed case, melodies are arranged for entertainment. (3) In the most refined case, music involves developed self-reflexivity and it has a profound and beneficial influence on the surroundings

When a person is affected by external things, a certain mood is produced in them, and they are prone to produce music that expresses such emotions. Six emotions are distinguished (see 1.2; cf. Cook 1995: 27–8; 1.2): sorrow, happiness, joy, anger, reverence, and love. Each produces a specific kind of music: exhausted and withering (sorrow), spacious and leisurely (happiness), expansive and scattering (joy), coarse and violent (anger), straightforward and upright (reverence), and harmonious and gentle (love). The authors emphasize that those emotions do not reside in the human nature, but they are responses to affectations from external world. In the Western world, we are familiar with the idea that music in major key is associated with joy, and music in minor key with sorrow. Film music has turned the management of emotions into a refined technique. The general idea is the same: certain kind of music induces certain emotions, which in turn are prone to be expressed in music.

Also, the timbre of different instruments is deemed to elicit certain bodily and emotional reactions. Some of them may be universal, for example the way drumbeat alters the physiological state and can induce a trance that can be useful in driving soldiers to battle.[8] Others may be more culture-specific, when, for example, the bells are associated with men in battle, the chime stones with soldiers on the borders, string instruments with ideal-inspired people (in part 8; see Cook 63–4). As we see in next section, this fact can be useful for governing a society.

7.6 Social Embeddedness: Collective Transformation of Emotions

One factor that determines the mood is the political situation. The way people are governed is common to the population of a whole country, and therefore a general mood or dominating emotion is formed. Again, this finds expression in music: the *Record of Music* claims that music of a well-governed era is peaceful, that of a chaotic era is resentful, and that of a lost state is mournful (1.3). The dominant style of music expresses the political climate. This connection can be used both ways: if we know the political situation, we can predict the musical style of a country; and from a musical style, we can make inferences to the quality of the government.

This brings into focus the social embeddedness of cognition, and first the embeddedness of a person's emotions in the society at large, and its political and economic situation. If we describe affectivity in terms of a dynamical systems theory, as Giovanna Colombetti's does (2014), then emotions (or emotional episodes, as Colombetti calls them) can be seen as a certain self-organizing pattern of the organism (2014: 53). This pattern can be described in terms of attractors that form the affective phase portrait. As the child grows, some of the attractors bifurcate, forming a more complex system of available affective patterns. And this process takes place in interactions with other persons and inside a society that more or less influences the process of affective maturation (see Colombetti 2014: 66–9). Emotions are always intertwined with cultural and interpersonal factors and are intricately embedded in our social field.

Certain emotions, moods, and political situations of a society naturally find expression in different sound patterns. This relationship can be actively exploited since certain sounds and music elicit emotions and moods in large groups of people. Knowing this, it is possible to influence the political situation. It is even necessary, because otherwise the moods created in common people upon different stimuli are unstable, erratic, chaotic.

> Now the people have natures [consisting] of blood, energy, heart, and mind, yet do not have any constancy of sorrow, happiness, joy, and anger. These arise in motion in response to being affected by [external] things, and then do the arts of the heart/mind take shape. (5.1; Cook 1995: 57, translation modified)
> 夫民有血氣心知之性，而無哀樂喜怒之常，應感起物而動，然後心術形焉。

In order to regulate societal emotions, the rulers use "arts of heart/mind" (*xinshu* 心術).[9] We can see here a direct link between mechanisms of the mind and social engineering. Music, together with the rituals, is one of the most powerful arts of the heart/mind and can be used both individually and collectively.

> Music—it is what sages delight in, and it can be used to make better the hearts of the people. Its effect on people is deep; it can alter habits and change customs. Thus the former kings made manifest their teachings therein. (4.6; Cook 1995: 57)
> 樂也者，聖人之所樂也，而可以善民心,其感人深，其移風易俗，故先王著其教焉。

The *Record of Music* makes it clear that music can be used to shape society, particularly by a process involving the shaping of the heart/mind through music.

By the choice of their music, rulers can modify society in a specific and reliable way, as certain characteristics of music produce a certain mood in the populace (5.1; cf. Cook 1995: 57). For example, a quick and overflowing music with sudden changes produces licentious and chaotic mood, but a slow music with simple rhythm makes people healthy and happy. A measured and subtle music where sounds fade away induces a pensive mood—we can think, perhaps, of the sounds of *qin* zither (which in its contemporary form developed after the writing of this text, probably after the start of common era) that was used by literati as an important tool for self-cultivation. Then, a coarse and violent music with abrupt starts and vigorous exertions makes one resolute and steadfast, but a "broad and rich, well-rounded" music "marked by consonances and harmonious motion" makes one affectionate and loving.

Even certain individual notes are related to certain aspects of the society:[10]

> The Way of sound and music connects with administration. *Gong* is the ruler, *shang* is the minister, *jue* is the people, *zhi* is the affairs, and *yu* is the things [of production]. If these five are not chaotic, then there will be no discordant melodies. (1.4; Cook 1995: 29–30; 1.3–1.4)
> 聲音之道,與政通矣。宮為君,商為臣,角為民,徵為事,羽為物。
> 五者不亂,則無怗懘之音矣。

If any of the musical instruments is chaotic and the tone is incorrect, then there will be a problem in a certain part of the society, and it will be "out of tune," or disharmonious. If all of them are chaotic, then "the extermination and passing away of the state will occur in no time at all" (國之滅亡無日矣, Cook 1995: 31).

The *Record of Music* establishes a systematic correspondence between: (1) the type of instruments;[11] (2) their sounds; (3) the effect they have on individuals (making them alert, able to discriminate between right and wrong, honest, prone to be united with others, and be motivated); (4) how these individual responses can be used in a collective endeavor, especially war (making them ready to fight and determined to face death, abide by the orders, act and attack as a cohesive unit); (5) finally, a fifth layer is added, that of the ruler, who for every instrument and sound is reminded of a particular type and function of subjects (soldiers and

Table 1 Correlation between music, emotions, and social roles in the *Record of Music*
© Margus Ott

Type of instrument	Sound	Individual effect	Collective aim	Ruler thinks of subjects who…
bells	clanging	alertness (*hao* 號)	set up for combat	serve in battle
stone	ding-ding	distinction (*bian* 辨)	determination to go to death	died in the frontiers
silk	mournful	honesty (*lian* 廉)	establish integrity	have integrity and propriety
bamboo	blending	coming-together (*hui* 會)	gather together multitudes	shepherd and gather people
drums	clamorous	motivation (*dong* 動)	advance multitudes	serve as military commanders

generals; their virtues of going to battle, face death, and not to desert or disobey orders). (See 8.11–16)

Certain sounds elicit certain emotions and these, in turn, are endowed with social meaning and are embedded in a social setting.

The idea that major and minor keys, and keys based on different notes, have different characteristics is something familiar to the Western culture,[12] but it has been mostly limited to the aesthetic sphere and it did not rise comparable philosophical and political interest. Under the influence of Pythagoras, the Western mind focused more on the mathematical numerical correlations between different sounds (based on the correlations between the length of the string and its pitch),[13] so that philosophical interest in music was driven in a completely different direction, namely toward a disembodied sphere of mathematics. Conscious and systematic use of music for political goals seems to be a more modern phenomenon in the West. Music has been an important tool for designing the emotional background of the people in totalitarian regimes,[14] and in democracies (see Massumi 2005), it has been used for mass mobilization (e.g., the so-called Singing revolution in Estonia in 1988), and it is especially important in the entertainment arts (e.g., the film industry, where the emotional impact of a horror film, thriller or romance comes largely from the soundtrack). In all those cases it has been acknowledged that music does influence us deeply, emotionally, that it can create a certain mood in a group, create enthusiasm, anger, sorrow etc. It may happen without conscious control or consent: I can be induced to sorrow by the soundtrack of a bad movie that I do not like. This points to a danger in this kind of embodied approach: society is fashioned without discussion, argumentation, dispute; and attitudes and moods may be induced surreptitiously.

7.7 Ontology of Energy and Veins

The *Record of Music* employs two terms that deserve special attention: energy (*qi* 氣) and veins (*li* 理).[15] These are some of the most refined concepts for an embodied approach to the world. "Energy" can be understood as the power of existence of a thing or a being. In Chinese philosophy it is often understood as an interpenetrating substance from which all things are contracted, condensed, or coagulated. "Veins" (also translated as "coherence," "principle," "structure," etc.) refers, according to the traditional etymology of the character 理, to the lines running through a piece of jade[16] (that appears in the left side of the character), and according to a historically more correct etymology, to a village (*li* 里) seen from above, showing its articulations of streets or channels. The word refers to the inner articulations of a thing (that later acquired also normative meaning, how things *ought* to be, hence the traditional translation of it as "principle"). The concepts of energy and veins were developed most notably in the Song dynasty (960–1279) Neo-Confucianism movement, where such ideas became central concepts. Although they are not yet so developed in the *Record of Music*, we can test their affordances as concepts.

In talking about designing emotions, the authors of the *Record of Music* say there is a good flow of energy and a bad, impeded flow of it. Specifically, they say that different kinds of music elicit energy that either "goes along" (*shun* 順) or "goes against" (*ni* 逆) its natural course (in the citation below they are translated by Cook as "favorable" and "contrary"). They give birth to, respectively, harmonious and licentious music. The licentious music might perhaps "go along" with human desires, but it goes against the "lot" or "role" (*fen* 分), or the heavenly veins, of human beings:

> If depraved sounds affect men, then a contrary energy comes in response; when contrary energy acquires form, licentious music arises. If upright sounds effect men, then favorable energy comes in response; when favourable energy acquires form, harmonious music arises; the initiator and the follower respond to each other, the round and deflected, the crooked and the straight, each goes back to its lot; and the veins of all things all interact with each other according to their class. (6.1; cf. Cook 1995: 59, Legge, § 31, Guidi 85–6)[17]
>
> 凡奸聲感人，而逆氣應之；逆氣成象，而淫樂興焉。正聲感人，而順氣應之；順氣成象，而和樂興焉。倡和有應，回邪曲直，各歸其分；而萬物之理，各以其類相動也。

This passage continues the idea that music affects a person's mental and emotional state. Of course, this idea can be taken to oppressive consequences, if those in power are able to tie the ideal of good music to certain particular forms. Indeed, this is done both in the *Record of Music* and already in the *Analects*, where the music of a certain region is denounced as bad (3.25, 15.11, 17.18). This kind of thought is politically suspicious and easily plays into the hands of those who simply want to perpetuate certain cultural forms. And this may harm the requirement of preparing the best channels for energy to flow.

To be faithful to the content of this idea, however, it must be detached from its historical goals and uses. It is legitimate to ask: which kind of veins or articulations (or, more specifically, which kinds of music) are best suited for the energy to flow in the best way? There cannot be a definite answer, but there might still be some hints that could help to choose.

It is said in the text that when the energy that goes along (or "is favorable") acquires form, it makes everything to "go back to its lot" (歸其分), so that "the veins of all things interact with each other according to their class" (萬物之理, 各以其類相動).[18] Again, this can be taken in a conservative fashion that "everyone should know his/her role," all persons and things should have a pre-established place. But this phrase can also be interpreted in a wider sense, that every person should be in contact with their field of individuation (the "lot" or "partition" *fen* 分 can be taken also in this sense), and not to be attached to particular forms, but on the contrary, to counter-actualize[19] them, and revirtualize the actual.[20] In this sense, it would be an appeal to interact not (only) on the actual level of juxtaposing things but further "upstream," in the intensities and the interpenetrating (cf. above, 2.12).

Energy and veins are good candidates for developing an embodied philosophy, as embodied existence always has a certain power of existence as well as certain articulations. It is namely in embodied interactions with the world that we exercise our energy and find its scope, and also discover and develop important articulations of our body and other bodies, beings, and environments. For instance, when I learn to swim, I deploy a certain power of action, of affecting my environment and being affected by it, and by doing this I discover the ways the articulations of my body match the environment of water. The veins would describe the lifeworld of a being, its enactive Umwelt (see Uexküll 1926, 1957). The concepts of the energy and the veins have also the advantage that they do not presuppose a human subject or even a living being, but can be applied to any entity, situation, or event, since these all have a certain power by which they endure and maintain certain articulations or "veins." There cannot be a force or power without any distinctions, and neither can distinctions be upheld without a certain energy (for more on this, see Ott 2021).

7.8 Self-cultivation According to Energy and Veins

In principle, good music helps people to direct their energy according to their innermost articulations or veins (*li* 理), and bad music diverts it. Thus, the exemplary person discards licentious music and proceeds to perfect themself through music, dance, and the auxiliary arts:

> After this [the exemplary person] manifests [the inner feeling] by the modulations of note and tone, the elegant accompaniments of *qin* and *se* lutes, the movements with the shield and battle-axe, the ornaments of the plumes and ox-tails, and the concluding with *xiao* and *guan* flutes. It excites the brilliance of complete virtue and stirs up the harmonious action of the four [seasonal] energies, displaying the veins of all things. Thus when Music is carried out, human relations are clarified, ears and eyes are perspicacious, blood and energy are harmonious and even, habits are altered and customs are changed, and all under Heaven is peaceful. (6.3; cf. Cook 1995: 59, 6.2, Guidi 2005: 86)
>
> 然後發以聲音，而文以琴瑟，動以干戚，飾以羽旄，從以簫管。奮至德之光，動四氣之和，以著萬物之理。故樂行而倫清，耳目聰明，血氣和平，移風易俗，天下皆寧。

Not only does music influence people's moods and political energies but it also promotes physical well-being and enables better contact with one's surroundings. Through music, the exemplary person may excite "complete virtue," or potency, and the movement of four seasons, allowing it to resonate with the inner articulations, or veins, of all things, and harmonize them. It might be a kind of intuitive knowledge, similar to the one we shall see in the next chapter where we discuss Zhuangzi.

It is interesting to note the distinction between the inner emotions *qing* 情 and outward-driven desires *yu* 欲. Basically, they are parts of the same process: outer things affect me, stirring the mind into motion; the mind in motion is a feeling or emotion; if we consider its relation to the object that put it into motion, it is desire. In this sense, desire is natural and necessary for human life. It is negative only when it becomes excessive and obsessed, overly attached, or addicted to things. The point is not that all the sensible world, including feelings, is illusionary or noxious and we should free ourselves altogether of the desire or "thirst" to exist, but only that this excessive attachment distorts our natural "veins"; and by being artificially fixed upon a thing for too long, it inhibits our changing, transformation.

> Thus it is said that music is happiness. The exemplary person delights in obtaining the Way; the little man delights in obtaining the desires. If the Way is used to restrain desires, then there is happiness without chaos. If through desires the Way is forgotten, then there is confusion without happiness. That is why the exemplary person returns to the inner emotions in order to harmonize their will and expands the music in order to accomplish their teachings. When the music has free course and the people direct themselves to the [good] direction, then we can see the potency. (6.6–7; cf. Cook 1995: 59, Guidi 2005: 87–8)

故曰：樂者樂也。君子樂得其道，小人樂得其欲。以道制欲，則樂而不亂；以欲忘道，則惑而不樂。是故君子反情以和其志，廣樂以成其教，樂行而民鄉方，可以觀德矣。

Desires should be restrained to and in accord with the Way, and then they bring joy. But if they are separated from the Way as their genetic ground, there is confusion or delusion without real joy. There are two different meanings of joy. One meaning of joy is limited joy, an enjoyment of the object of desire to the detriment of the person.[21] Another meaning of joy is an unlimited joy, which is not impeded by the objects or forms which stirred it up, and keeps contact with the generative force or potency that maintains the transformation of forms and their libidinal investment.[22] This latter joy means a return to the inner emotions or to the emotional core (*qing* 情) that is the heart/mind in motion.

7.9 Enacted Knowledge

Certain moral moods and attitudes are acted out in music and dance. Sometimes it is done through a reference to history.[23] In the *Record of Music*, it is even said that "Music symbolizes accomplished events" (Legge 1885: §44; 夫樂者，象成者也, cf. Cook 1995: 65). In the text, Confucius proceeds to interpret a dance, wherein he explains the dance's symbolic meaning and how it commemorates the Zhou conquest of Shang (*c.* 1045 BC):

> The holding of shields and standing upright symbolizes the affair to be undertaken by King Wu; the waving and stamping symbolizes the aspirations of Jiang Tai Gong; and the breaking-up of the rows and sitting down of the dancers symbolizes the transition into the civil rule of Zhou Gong and Shao Gong. (translation slightly modified; cf. also Legge 1885, §44; 9.2; Cook 1995: 65)
> 總干而山立，武王之事也；發揚蹈厲，大公之志也。《武》亂皆坐，周、召之治也。

Reliving the Zhou conquest presumably reaffirms collective identity and transports one to the times of those sage rulers and makes one to participate in their virtue. Through sympathetic enactment, the performance transforms the spectators:

> In listening to the singing of the Ya and the Song, the aims and thoughts receive an expansion. From the manner in which the shields and axes are held and brandished, and from the movements of the body in the practice with them, now turned up, now bent down, now retiring, now stretching forward, the

carriage of the person receives gravity. From the way in which [the pantomimes] move to their several places and adapt themselves to the several parts [of the performance], the arrangement of their ranks is made correct, and their order in advancing and retiring is secured. In this way music becomes the lesson of Heaven and Earth, the regulator of true harmony, and what the nature of man cannot dispense with. It was by music that the ancient kings gave elegant expression to their joy; by their armies and axes that they gave the same to their anger. Hence their joy and anger always received their appropriate response. When they were joyful, all under heaven were joyful with them; when they were angry, the oppressive and disorderly feared them. In the ways of the ancient kings, ceremonies and music may be said to have attained perfection. (10.7; Legge 1885, §49)

故聽其雅、頌之聲, 志意得廣焉; 執其干戚, 習其俯仰詘伸, 容貌得莊焉; 行其綴兆, 要其節奏, 行列得正焉, 進退得齊焉。故樂者天地之命, 中和之紀, 人情之所不能免也。夫樂者, 先王之所以飾喜也, 軍旅鈇鉞者, 先王之所以飾怒也。故先王之喜怒, 皆得其儕焉。喜則天下和之, 怒則暴亂者畏之。先王之道, 禮樂可謂盛矣。

A similar passage can be found in Xunzi's chapter on music:

Hence, when we listen to the sounds of the *Odes* and *Hymns*, our aspirations and sense of purpose gain breadth from the experience. When we observe the way the shields and battle-axes are brandished and the repetitive episodes of the dancers gazing down and lifting their faces up, bending and straightening their bodies, our demeanor and bearing acquire dignity from it. When we observe their ranks move within borders of fixed areas and their coordination with the rhythm and meter of the music, the arrangement of our own ranks is corrected and our advances and withdrawals are made uniform. Thus, in musical performances, the ranks moving forward is the way to suggest punitive expeditions and punishing offenders and their stepping back the way to suggest saluting and yielding. (Xunzi 1999: 651–3)

故聽其雅頌之聲, 而志意得廣焉; 執其干戚, 習其俯仰屈伸, 而容貌得莊焉; 行其綴兆, 要其節奏, 而行列得正焉, 進退得齊焉。故樂者、出所以征誅也, 入所以揖讓也。²⁴

The ordered dance arrangements instill certain psychological dispositions (gravity, dignity) and social ideals (order, stability). Attending the ceremony, one's ideas are expanded, and the physical movements obtain symbolic power (as we saw above in 3.5 in the case of Kuranko rituals). The opposing movements of going forward and stepping back represent the duality of punishing and yielding, which correspond to anger and joy. While Han Feizi discussed punishments and rewards through laws, here this duality is given artistic representation. Han Feizi tapped into human motivation by their rational calculation, but here this is achieved through emotional involvement and understanding immersion in ritual and artistic participation. The ritual is given a further expansion by claiming that it reflects the order and harmony of the nature (Heaven and Earth). Therefore, the dance works at different levels at the same time: the individual dancer, their group of dancers, the community they belong to, the ancestors whom they represent, the whole cosmos.

Not only are certain attitudes enacted through dance and music but they also receive expansion, refinement, and sublimation. Factually, music and dance were parts of the same ceremonies, but conceptually, in this text, music (*yue* 樂) is connected to joy (*le* 樂; same sinogram, but different pronunciation), and ax-dance is related to anger. These correspond, respectively, to culture and war, self-refinement and self-preservation. Through the choreography of dance and the character of music, individual emotions are acted out and integrated into a collective ritual.

Xunzi also stresses that certain meanings are enacted and diffused in dance and music:

> How can we know the idea of the dance? I say the eyes do not see it and the ears do not hear it. Rather, it happens only when the order of every episode of gazing down and lifting up the face, of bending and straightening, of advancing and retreating, and of retardation and acceleration is executed with proper, restrained control; when the strength of bone and flesh has been so thoroughly trained that every movement is in such agreement with the rhythm of the drums, bells, and ensemble that there is never an awkward or wayward motion; and when these, through constant practice, are combined into an ideal that is realized again and again. (Xunzi 1999: 663)
> 曷以知舞之意? 曰: 目不自見, 耳不自聞也, 然而治俯仰、詘信[伸]、進退、遲速, 莫不廉制, 盡筋骨之力, 以要鐘鼓俯[附]會之節, 而靡有悖逆者, 眾積意譁譁乎!

This enacted meaning is diffuse; it cannot be directly seen or heard, or tied to a specific word or proposition but is expressed in the whole of the dance itself. Meaning is expressed through proper articulations of dance and music (looking up or down, bending or straightening, advancing or retreating, retarding or accelerating) and there is a gradual and time-consuming improvement in apprenticeship (cf. above 2.11) of harmonizing one's movements and coordinating them with other dancers and musicians, resulting in the acquisition of grace.[25]

At the end of his chapter on music, Xunzi gives a detailed description of wine ceremony, how is it articulated and what distinctions are made. Host pays a special attention to the chief guest; while he engages all guests in a ritual exchange, with the chief guest, it is longer and more complex. Wine drinking is interspaced with musical performance; wine is offered to the main guest who gives it to his attendant, who in turn gives it to all other guests in the order of seniority. Finally, after the formal part, all enjoy together drinking. Xunzi then concludes his long description with the following words:

> Being clear about the distinction between noble and base, keeping distinct those to be exalted and those to be diminished; being congenial and enjoying oneself without dissipation; observing the distinctions between junior and senior without leaving anyone out; and being content and at ease yet in no way becoming disorderly—these five patterns of conduct are sufficient to rectify the individual and to make the country tranquil. (Xunzi 1999: 667)
> 貴賤明, 隆殺辨, 和樂而不流, 弟長而無遺, 安燕而不亂, 此五行者, 足以正身安國矣。

As in the case of the Kurankos (see 3.5), we can see that certain moral values are instilled by this kind of ritual behavior, especially moderation and honoring of superiors and elders. The ceremony by itself requires patience: you cannot get drunk immediately, but your acts are sequenced in ritual exchanges and interspaced with musical interludes. By the very nature of the ritual sequence, it thus inculcates moderation and self-control.[26] The exchange on which one dwells longer and in a more nuanced way, is inherently more important, since one has to pay more attention and make more effort. The distinctions in ritual behavior according to the status and age of the persons, iconically represents this difference in importance. Also, you can interact more with persons who sit closer to you, so that the ones you seat closer to the host are honored more. So, you act out honoring, and this attitude will also permeate your mind. Distinctions are made, but at the same time nobody is left out.

Regulating and distinguishing are the most important functions of rituals for Xunzi (see also in *Xunzi* the preceding Chapter 19 on rituals). In the *Record of Music*, this idea of distinction-making in rituals is taken a step further, together with the idea of cohesion attributed to the music. "Rituals" and "Music" (that are also chapters in the *Xunzi*) are the focus of a very refined ontological speculation in *The Record of Music*, explored in the next section. *The Record of Music* elaborates on Xunzi's phrase "Music unites and makes common; rituals separate and differentiate" (樂合同, 禮別異).[27]

7.10 Music and Rituals: Integration and Differentiation

Large parts of the *Record of Music* are dedicated to sophisticated, parallel discussions on music and ritual. Exploring this pair provides a nuanced presentation of the embodied, embedded, and emotional dimensions of cognition in particular and existence in general. This adds ontological depth to the embodiment theory.

The focus of music is said to be on the inside and that of rituals on the outside:

> Music comes out from within; ritual is made from without. (2.3; Cook 1995: 43; 2.2, translation modified)
> 樂由中出, 禮自外作。

> Thus, music is that which moves inside, and ritual is that which moves outside. (10.3; Cook 1995: 67, translation modified)
> 故樂也者, 動於內者也; 禮也者, 動於外者也。

Music and rituals move in opposite directions. Music, on the one hand, is that which is born from a stirring of the heart/mind and finds expression on the outside, in the songs and music. When people feel happy, they spontaneously start to sing and dance, and sad feelings may find expression in melancholic songs. Rituals, on the other hand, start from the outside, through ritual interaction with others, and transforms the inside. For a long time, you rehearse a ritual script: this disciplines the body and hence also the mind. Also, certain implicit moral ideas are instilled in some rituals (e.g., bowing to an elderly person or to the spirit tablet of an ancestor), the full meaning of which may come explicitly to the consciousness much later.

In very broad terms, music is related to integration and rituals to differentiation:

> Music serves to integrate; ritual serves to differentiate. With integration there is mutual closeness; with differentiation there is mutual respect. When music gains the upper hand there is homogeneous stream.[28] When ritual gains the upper hand there is falling apart.[29] To unite the emotions and to polish external appearances—these are the affairs of ritual and music. (2.1; Cook 1995: 42, translation modified)
> 樂者為同, 禮者為異。同則相親, 異則相敬, 樂勝則流, 禮勝則離。合情飾貌者禮樂之事也。

We can first take it in the social sense: music is responsible for cohesion and rituals guarantee distinctions.[30] Indeed, when we sing or dance together, a bond forms between us; we may even feel our subjectivities to merge, and to become one body. Rituals, on the other hand, maintain distinctions: they regulate how persons are distributed in space, how actions are sequenced and articulated.

But in these social aspects we can see the expression of two general aspects of existence: integration and differentiation. Both aspects require the other. Real time and space (as distinguished from imagined ones) are both integrated and differentiated. Without differentiation, they would collapse and without integration they would fall apart. It is true on all levels of entities.[31]

Music and rituals must work together, and if they do, then music begets harmony and rituals beget flexibility:

> Music reaches the utmost of harmony; rituals reach the utmost of flexibility. If one is harmonious inside and flexible outside, then the people will observe their facial expression and not contend with them; the people will look at their behavior and appearance and will not be careless or inattentive. Thus, if potency shines and moves inside, the people are sure to listen; if the veins are displayed outside, the people are sure to follow. Thus it is said: "When you expand the Way of rituals and music, take it up and put it into practice, then nothing will be difficult under Heaven." (10.3; cf. Cook 1995: 67, tr. mod.)
>
> 樂極和, 禮極順, 內和而外順, 則民瞻其顏色而弗與爭也; 望其容貌, 而民不生易慢焉。故德輝動於內, 而民莫不承聽; 理發諸外, 而民莫不承順。故曰: 致禮樂之道, 舉而錯之, 天下無難矣。

It is said in the *Analects*: "The exemplary person harmonizes and does not make identical; the small person makes identical, but does not harmonize" (君子和而不同, 小人同而不和, 13.23), where the distinction is between "to make identical" (*tong* 同) and "to harmonize" (*he* 和). Integration without differences creates a homogeneous flow; it makes identical, like the small or petty person who is not able to make distinctions. Together with differentiation, however, it produces harmony. Similarly, differentiation without integration falls apart, but together with integration it gives flexibility: the distinctions and differences are integrated, so that they are not constrained by a single form or rule, or a limited number of them. Differences influence and interact with each other (are "integrated"), so that they incessantly transform each other, in the end providing for flexible behavior. The word for flexibility here is *shun* 順, meaning "to follow; to obey" (that we saw above in 7.5). Yet, this following or obeying cannot be blind submission, because in that case, there would be an excess of integration (cancelling of my own and other person's subjectivity), and not the dynamic dialectics of integration and differentiation that is required by the text.

7.11 Free Space

To obtain an optimum result, music and rituals themselves must balance between having a certain form and refraining from overfilling these forms. Music and rituals should not be too complicated and they should accommodate enough empty room:

> For this reason, the prospering of music [at the sacrifice] is not [a matter of] reaching the extreme in melodies; the ritual of the communal ancestral sacrifice is not [a matter of] extending to the utmost in flavors. The *se* in the Temple to King Wen had red [-boiled] strings and sparse holes [in the bottom], and with one singing and three sighing, there would be left-over music. In the Ritual of the Great Ancestral Sacrifice, water (lit. "black wine") was held highest and raw fish was put on the offering stands; the great thick-soup was not mixed [with spices, etc.], and there would be left-over flavors. (1.9; Cook 1995: 34; 1.6, translation modified)
>
> 是故樂之隆, 非極音也。食饗之禮, 非致味也。清廟之瑟, 朱弦而疏越, 壹倡而三嘆, 有遺音者矣。大饗之禮, 尚玄酒而俎腥魚, 大羹不和, 有遺味者矣。

If music and rituals are too complex, too stuffed with forms, they hamper the free movement of spirit for those participating.[32] This is the art of implication, and if understood rightly, it is not "less" but "more," because if the music is too much filled with notes, chords, melodies, with few pauses, then it becomes easily identical with what is performed, with the actual melodies (with simple "melodies"), whereas if you leave more "space" in music, then you sense also what is not there, all the implied music (so that it becomes music in the strong sense of the word). Of course, it is easier to impress listeners with overfilled music than with sparse music, without the latter becoming tedious.[33] The same applies to taste. Dishes in most important sacrifice rituals have no added spices or salt. In this way the dish retains its capacity to receive all the tastes.[34] If it is made according to one taste (e.g., salty or spicy), then it is determined and constrained by it; it cannot revert to other tastes, and it has lost its totipotency. Whereas in ordinary dishes spices are added for the enjoyment of those different tastes, the sacrificial dish has to be congruous with the undetermined, undifferentiated, or interpenetrating state of nature.

The enjoyment of this sparse music requires intellectual and emotional engagement from the audience; people with an unrefined sense of music and emotion feel bored like marquis Wen:

Marquis Wen of Wei asked a question of Zi Xia: "When I put on my official robe and black hat and listen to ancient music, I only feel I will keel over [from boredom]. When I listen to the melodies of Zheng and Wei, I do not know what it means to be tired. May I ask, why is ancient Music like this and new music like that?" (8.1; Cook 1995: 61, translation modified)

魏文侯問於子夏曰:「吾端冕而聽古樂, 則唯恐臥; 聽鄭衛之音, 則不知倦。敢問: 古樂之如彼何也? 新樂之如此何也?」

Zi Xia then explains to the marquis the difference between the music that is capable of implication and the melodies that are not:

Zi Xia replied, "Now with ancient Music, [the dancers] advance and retreat in unison, and [the music] is made broad with an upright harmony. Instruments of strings, gourds, and reeds are all held together by [the rhythm] of *fu*-shakers and drums. The performance begins with the civil (drums) and is again brought to order at the end with the military (bells). [The music] is kept in order by *xiang*-shakers, and the tempo [of the dancers] is maintained by the *ya*-drum. At this point, the superior man discusses its meaning, and talks about the ancient. He cultivates himself on down to his clan, and evens out all under Heaven. This is the issuing forth of ancient music.

Now with the new music, [the dancers] advance and retreat in contracted movements, and [the music] overflows with lascivious sounds. It entrances [the listener] and does not cease. It reaches the point of clowns and dwarfs, and boys and girls frolicking together like monkeys, and [the distinction between] father and son is not known. At the end of the music, no discussion can be done, and the ancient can not be talked about. This is the issuing forth of the new music." (8.2; Cook 1995: 61)

子夏對曰:「今夫古樂, 進旅退旅, 和正以廣。弦匏笙簧, 會守拊鼓,
始奏以文, 復亂以武, 治亂以相, 訊疾以雅。
君子於是語, 於是道古, 修身及家, 平均天下。此古樂之發也。
今夫新樂, 進俯退俯, 奸聲以濫, 溺而不止; 及優侏儒, 獶雜子女, 不知父子。樂終不可以語, 不可以道古。此新樂之發也。

The so-called ancient music is regulated. There is an alternation of the "civil" and "military" and there are distinct functions of instruments and differentiated movements of the dancers. In this description, the stress is not so much on the sparseness or overfilling of the music but on its regulation. Music has certain articulations, or veins, and therefore it has an implied meaning. This requires a bit of cultural knowledge, as shown in the *Record of Music*, Part 9, where Confucius and Binmou Jia discuss the symbolic meaning of musical performance (cf. above, section 7.7). In general, it is namely due to these articulations that a melody becomes music in the higher sense of the word. Without these articulations, it is mere melody, like the so-called new music. In the new music, meaning is completely exhausted by its manifest form; it is pleasant, but there is nothing in it to talk about, because it doesn't have an implied reserve in its meaning. On a critical note, it may be said that Confucian observers were too attached to certain cultural forms and were incapable of detecting and appreciating the distinctions of the "new music." Without a recording of this ancient music, contemporary evaluations of the new music are impossible. It may have indeed been simple entertainment, or it may have been a new form of musical articulations to which the Confucians were simply apprehensive, just as many twentieth-century critics spoke ill of jazz or rock & roll when they emerged.

Rituals and music cultivate the person by "lessening" and "filling":

> Music moves inside and rituals move outside. Therefore, the rituals most importantly are about lessening and music about filling. Rituals lessen and go forth, with going forth it makes refinement. Music fills and returns, by returning it makes refinement. If the rituals lessen but do not go forth, then it withers away; if the music fills but does not return, then it indulges. Therefore, rituals have expression and music has return. When rituals reach expression, there is joy; when music attains return, there is calm. The expression of rituals and the return of music have the same meaning. (10.4)
> 樂也者, 動於內者也; 禮也者, 動於外者也。故禮主其減, 樂主其盈。禮減而進, 以進為文: 樂盈而反, 以反為文。禮減而不進則銷, 樂盈而不反則放; 故禮有報而樂有反。禮得其報則樂, 樂得其反則安; 禮之報, 樂之反, 其義一也。

Ritual behavior is a certain simplification of behavior. Not all behavior counts as ritualistic, but only certain chosen sequences of action and speech. Yet, rituals should not be simplified up to complete disappearance. They must "go forth," be performed, find an expression, lest they be cancelled altogether (or "wither away"). Music "fills" and gives satisfaction, but it must also "return," leading to introspection (*fan* 反). Introspection is not fostered through mere melodies, and without it music is simple, lascivious entertainment. With these complementary functions—to go forth and to return—the person is refined and culture promoted, and joy and calm achieved. Joy forms a pair with calm (*an* 安), and this pair of joy and calm is related to two other pairs of notions in ritual and music: expression and introspection; going forth and returning.

To understand the joy-calm notional pair, think of the words of Spinoza. He says that when the spirit contemplates itself and its power of action, it is joyful (Ethics 3p53; cf. below 8.7). On the one hand, the power of action, which is a certain expression or going-forth, and in its most refined form it would be a smooth, natural, free action, or movement. On the other hand, there is the contemplation of that power of action, which is nothing but the interpenetrating aspect of the action or of the situation itself, without prescribing any concrete form for the future and without remorse from things past. In this way, contemplation is "calm"—one is mindful to the situation, to one's power, and to the affordances of the world. And when one pays attention to this calm presence to or contemplation of one's power of action, one is joyful. It does not depend on the absolute level of that power and is accessible even at the deathbed when all powers for action are fading—because joy arises from the simple interpenetrating aspect of those powers themselves.

This sufficiency of the consciousness that contemplates the situation and is adequate to it, does not contradict the power of implication. It may indeed seem that implication imposes something "more" that is not explicitly posited in the situation, and so it would seem inadequate to the situation and to one's power to be in it. But calm contemplation does not cancel implication; on the contrary, contemplation requires it. Without implication and its potential, consciousness would be exhausted by its contents, and it would only "go forth," without "returning." It is this returning or reflective capacity that is the root of all implication and enables one to pack more into the experience than is given on the surface of actualized forms.

7.12 Simplicity and Ease

Music is related to being still and easy, and rituals are related to refinement and simplicity.

> Music comes out from inside; rituals are made from outside. Music comes out from inside; thus it is still. Rituals are made outside; thus they are refined. Great Music must be easy; Great Ritual must be simple. (2.3; Cook 1995: 43, translation modified)
> 樂由中出, 禮自外作。樂由中出故靜, 禮自外作故文。大樂必易, 大禮必簡。

Music is said to be still, but wasn't it said before that music comes out when the heart/mind is affected by external stimuli and starts to move (and movement *dong* 動 is the contrary of stillness *jing* 靜), producing an emotion that naturally expresses itself in sounds and music? But the heart/mind, before being stimulated, is still. When a human is born, they are still, and that is their nature. It is namely because of this that their heart/mind is able to be moved, and to be affected by movement. If the heart/mind already moved in itself, this would inhibit its capacity to be moved by external modulators (cf. above, 7.2). In a similar way, the origin of sounds cannot be soundy. Only stillness lets the music to be heard.[35]

Music in the higher sense of the word, discussed in the *Record of Music*, is those melodies that are in contact with this stillness as their origin and are able to "return." If the music lacks this, it is a mere conglomeration of melodies that has severed this link with original stillness and only goes forth, without returning. A counterpart to this stillness is the refinement (*wen* 文) by rituals: it becomes the basis of human culture (*wen* 文). Rituals give interpersonal articulations that can, in principle, foster smooth social interaction. They channel the external stimuli in a beneficial way. Without them, the internal stillness of the mind would receive bad articulations and develop bad, untamed, willful habits. As it is said in the *Analects* 2.15:

> If you learn without thinking about what you have learned, you will be lost. If you think without learning, however, you will fall into danger. (Slingerland 2003a: 13)
> 學而不思則罔, 思而不學則殆.

If you learn and do not think, then you do not connect what you have learned with your own person, and you will be lost in empty scholasticism. But if you only think and do not learn, you will remain an uncouth ruffian unable to navigate properly social relations and you will therefore face danger. The latter problem arises from the lack of rituals.

On the topic of ease and simplicity (cf. ease and joy in 4.11), two accounts of knowledge—the disembodied and the embodied—give rise to two different forms of ease or simplicity. One kind of easiness is technical type. With knowledge of certain mathematical formulas, for example, it is *easy* to solve certain algebra problems. With knowledge of a code of law, it is easier to prosecute a case. With a compass, it is easier to draw an accurate circle. With an electric screwdriver it is easier to drive in a screw. With a calculator it is easier to compute. The basis of this kind of easiness is a technical facilitation of life, a modulation of forces, so that more effect can be achieved with less effort. That is what technology is for: lever and pulley help to hoist things, bicycle helps moving around, and computer facilitates complex calculations. In the mental realm, certain artifacts (mathematical formula, code of law, etc.) serve as external fulcra for the mental effort, making the work easier. This is the ease and simplicity of a disembodied type, arising from external materials or mental tools, technical devices for transmission of force and intellect in order to enhance efficacy. (Cf. below, 8.4.)

Another kind of easiness is an embodied type of grace and mastery that is acquired by a painter, acrobat, swimmer, dancer, or musician, who has attained the "flow" (Csikszentmihalyi 2014), "scenic sensibility" (Stanislavski 2010), "*satori*" (D.T. Suzuki 1996), or "free and easy wandering" (Zhuangzi, cf. above, 2.11, and below, 8.8). This easiness comes from mastering technique so that actions may be performed without much intentional thought. A masterful flutist will know how to play a tune without having to consciously think of the position of fingers. The flutist masters the instrument, but it is not a one-directional relation. The flutist is also modulated by the flute, audience, room, musical piece. There is a dialogue, a feedback, or "back-talk" from the instrument and surroundings (see Schön 1983: 79). The identity of the flutist is not left unaffected by the instrument, but they together form a complex and dynamic system that overflows to the surroundings.

Of course, the same is true for any tool, but it is a question of emphasis: in case of technical involvement, the focus is more narrowly on the result that can also be quantified and estimated, *how much* does it make action easier than without the use of tools, or with the use of less developed technology. In case of embodied mastery, the emphasis is on the process itself and its expressive power of the graceful performance.

Similarly with technical performance, embodied mastery requires certain tools (for example, the flute), environments (a place for performing), and traditions (the musical tradition). After a period of training, one's body, tools, environments, and other factors are integrated, and the performance becomes fluent. Here, the focus is on this fluency that is a phase transition into qualitatively different mode of action where everything fits, an aspect of performance stops being isolated (where is my finger? what note was it?) and appears in the context of other aspects and integrated with them. The butterfly of easy, lively, and graceful action breaks free from the chrysalis of training.

These two kinds of easiness are not necessarily exclusive to each other; a technically efficient performance may be also graceful. It is just that one focuses on external effectiveness and the other on immersed grace.

7.13 Cosmic Purport

Music and rituals have a cosmic purport:

> Great Music shares a common harmony with Heaven and Earth. Great Rituals share a common articulation with Heaven and Earth. There is harmony, thus

the "hundred things" do not suffer loss; there is articulation, thus [there are] sacrifices to Heaven and to Earth. In the bright [sphere] there are Ritual and Music; in the dark [sphere] there are ghosts and spirits. (2.5; Cook 1995: 44; 2.3, translation modified)

大樂與天地同和, 大禮與天地同節。和故百物不失, 節故祀天祭地, 明則有禮樂, 幽則有鬼神。如此, 則四海之內, 合敬同愛矣。

Music and rituals on the manifest side, "the bright sphere," are connected to the latent, virtual side, "the dark sphere," of ghosts and spirits. Action in the actual, clear, and juxtaposed world has repercussions in the virtual, dark, and interpenetrating world. Music and ritual change the interpenetrating side of being, the potency from where everything is unfolded. In a religious sense, music and ritual connect to the spirits of the ancestors, heavenly and earthly spiritual forces, and implicated agents who remain in the virtual and do not actualize themselves as properly spatiotemporal beings (and therefore they could be measured or timed).[36]

It is important to access the interpenetrating aspect of music and ritual; only then is one able to create them:

> Thus those who know the core feeling of rituals and music can create; those who understand the patterns of rituals and music can transmit. Creators are called sagely; transmitters are called enlightened. Being enlightened and sagely refers to transmitting and creating. (2.8; cf. Cook 1995: 46; 2.4)
>
> 故知禮樂之情者能作, 識禮樂之文者能述。作者之謂聖, 述者之謂明; 明聖者, 述作之謂也。

Music and ritual come from "core feeling" (*qing* 情), that is, the interpenetrating side of the person. If one is familiar with this ontological aspect, one is able to create new forms of ritual and music. But if one only follows their forms, one is at best only able to copy and reproduce preexisting forms, to transmit them. This is a very important aspect of self-cultivation: how to become creative; how to attain grace, smoothness, and ease of action; and how to reach beyond given forms to their generative sources.

Music and ritual are connected to cosmic and social patterns:

> Music is the harmony of Heaven and Earth. Rituals are the order of Heaven and Earth. Harmony, thus the hundred things all transform; order, thus the myriad things are all differentiated. Music is created from Heaven, Ritual is constructed through Earth.[37] If there is excess in the construction [of rituals], there is chaos. If there is excess in the creation [of music], there is violence. Only after having a clear understanding of Heaven and Earth is it possible to make rituals and music prosper. (2.3–2.4; Cook 1995: 46, translation modified)

樂者，天地之和也；禮者，天地之序也。和故百物皆化；序故群物皆別。
樂由天作，禮以地制。過制則亂，過作則暴。明於天地，然後能興禮樂也。

Music, as the integrative function, is related to harmony (*he* 和), and ritual, as the differentiating function, is related to ordering, sequencing (*xu* 序). Together, these aspects uphold the transformation (*hua* 化) of things, so that they maintain their otherness, or distinction (*bie* 別). An interesting contrast is drawn between making or creating (*zuo* 作) from heaven and constructing or designing (*zhi* 制) from earth. This refers to the two aspects of creation: one is the interpenetrating and virtual[38] aspect (heaven), and the other is juxtaposing and actual aspect (earth). All making, forming, or creating proceeds from the virtual Heaven, whence the actualization starts, but it "uses Earth" (*yidi* 以地), being continually in feedback from the already actualized. Earth in this sense is not any particular actual form but the form or level of actuality itself. If one delves too deeply into the virtual, this leads to the loss of all forms, like the "homogeneous flow" mentioned above, and if one focuses too much on the actual, this leads to the violent clash between forms, as they are individually and collectively separated from their origin and are therefore not flexible, adapting, or accommodating.

7.14 Conclusion

In this section, we returned to the contextualizing strand of Chinese tradition, to a Confucian response to decontextualizing tendencies. We discussed some themes of embodiment in Mencius and Xunzi, who in different ways promoted knowledge as embedded and enactive.

Then, in the *Record of Music*, we discussed in more detail the same topics of embodied, enacted, emotive knowledge, and existence as in Confucius. The *Record of Music* represents one of the most advanced philosophical developments of an embodied type of thinking, one of the furthest "ramifications" of it:

First, in the *Record of Music*, important epistemological ideas are presented. It is said that mind is initially still, and that it starts to move on the influence from external things. When external things influence me and my heart/mind starts to move, it creates simultaneously an emotional coloring and ideational content. Therefore, all external knowledge has an emotional and embodied background. But the essence or "root rhizomatic body" (*benti* 本體, to use a traditional

Chinese concept) that accommodates this movement is tranquil, still, "empty," interpenetrating. And the way music influences us is paradigmatic, since music has a deep influence on people. It creates particularly strong emotional coloring. And this fact can be used for both self-cultivation and social design. Certain types of music induce certain moods in people and affect society with certain dispositions.

Second, an interesting aesthetics is developed, where music has to accommodate silence and maintain a connection with its source in the virtual, interpenetrating realm or "Heaven." Music should maintain at its center an empty or free space, and not be overfilled, as simple popular melodies are. Sparse music, where sounds are emphatically in relation with silence, can remain in contact with the interpenetrating ground of music. Music is also a good case upon which to study the different modes of embodied activity. First comes a phase of learning and rehearsing, and then at some happy moments, everything fits into place and one obtains a "flow," a simple, easy, and perfect way of performance (we are going to see some further examples in the next chapter). This kind of easiness can be distinguished from a technical ease of performance, when one uses certain tools that make the more performance powerful and efficient.

Third, in the *Record of Music* there are hints toward a philosophy of "energy" (*qi* 氣) and "veins" (*li* 理), developed more thoroughly in the Song dynasty (960–1276) Neo-Confucianism. In these terms, every entity or event can be treated in terms of a certain power to exist ("energy") and certain articulations ("veins"), both internal and external articulations (how a thing is articulated and how these articulations match other things and environments).

Fourth, the *Record of Music* presents an ontology of integration and differentiation, where music and ritual stand for integration and differentiation, respectively. Although in themselves they are related to the concrete, embodied experience of music and rituals, in this reflective development they obtain a broad social, cosmological, and ontological significance. Every thing, being, or event can be analyzed in terms of integration and differentiation. It offers guidance for self-cultivation, where these two aspects should complement each other. One should unite with other beings and situations through one's differences, to maintain these differences in every assemblage that one makes with other things, beings and people. One should remain different yet integrated, and united yet differentiated. It has hence a deep ontological and cosmic purport.

Fifth, the ontology of integration and differentiation points toward an ethics where special attention is devoted to maintaining both aspects. It is valid both for individual self-cultivation and for social design. The *Record of Music* deals more with the latter (and *Zhuangzi*, which we are going to see in the next chapter, deals more with the former). It is shown how with the help of music and rituals it is possible to keep the society integrated and differentiated at the same time, so that it would maintain its regenerative, transformative power. Although the Confucian authors of the text certainly cherished traditional cultural forms, according to the inner logic of the ontology sketched in the text, those forms are not so important in themselves, but as necessary supports for maintaining music and rituals that represent, broadly speaking, integrating and differentiating forces. This is one of the finest ontologies based on embodied foundations.

8

A Daoist Development of Embodiment: Zhuangzi 莊子

8.1 Introduction

This chapter discusses parts of *Zhuangzi* 莊子, a book that takes its name from Zhuang Zhou 莊周 (*c.* 370–*c.* 289 BC) and which was compiled over a long period of time by several different authors.[1] Zhuangzi's starting point is an embodied, embedded, enactive, extended knowledge and practice. He starts from a reflection on skillful embodied practices and then arrives at very deep ontological and epistemological ideas. He takes contextualization to the extreme, where "context" is the change, the decentering, and the transformation of everything. It is not random but proceeds as an unfolding of interpenetrating relations and differences.

8.2 Knack in Performance

In *Zhuangzi* there are a lot of stories that address the question of embodiment and bodily practices, and a good starting point is Wheelwright Flat.

> Duke Huan was reading in the upper part of his hall and Wheelwright Flat was hewing a wheel in the lower part. Setting aside his hammer and chisel, the wheelwright went to the upper part of the hall and said to Duke Huan, "This book Your Grace is reading—may I venture to ask whose words are in it?"
> "The words of the sages," said the duke.
> Are the sages still alive?
> "Dead long ago," said the duke.
> "In that case, what you are reading there is nothing but the chaff and dregs of the men of old!"
> "Since when does a wheelwright have permission to comment on the books

I read?" said Duke Huan. "If you have some explanation, well and good. If not, it's your life!" (Watson 1968: 152, Ch. 13[2] ; Translation based on Mair 1994: 128)

桓公讀書於堂上,輪扁斲輪於堂下,釋椎鑿而上,問桓公曰:「敢問公之所讀者何言邪?」公曰:「聖人之言也。」曰:「聖人在乎?」公曰:「已死矣。」曰:「然則君之所讀者,古人之糟魄已夫!」桓公曰:「寡人讀書,輪人安得議乎! 有說則可,無說則死。」(13/36/68–71)[3]

This first half of the story is very dramatic: it is a question of life and death. Duke Huan of Qi (r. 685–643 BC) was the most powerful person in China at his time, recognized as hegemon. Wheelwright Flat[4] is most probably a fictitious person. He embodies a paradox: he makes round wheels, but his name is "flat."[5] That a common wheelwright would casually go to chat with the hegemon was absolutely unthinkable, and this adds a humorous tone to the situation. In the following we will see that he is not only skillful craftsman but also very dexterous in speech.

Note the metaphorical dynamics of the story: in the beginning, the duke who is reading books is upstairs and the wheelwright is downstairs. Duke represents discursive knowledge, and Wheelwright Flat represents embodied knowledge. According to the spatial metaphor UP IS GOOD (Lakoff and Johnson 1980: 16), initially the discursive is more important than the embodied. But then the wheelwright puts his work aside and ascends the stairs to the duke, so that he is now on the same level with duke. The wheelwright starts to talk; so, it seems that the whole "upper quarters" is the realm of discourse, into which the wheelwright, having embodied knowledge, introduces a disruptive, subversive, defying element.

Wheelwright Flat said, "I look at it from the point of view of my own work. When I chisel a wheel, if the blows of the mallet are too gentle, the chisel slides and won't take hold. But if they're too hard, it bites in and won't budge. Not too gentle, not too hard—you can get it in your hand and feel it in your mind. You can't put it into words, and yet there's a knack to it somehow. I can't teach it to my son, and he can't learn it from me. So I've gone along for seventy years and at my age I'm still chiseling wheels. When the men of old died, they took with them the things that couldn't be handed down. So what you are reading there must be nothing but the chaff and dregs of the men of old." (Watson 1968: 152-3)

輪扁曰:「臣也,以臣之事觀之。斲輪,徐則甘而不固,疾則苦而不入。不徐不疾,得之於手而應於心,口不能言,有數存焉於其間。臣不能以喻臣之子,臣之子亦不能受之於臣,是以行年七十而老斲輪。古之人與其不可傳也死矣,然則君之所讀者,古人之糟魄已夫。」(13/36/71–4)

Wheelwright Flat explains how the blows of his mallet have to adapt to be exactly adapted to the wood he is working on; they can be neither too gentle nor too hard.[6] Wheelwright Flat means that his knowledge is both contextual, depending on the precise qualities of the wood, and the state of the chisel (which becomes gradually blunter during the work, so that the strength of the blows also has to change accordingly) and embodied (adapting the hardness of blow or tightness of spokes), for it "is something you sense in your hand and feel in your heart" (Mair 1994: 129) or "you can get it in your hand and feel it in your mind" (Watson 1968: 153) (得之於手而應於心). A skilled hand and knowledgeable heart/mind are not opposed to each other like theory and practice, for the heart/mind "responds" (*ying* 應) to the achievement (*dé* 得) of the hand. The question is not about how to make theory[7] from practice, but how to follow bodily activity with the mind, so that it is truly knowledge of and from embodiment.

A central focus of the Wheelwright Flat story is that this kind of embodied knowledge cannot be adequately expressed in words (*kou buneng yan* 口不能言). There is a "knack" (*shu* 數) about it that resists verbalization or, if it is put into words, is understood only by those who have obtained the knack independently, in their own embodied knowledge. This explains why Wheelwright Flat says he could not teach his own son his skill, why he was not able to explain (*yu* 喻) it to his own son, and the son is not able to receive (*shou* 受) it from him. Someone might explain and show a bodily movement, but it is not understood until performed by the person themselves. Embodied knowledge can only be acquired by each person in their own body. The wheelwright may explain and show, but that does not guarantee that the apprentice is able to grasp it themself (cf. above, 2.11, 4.12, 5.4). This is directly opposed to "bookish" learning, where it is possible to transmit knowledge not only through direct instruction but also over great spatial and temporal distances.[8]

At first glance it might seem that Wheelwright Flat has practical knowledge, as opposed to Duke Huan's theoretical knowledge. This seems a very natural distinction and it is worth to linger on this a bit longer. This distinction owes a lot to Aristotle. In the beginning of "Metaphysics" (Aristotle 1998: 4–6) he defines the three main characteristics of theoretical knowledge are that it is general, concerns cause, and is prone to be verbally transmitted and taught. Aristotle acknowledges that practice may be needed, for example, in medicine, and that for some purposes theoretical knowledge is not sufficient. He does note, however, the superiority of theoretical knowledge: "we think also that the architects (*architektonas*) in each *technē* are more honourable and know in a truer sense and are wiser (*sophōteros*) than the manual artisans (*cheirotechnōn*), because they know the causes of the things that are done (981a30-b2)." Power relations come into the definition of theoretical knowledge. The architect does not himself toil but makes others work, who might be ignorant of the general plan; indeed, Aristotle compares them to inanimate things (from a modern perspective, we could indeed say that most of their work could be done by machines). It goes even deeper:

> At first he who invented any art whatever that went beyond the common perceptions of man was naturally admired by men, not only because there was something useful in the inventions, but because he was thought wise and superior to the rest. But as more arts were invented, and some were directed to the necessities of life, others to recreation (διαγωγήν), the inventors of the latter were naturally always regarded as wiser than the inventors of the former, because their branches of knowledge did not aim at utility. Hence when all such inventions were already established, the sciences which do not aim at giving pleasure (ἡδονὴν) or at the necessities of life (τἀναγκαῖα) were discovered, and first in the places where men first began to have leisure. This is why the mathematical arts were founded in Egypt; for there the priestly caste was allowed to be at leisure (σχολάζειν). (Aristotle 1908)

Here Aristotle adds a fourth and fifth element, lack of utility[9] of the highest knowledge, and the idleness of the ruling class who are able to dedicate themselves to purely theoretical investigations.

Wheelwright Flat presents a direct opposite idea(l) of knowledge in all these five points. His knowledge seems to concern the particular, he does not mention causes,[10] and he is unable to put it into words or teach it to his son. Also, he is not leisurely, and his trade has usefulness.

Yet, it would be a mistake to conceive of Flat's art in terms of what Aristotle calls practice, because it involves a completely different logic. Whereas Aristotle develops decontextualized knowledge, Zhuangzi develops contextualized knowledge. It is true that Flat has developed his art on one skill, but it is not a particular to be subsumed under some universal. That would be the order of the explicit. Wheelwright and other similar characters in *Zhuangzi* develop implicit knowledge, the "knack." It has its generality and is different from the knowledge of a beginner. The expert knowledge of the wheelwright envelops knowledge of different materials, tools, wheel-types, and surely also social knowledge of marketing his product. In fact, the distinction between simple expert knowledge of a craft and the same craft as a "way" (*dao* 道) consists namely in that wayfarers do not stop the implicated knowledge strictly at their craft but imply the whole universe in it. The general way is expressed in that craft as a singular way.

This means that the different causes at work in his craft are also implied, and perhaps a more genuine notion of causation is involved here. When you explicitly extract a cause, then it will always be only a partial reason of the effect. When in snooker the cue ball knocks a red ball into a socket, what is the cause of red ball moving to the socket? There is the impulse of the cue ball; their elasticity of the balls; properties of the table; gravity; muscles of the player who stroke with the cue, room that houses the event, Earth, Milky Way. There is always an infinity of causes involved in every event. For practical purposes we eliminate most of them and consider only a handful, but this gives a partial and simplified knowledge. Even the will to extract a certain number of causes deforms the understanding, and the most genuine understanding of causality is when you resolutely refrain from extracting one or some causes but try to imply them all in your activity. For *practical* purposes simplification is justified, but in a philosophical context it is not so justified.

Verbalization and teachability differ in knowing-what and knowing-how. Aristotle bases his theory upon knowing-what, and this knowledge can be put into words more directly and conveyed by verbal teaching. In one history lesson, a lot of facts can be taught. And for the exam in history, it is possible to learn those facts in a short period of time, maybe even in one night. Progress in wheelmaking or, say, piano playing is much more gradual. It takes constant repeated rehearsal to learn the art (there is a rule of thumb of 10,000 rehearsals for acquiring proficiency). And you cannot zip it up so easily. You may work hard the night before the assessment in carpentry or piano, but without previous practice over a considerable period, you will fail. It is not that carpentry or piano could not be talked about and taught, but the discourse is more indirect, implicating, hinting. The apprentices should find the right action in their body, and only then will they understand what was meant with the verbal guidance of their teacher.

In Wheelwright Flat's example, his trade has also practical value, since it produces wheels that can be used. In principle, any practice can be developed in the embodied direction, whether it produces something usable or not. Aristotle's description of the highest knowledge as impractical and the pursuers of this knowledge as leisurely is directly related to social power structures: the one in charge of masons does not lay stones himself, but commands those who lay stones. A white-collar employee makes designs, and a blue-collar worker executes them. A scientist formulates the most abstract description of the universe, and an engineer builds machinery that scientists need. The more cognitive work of white-collar workers and scientists is valued more than the manual work of blue-collar workers and engineers. The latter are meant to provide input to science (lab equipment) and execute output from it (new tools and technology). In reality, the relation of these two kinds of work is much more complex, and manual workers and engineers have an independent source of knowledge from bodily interaction and familiarity with things and materials.

In Aristotle's scheme, philosophers who ponder on questions with least direct practical usefulness are the highest. But such abstract, general, discursive knowledge highlights only a certain part of reality, leaving the rest in obscurity. It may then bring another aspect out of obscurity to the clarity of consciousness, but again on the background of some obscure implicit knowledge. Logically, all of it cannot be brought to clarity; there always remains an obscure ground of knowledge. Zhuangzi's Wheelwright Flat (and other similar characters) wants to relate with this obscure ground, to integrate it with the clarity of consciousness. Being a member of an elite class of idle exploiters would rather hinder this endeavor. You would have to bother yourself with commanding, labor your mind with setting goals for others, controlling them, and worrying about their possible insubordination. For Zhuangzi, Aristotle's idleness would not be idle enough. You would have freed your body from toil, but you would labor your mind. You should also free your mind, and this goal is even more important, and it can be achieved, in principle, in any social condition and in any occupation.

8.3 Stages of Practice

Motifs of embodiment and contextuality are expressed in one of the most famous stories of *Zhuangzi*, about Cook Nail in the 3rd chapter. Cook Nail cuts up an ox and his graceful movements resemble a dance. Lord Wenhui was watching this and praised the cook for his skill. Cook Nail replied:

> "What your servant loves is the Way, which goes beyond mere skill. When I first began to cut oxen, what I saw was nothing but whole oxen. After three years, I no longer saw whole oxen. Today, I meet the ox with my spirit rather than looking at it with my eyes. My sense organs stop functioning and my spirit moves as it pleases. In accord with the natural grain, I slice at the great crevices, lead the blade through the great cavities. Following its inherent structure, I never encounter the slightest obstacle even where the veins and

arteries come together or where the ligaments and tendons join, much less from obvious big bones. A good cook changes his cleaver once a year because he chops. An ordinary cook changes his cleaver once a month because he hacks. Now I've been using my cleaver for nineteen years and have cut up thousands of oxen with it, but the blade is still as fresh as though it had just come from the grindstone. Between the joints there are spaces, but the edge of the blade has no thickness. Since I am inserting something without any thickness into an empty space, there will certainly be lots of room for the blade to play around in. That's why the blade is still as fresh as though it had just come from the grindstone. Nonetheless, whenever I come to a complicated spot and see that it will be difficult to handle, I cautiously restrain myself, focus my vision, and slow my motion. With an imperceptible movement of the cleaver, plop! and the flesh is already separated, like a clump of earth collapsing to the ground. I stand there holding the cleaver in my hand, look all around me with complacent satisfaction, then I wipe off the cleaver and store it away. (Mair 1994: 26–7, tr. mod.)

臣之所好者道也，進乎技矣。始臣之解牛之時，所見無非牛者。三年之後，未嘗見全牛也。方今之時，臣以神遇，而不以目視，官知止而神欲行。依乎天理，批大郤，導大窾，因其固然。技經肯綮之未嘗，而況大軱乎! 良庖歲更刀，割也; 族庖月更刀，折也。今臣之刀十九年矣，所解數 千牛矣，而刀刃若新發於硎。彼節者有間，而刀刃者无厚，以无厚入有間，恢恢乎其於遊刃必有餘地矣，是以十九年而刀刃若新發於硎。雖然，每至於族，吾見其難為，怵然為戒，視為止，行為遲。動刀甚微，謋然已解，如土委地。提刀而立，為之四顧，為之躊躇滿志，善刀而藏之。 (3/7/5–3/8/11)

Lord Wenhui comments that from this explanation he has learned how to nourish life (*yangsheng* 養生).

Since Cook Nail's performance resembles a dance, it is clear that he has perfectly embodied his art of butchering an ox. The cook's mind responds to the bodily activity. It has taken time to achieve. In the beginning the cook saw just an ox. With practice, after three years he lost sight of the ox as an unanalyzable whole. Finally, he says: "I meet the ox with my spirit rather than looking at it with my eyes," his sense organs "know how to stop" or focus (*zhizhi* 知止), and his spirit "likes to move" or "moves as it pleases" (*yuxing* 欲行). He perfects his knowledge: not toward disembodiment but toward more refined embodiment, at the end of which one can "forget the body," like a musician or a dancer, who attains a state of flux (see Csikszentmihalyi 2014) and reports being "one" with music or movement.

The embodied practice described here is context-sensitive. Cook Nail says that he follows the natural articulations or veins ("natural grain," in Mair's translation, *tianli* 天理, cf. above, 7.4) of the ox to cut it open. And also, when he meets a difficult point, he "stops" or focuses his vision (*shi wei zhi* 視為止) and slows down his movements (*xing wei chi* 行為遲), so that he is in perfect accord with the case at hand. Through his personal practice he becomes more adequate; he acquires an intuitive knowledge of the natural articulations of the ox. Often Cook Nail's slowing down at difficult places is interpreted as him dropping his "flow." But this would turn the "flow" into an unconscious state, which can only function in a quick, "hot" mode. This is unrealistic. When a musician is in a state of "flow," it does not mean that they perform unconsciously. Quite the contrary, it means a higher form of consciousness that is able to zoom in and zoom out of different parts of the piece without interrupting the flow. The "stopping" of the vision, in Chinese, does not necessarily mean an interruption, but it can mean a focusing or zooming in. While Cook Nail has achieved an interpenetrating understanding of the ox, himself, and the world, he is still anchored in the situation at hand, and receives feedback from it.

We can detect distinct phases in Cook Nail's study process: an analytic phase is followed by a new synthesis where he is able to recontextualize his knowledge. Another story involving stages of practice and finding natural articulations is found in the story of the master swimmer in Chapter 19. Confucius sees an old man in a river that is so turbulent that even fish and turtles cannot survive there. He fears that the person had committed suicide, and sends his student to pull him out. But the man comes out by himself, with his long hear loose on his back, and walks away, singing casually. Confucius hurries after him and says:

> "I thought you were a ghost, but now I see you are a man! Do you have a method that allows you to tread upon the waters?"
> "No, I have no method," said the old man. "I got my start in the given, grew in my nature, and reached completion in fate. I enter into the navels of the whirlpools and emerge with the surging eddies. I just follow the course of the water itself, without making any private one of my own. This is how I tread the waters."
> Confucius said, "What do you mean by getting your start in the given, growing in your nature, and reaching completion in fate?"
> "I was born on the land and thus I feel securely at home on the land. That's the given. I grew up with the water and thus I feel securely at home in the water. That's my nature. And I am thus and so but without knowing how or why I am thus and so. That's fate." (Ziporyn 2009: 81, tr. mod.)
> 「吾以子為鬼, 察子則人也。請問蹈水有道乎?」曰:「亡, 吾無道。吾始乎故, 長乎性, 成乎命。與齊俱入, 與汩偕出, 從水之道而不為私焉。

此吾所以蹈之也。」孔子曰:「何謂始乎故, 長乎性, 成乎命?」曰:「吾生於陵而安於陵, 故也; 長於水而安於水, 性也; 不知吾所以然而然, 命也。」(19/50/49–54)

Again, we have a practitioner whose performance is above the ordinary: the old man swims where even fishes and turtles could not pass, let alone humans. Confucius, seeing the man emerge from the water by himself, thought for a moment that he was a ghost (*gui* 鬼). In other stories, this kind of performance is related to the numinous, the spiritual (*shen* 神), or to "heaven" (*tian* 天). The old man explains his performance, and, as in Cook Nail's story, brings out three stages in the process of obtaining abilities that surpass the common human realm.

(1) He started (*shi* 始) from the "given" (*gu* 故), and he explains that it means that he was "born on the land" and felt "securely at home" there. This first stage is the facticity of being: everyone is born at a certain time in a certain place, with a certain genetic, social, and environmental background. No one starts as a blank slate, but the slate has already some articulations,[11] and development consists in developing them. Here, the swimmer explains that his starting point is on land; i.e., he has capacities for action in out-of-water environments.

(2) Next, he grew (*zhang* 長) in his "nature" (*xing* 性). He developed his given capacities and extended them to other environments: he moved to water and gradually matched the singularities of his body with those of the currents,[12] until he felt "at home in the water."

(3) Finally, he "reached completion" (*cheng* 成) in "fate" (*ming* 命).[13] This is a consummate phase where the swimmer has matched his body with the water so well that he is able to "follow the course of the water itself" (從水之道). He has formed an assemblage with the river. River forms a part of his body, and he is part of the river, where he does not "make any private of his own" (不為私). He does not retain a subjectivity separated from the river. This is further emphasized by his statement that he is thus and he does not know why he is thus: his knowledge is not external to his performance, but is expressed in that activity itself. The third stage is the phase transition where the swimmer has reached graceful action in swimming. He has achieved liberty in this new mode of self-expression and forgotten the technique in the sense that he has integrated its elements and integrated himself to his environment.[14]

In another story, a hunchback cicada-catcher explains how he acquired his skill. Similarly to previous cases, he presents a progression. He says that he started with juggling with balls. In the beginning with two balls, then with three and finally with five balls.[15] As swimmer's starting point was on land, and only then moves to water, here also the hunchback starts not directly with cicada, but with balls. In this way he trains his fine motor control and focus. Finally,

> I position my body as though it were an erect stump with twisted roots. I hold my arms as though they were the branches of a withered tree. The greatness of heaven and earth and the numerousness of the myriad things notwithstanding, I am aware only of the cicada's wings. I neither turn around nor to the side and wouldn't exchange the wings of a cicada for all the myriad things. How can I not succeed? (Mair 1994: 176–7)
> 吾處身也若厥株拘, 吾執臂也若槁木之枝, 雖天地之大, 萬物之多, 而唯蜩翼之知。吾不反不側, 不以萬物易蜩之翼, 何為而不得! (19/48/19–21)

Again, there is a phase transition from gradual progression toward dexterity to another state of mind where the action is infallible. This may have been the main goal from the beginning: it is possible that the hunchback was not so much after the cicadas (there would have been more efficient means to catch them), but that the main aim was, in effect, to train focus and reaction, and that the agile and fast cicadas were good training aids. Just as swimmer with the currents, the hunchback forms an assemblage with the cicadas. Confucius, who was talking to the man, explains to his disciples that this is how one should concentrate or "freeze" in the spirit (*ning yu shen* 凝於神).

Zhuangzi takes the ideas of embodied self-cultivation that were present in the culture (see above, Chapter 4) and develops them further, extending them to other contexts. Confucians limited this kind of refinement mainly to the social order and moral behavior (see Ch. 4), while Zhuangzians extend it to all environments, occasionally opposing social refinement, insofar as it inhibits a larger extension of embodied practice in more humble crafts (Zhuangzi talks about wheelwrights, rafters, cicada-catchers, ox-cutters, etc.), and to the natural environment (swimming, roaming). By perfecting an embodied practice, a person can obtain higher, more nuanced forms of self-integration, interaction with others (oxen, cicadas), and being embedded in the environment (water for the swimmer). The movement is not so much beyond the body as into it, into its nuances, and into its interactions with the environment.

In these stories from *Zhuangzi*, self-cultivation creates joy: the cook looks around in satisfaction; the swimmer comes out of the water and sings joyfully.

Joy is the sign of the "third stage." As noted above in 3.5, the lightening and easying effect of the ritual is very important among the Kurankos. It is a common experience that when a skill is practiced to perfection, so that it becomes natural, we feel happy. At the same time, it is important to note that these stories are not limited to just perfecting a skill. All of these "skill" stories in the *Zhuangzi* stress that the practitioners go beyond a mere skill or craft, and that they have reached the Way, the Dao.[16] Here, this notion refers to the "third phase" of practice, a phase transition into mastery where aspects of the practice have become well integrated and where the practitioner is integrated to the environment. On the other hand, this enables finer distinctions and differences to emerge: the practitioners perceive minute details in their surroundings. And it then becomes also more meaningful to others. As lord Wenhui says who observed Cook Nail's performance, that he learned how to nourish life, or Confucius brought cicada-catcher as an example to his students for how to concentrate. A particular practice becomes universally meaningful, a single way expresses the overall Way.

8.4 Danger of Mechanical Mind in Extended Cognition

The knowledge of the skillful masters in the *Zhuangzi* extends to things, materials, and environment. Take Cook Nail, and his supernatural knife that needs not be sharpened. He does not apply certain forces to the knife as an object, so that the knife, in turn, would have a certain effect on the body of the ox. Instead, the knife is part and parcel of his activity; his intention is at the tip of the knife. For the swimmer in the section above, the environment of the water, its whirlpools, and eddies are not external objects of his knowledge, but seem to form part of his body, so that the knowledge emerges from the interplay between the swimmer's body and the flow of water. The knowledge is not *inside* the swimmer but rather *between* him and the water. Or, to put it another way, it is *in* the assemblage of swimmer and currents. The same applies to the woodworker discussed in the next section.

Confucius' knowledge (see 4.6) extends to ritual objects, and Mozi uses the examples of compass, square, and other tools to make the case for objectified knowledge (5.2). The mention of tools and materials in the *Zhuangzi* is something of a hybrid of these two. On the one hand, the tools that the masters use are indeed useful tools of craftsmen and workers: knife, axe, raft, etc. And the master craftsmen use them with great dexterity.

Yet, the emphasis is not on their mechanical efficacy but rather on their efficacy for self-cultivation (and in this sense similar to Confucius' ritual items). To make this point, in Chapter 12 of *Zhuangzi* there is a story of Confucius' student Zigong seeing a man working in his garden, bringing water with a jar and spending great effort. Zigong wants to spread technical innovation and tells the man that there is a device called wellsweep with which he could do the job much more easily. The gardener replies:

> I have heard from my teacher that where there are mechanical devices, there are sure to be mechanical affairs, and where there are mechanical affairs, there are sure to be mechanical minds. When one harbors a mechanical mind in one's breast, its pure simplicity will be impaired. When pure simplicity is impaired, the spiritual nature will be unstable. He whose spiritual nature is unsettled will not be supported by the Way. (Mair 1994: 111, tr. mod.)
> 吾聞之吾師：『有機械者必有機事，有機事者必有機心。』機心存於胸中，則純白不備；純白不備，則神生不定；神生不定者，道之所不載也。(12/31/55–7)

The gardener's goal was not efficacy in the cultivation of his garden but efficacy in cultivating his mind (cf. 7.12). The jar was not simply a technical device to achieve a goal but part of his practice. If one pays too much attention to the technical efficacy, then one will have a "mechanical mind" (*jixin* 機心) and it would impede a shift to the third phase of practice. Mechanization and objectification were the goals of Mohists and Legalists, as well as twentieth-century Western cognitivists (see Dupuy 2009). The goal of the old man in Zhuangzi's story was self-cultivation, to obtain and maintain the pure simplicity of his mind and his "spiritual nature" or "spiritual life" (*shensheng* 神生).[17] For the author of this story who is close to the "primitivist" strain of the *Zhuangzi*, complex mechanical devices lure one to external concerns. With the help of machines you may have more leisure time, but if your goal is self-cultivation, then you do not need necessarily additional leisure and you can as well cultivate your mind while doing some useful work.

8.5 Other-relation

The aspect of other-relation (see 2.9) is present in the story of Cook Nail, where the cook meets the ox "in the spirit." It is also central to the story of Woodworker Praise, who makes wooden bellstands so well that they seem to be made by a spiritual being. When asked what art does he have, he replies:

What art could I possess? However, there is one thing. When I am getting ready to make a bellstand, I dare not waste any of my energy, so it is necessary to fast in order to calm my mind. After fasting for three days, I no longer presume to harbor any thoughts of congratulations and rewards, of rank and salary. After fasting for five days, I no longer presume to harbor any thoughts of censure or praise, of skill or clumsiness. After fasting for seven days, I abruptly forget that I have four limbs and a body. At that time, I have no thought of public affairs or the court. My skill is concentrated and all external distractions disappear. Only then do I enter the mountain forest and observe the heavenly nature of the trees till I find one of ultimate form. Only after the completed bellstand manifests itself to me do I set my hand to the work. Otherwise, I give up. Thus is heaven joined to heaven. This is what makes one suspect that my instruments were made by a spiritual being. (Mair 1994: 183, Ch. 19, tr. mod.)

何術之有! 雖然, 有一焉。臣將為鐻, 未嘗敢以耗氣也, 必齊以靜心。齊三日, 而不敢懷慶賞爵祿; 齊五日, 不敢懷非譽巧拙; 齊七日, 輒然忘吾有四枝形體也。當是時也, 無公朝, 其巧專而外骨消; 然後入山林, 觀天性; 形軀至矣, 然後成見鐻, 然後加手焉; 不然則已。則以天合天, 器之所以疑神者, 其是與? (19/50/55–9)

Woodworker Praise explains that before setting out to select the right tree, he fasts (*zhai* 齊) and calms his mind (*jingxin* 靜心), during which process he gradually discards thoughts about rewards and praise.[18] After seven days "I abruptly forget that I have four limbs and a body" (輒然忘吾有四枝形體也). This does not mean so much that he has transcended the body but rather that he has integrated it so well that it does not manifest separate parts like limbs or "branches" (*zhi* 枝), nor as a body with a certain form (*xingti* 形體). Then his "skill is concentrated, and all external distractions disappear." The effect of this preparation is not a numbness or insensitivity of the body but, rather, it is a heightened sensitivity to the environment. At that point, Woodworker Praise sets out for the forest, and just as Cook Nail does not look at the ox with his eyes but is able to follow the "heavenly veins" of the ox, so too the woodworker does not look at the trees with his eyes, but "observes the heavenly nature of the trees" (*guan tianxing* 觀天性). Of course he must use his eyes, but he is not limited to the external or extensional data. Due to his sensitivity he is able to "understand" a tree's inner nature or "heaven."

"Heaven" (*tian* 天) is a central concept in the *Zhuangzi* and is often opposed to the "human" (*ren* 人): "The heavenly is within, the human is without" (天在內, 人在外, Ch. 17, "Autumn Floods," Mair 1994: 158). It would be tempting to relate "heaven" with embodied and "human" with disembodied knowledge, but they rather seem to be connected to two different stages in the acquisition of knowledge. "Heaven" would be the perfected, spontaneous outcome (stage 3) and also perhaps the initial, natural spontaneity (stage 1), and "human" would refer to the intermediate phase (stage 2) of analysis, recomposition, and effort. In any case, the inner "heavens" of different beings communicate with each other, so that "Heaven is joined to Heaven"; with his own "heaven" the woodworker matches the "heaven" of a tree (以天合天). The woodworker has attained his own spontaneity or "heaven" and thus has an intuitive grasp of other beings. In this way he extends his consciousness, making his selfhood and the "self" of other things and beings become intertwined and interpenetrating.

This connection with other things also facilitates the shifting of perspective, seeing things from other beings' viewpoint:

> If people sleep in damp places, they develop lumbago or even partial paralysis. But would the same thing happen to a loach? If people dwell in trees, they will tremble with vertigo. But would the same thing happen to a gibbon? Of these three, which knows the proper place to dwell? People eat meat, deer eat grass, giant centipedes savor snakes, hawks and crows relish mice. Of these four, which knows the proper food to eat? Gibbons go for macaques as mate, moose will interact with deer, loaches cavort with fish. Mao Qiang and Xi Shi were considered by men to be beautiful, but if fish took one look at them they would dive into the depths, if birds saw them they would fly high into the sky, if deer saw them they would run away pell-mell. Of these four, which knows the correct standard of beauty for all under heaven? (Mair 1994: 20–1, tr. mod.)
>
> 民溼寢則腰疾偏死, 鰌然乎哉? 木處則惴慄恂懼, 猨猴然乎哉? 三者孰知正處? 民食芻豢, 麋鹿食薦, 蝍且甘帶, 鴟鴉耆鼠, 四者孰知正味? 猨, 猵狙以為雌, 麋與鹿交, 鰌與魚游。毛嬙、麗姬, 人之所美也, 魚見之深入, 鳥見之高飛, 麋鹿見之決驟。四者孰知天下之正色哉?

We discussed above that Confucius' Golden rule involves taking the position of another person (4.7), and Mozi used a decontextualized general rule of universal care (5.3). Zhuangzi has a less anthropocentric approach, sympathetically taking on the viewpoint of any creature, creating a lifeworlds theory of different living beings that resembles the Umwelt theory of Jakob von Uexküll (cf. 2.3). This Zhuangzi's view does not result in a universal undifferentiated care as in Mozi; each creature still has its preferences. Even if it does not find conspecifics, it will look for creatures similar to it: a gibbon will recognize a macaque as kindred, and a moose will interact with a deer.[19] So, Zhuangzi's version of other-relation has much wider extension than either Confucius' or Mozi's. On the other hand, it still maintains distinctions (the main Confucian complaint against Mohist universal care was that it destroys distinctions): it is natural to feel attracted to someone from your own species, and the axiological space of an embodied being is not random. But one should be aware that *everyone* has their own viewpoint and preferences, so that one should beware of taking their own personal or species-dependent preferences as something universally valid. This knowledge can dislocate a naïve attachment to one's form as a species or an individual. All actualized forms and their distinctions are but anchoring points to an actualization process. If one ascends this process, toward the virtual, one can find a "spiritual" or "heavenly" connection with other beings and things.

In these Zhuangzian stories, people with a masterful understanding of certain creatures (cicadas), things (carcasses of oxen), materials (wood), and environments (water) are often featured as teachers. Their knowledge is different from a decontextualized, objective, third-person analysis of things, such as things taught in classrooms or analyzed in labs. The main difference is that in Zhuangzi's stories, the knowledgeable body and its activity are involved in the knowledge itself. Of course, all decontextualized knowledge must also be finally contextualized. For example, in a scientific experiment there are somewhere embodied scientists who read and interpret the results, and engineers who build and operate the equipment; and they all do this in the meaningful context of their lifeworld. But the difference with contextualized knowledge is that in decontextualized knowledge the fact of embodiment is not *directly* involved in the content of knowledge. In a contextualized knowledge, as we saw in case of Zhuangzi's master-performers, bodily activity is directly part of their knowledge and shapes it. The progress in knowledge is then a deeper understanding both of things and environments, and of themselves.[20] They have discovered the ways in which certain things and environments behave in conjunction with their body.[21]

This does not mean a dissection or analysis of a thing, a process, or an environment (although Cook Nail does dissect[22]) as something actualized and ready-made, but rather, it is an investigation how do they evolve when one interacts with them. It is about the discovery of the singularities of those things, processes, and environments (cf. 4.2). If Cook Nail were to simply conduct an objective analysis of some carcass, measuring its metric properties and planning incisions, he would not be able to reach such a rich, deep, and full understanding of the behavior of these materials, and quite certainly would not be able to cut with such mastery. To take Merleau-Ponty's example of the organ (1945: 180–1; cf. 2.3 above): these instruments are so different from one another that a "metric" understanding of one or more organs would not help a player to play them all. Organists develop a different kind of understanding that is more topological and concerns rather the *relations* between certain important parameters of the instrument. That is why an experienced player can approach any type with some familiarity. It is not so much the precise distances between keys, pedals, registers, that count, but their relations. An organ has a phase space that is determined by all the relevant ways it can change, its "degrees of freedom": one dimension for every key, pedal, etc. A musical score establishes singular points in this phase space, which would govern the process of actualization for that piece of music. The musician has, in relation to the instrument, their own phase space and their ability to actualize the score, and with only a little habituation with a new instrument, the organist is able to match effectivities of body to the affordances of the organ.

At a certain point of the embodied practice there happens a phase transition into a different, distinct mode, which denotes a certain freedom from metric, actualized forms of one's body and of other things, processes, and environments, providing access to singularities that are more "interpenetrating," but in themselves distinct. Cook Nail, or a master organist, can intuitively grasp singularities that perplicate each other. Each could unfold them in an activity that is not hampered by actual forms but supported by those forms that have been already actualized and elicit change and transformation. It is wrong to consider the master-performers as blindly following a program and think that it is a lapse in cook Nail's otherwise masterful performance when at difficult places he "stops" or slows down. It would imply that a performer is an automat that thoughtlessly rushes through the performance with no input from the environment. On the contrary, it is a credit to cook Nail's mastery that he adapts to concrete situations at hand. All the masters described in previous citations can adapt to a difficult place in the carcass, movements of the cicadas, or the ever-changing flows of water in case of the swimmer.

The swimmer calls this new phase of performance "inevitability," "necessity," or "fate" (*ming* 命). It does not mean the opposite of freedom, but a mode of acting where freedom and necessity cannot be distinguished. The swimmer makes a certain move, and it is the only one, or the best one, to be made in that situation. A freedom where one can still "choose" between two or more options is a low degree of it. This low-intensity freedom engages a leisurely state, wherein one imagines "options." One's existence then englobes this imaginary bifurcation, but one does not really invest in either. One's power of activity and freedom are not at their maximum. This is the situation of performers in the second stage, when they still develop their skill. Arriving at mastery, at the third stage, they have no "options"; they do not pause to reflect, but their reflection is ongoing, mirroring the situation at hand and enabling immediate adaptations.

In some modern developments of science, these more interpenetrating levels have been considered, for example, in the dynamic systems theory, whose concepts have been occasionally discussed in this book (cf. DeLanda 2002). The description of a system in terms of phase space, singularities, and trajectories refers to inner articulations of a system that are not actual, but virtual and intensive. A singularity cannot be seen under a microscope, yet it is perfectly real, and can be investigated in a scientifically rigorous way (e.g., the different distinct types of flows in a container). In this way, the scientific study that usually takes place in the mode of disembodiment and decontextualization wins back something of bodies and contexts themselves, as it investigates the actualization of the system in view of its internal topological articulations. It is not an objectifying attitude that imposes external metric coordinates to it, and therefore, these concepts may be useful also in the contextualizing and embodying line, when making sense of Zhuangzi's skillful masters.

8.6 Sitting and Forgetting

There is another description of stages through which a peculiar skill of forgetting is developed. In it, a fictional dialogue is staged between Confucius and his favorite student Yan Hui. Yan Hui tells Confucius that he is making progress and explains, with a clearly humorous intent from the part of Zhuangzi, that he has "forgotten" rites and music that were central Confucian self-cultivation methods. Confucius, again humorously, approves, but says that this is not enough. Another day Yan Hui comes back and tells Confucius that he has forgotten humaneness and righteousness that were the loftiest Confucian ideals. Again, Confucius approves, but says that this is not enough. Then,

> Yan Hui saw Confucius again on another day and said, "I'm making progress."
> "What do you mean?"
> "I sit and forget."
> "What do you mean, 'sit and forget'?" Confucius asked with surprise.
> "I slough off my limbs and trunk," said Yan Hui, "dim my intelligence, depart from my form, leave knowledge behind, and become integrated with the Great Interpenetration. This is what I mean by 'sit and forget.'"
> "If you are integrated," said Confucius, "then you have no preferences. If you are transformed, then you have no more constants. It's you who is really the worthy one! Please permit me to become your follower." (Mair 1994: 63–4, translation modified)

他日復見,曰:「回益矣。」曰:「何謂也?」曰:「回坐忘矣。」仲尼蹴然曰:「何謂坐忘?」顏回曰:「墮肢體, 黜聰明, 離形去知, 同於大通[23], 此謂坐忘。」仲尼曰:「同則無好也,化則無常也。而果其賢乎! 丘也請從 而後也。」(6/19/91–3)

Zhuangzi switches the common student-teacher roles, like in the case of Wheelwright and Duke Huan. In the beginning, Confucius is the teacher and instructs his student Yan Hui, as it was historically the case. By the end, the latter's ability to understand "sitting and forgetting" impresses Confucius so much that Confucius asks to become Yan Hui's student. Sitting and forgetting (*zuowang* 坐忘) is a common term for Daoist meditation even nowadays (Kohn 2014: 134). To "sit" means to cut all the usual activities and remain still, while sitting. To "forget" means not to follow the contents of the psyche but to let them go. The result is the apotheosis of embodiment. But how can it be so? Doesn't Yan Hui speak of "sloughing off limbs and trunk" (*duo zhiti* 墮肢體)? Similarly, Woodworker Praise "abruptly forgets that he has four limbs and a body." Is it not a negation of the body?

Living beings on the one hand incessantly form: obtain new matter for their bodies, and integrate new information in their psyche. On the other hand, they at the same time unform: discard matter, and suppress the past experience in order to accommodate the new. Human beings are especially complex and the requirements of forming and unforming are very high. We mostly pay attention to the forms and hope that unforming happens naturally by itself. Yet, unforming is often impeded and we become too rigidly attached to certain forms: for example, food, alcohol, sex, riches, or fame, which then become vices of gluttony, alcoholism, lust, greed, and ambition (*Ethics* 3p56sc, Spinoza 2002: 308). It happens also in uncountable more inconspicuous ways; our mind being invaded by images of things, and we become thing-like. We then become less capable of responding adequately to the current situation.

The aim of "sitting and forgetting" is to introduce a delay in psychophysical busying around, and to turn one's body like a "withered wood and mind like dead ashes" (形固可使如槁木, 而心固可使如死灰, Ch. 2), and to "lose one's counterpart" (喪其耦, Spinoza 2002). It is a kind of phenomenological epoché, where phenomena, cultural forms, and attitudes continue to flow, but are not given "consent," and judgment about them is deferred, allowing one to "forget" their habitual relations to the person, and simply "observe" them. The habitual bundle of habits and reactions is loosened, presenting more nuances and articulations. This also means that force or energy of existing is not squeezed into the habitual veins (by affirming that one is like this or that, is interested in this or that, wants to obtain this and that, etc.), so that energy becomes more free, nuanced, adjusted, and adapted to the situation.

It is legitimate to give a religious and mystic interpretation of the text saying that Zhuangzi aims at transcending the material body through meditative practice. But another interpretation is possible: what disappears is not the "material body" but a certain *form* of it, namely body as form. The text would then not be directed against the body, but against a certain mode of both body and mind. Yan Hui says: "[I] dim my intelligence, depart from my form, leave knowledge behind" (黜聰明, 離形去知). Here "form" means the body, but the term may be generalized and a distinction made between, on the one hand, form (*xing* 形) of mind and body, and on the other hand, interpenetration of mind and body (*tong* 通).

What does it mean, then, when Yan Hui says, "slough off limbs and trunk" or "forget four limbs and body"? Certainly it does not mean that the body of Yan Hui or Carpenter Praise would disappear, or that they would lose any organization of their mind and go insane. Rather, Yan Hui seems to denote a certain attitude toward the actual organization of one's body and mind. First, the interruption of the sitting and forgetting thaws up certain fixations of the intention, so that one is less obsessed by the "forms," or actualized things. Second, it does *not* mean a transcending of the body how it is, but affirming its facticity, affirming embodied existence (in a certain place and time). Third, philosophically speaking, it means to connect actualized psychophysical forms with their "interpenetrating" phase, or their generative ground from where they are produced. In an ordinary embodied existence, one is already on this interpenetrating level, but with the help of sitting and forgetting, they can take it into account more fully, and to live in contact with their forces. This, according to Spinoza's definition, is joy.[24] Sitting and forgetting takes this kind of embodiment one step further, thawing up the disembodied chunks in embodied experience, abstaining from simply agreeing with the established forms ("rites" and "music," "humaneness" and "righteousness," fear of death, yearning for fame), and letting more nuanced articulations transpire, so that the force channeled into them can move more freely.

The previous stories of skillful masters are directed at the cultivation of self. These stories do not simply present an understanding of knowledge and action, but they also show how knowledge and action can be developed and refined in an embodied framework. In the story of Yan Hui, it is most evident. Yan Hui "simply sits."²⁵ Yan Hui is able to directly deal with the self—and other-relation, without needing to engage in a bodily activity other than sitting. Although it is the most contextualizing and embodying attitude of the Zhuangzian stories, Yan Hui is also liberated from the contingencies of body and context—showing how the maximum of contextualization can also lead to a maximum of decontextualization.

8.7 Transformation

Embodiment is as much temporal as it is spatial. Embodied existence incessantly changes, always remaining in a state of transformation. The *Zhuangzi* presents some very vivid descriptions of bodily transformations. For instance, in Ch. 18 a willow suddenly sprouts from a person's elbow. He does not resent the change, and explains:

> Why should I resent it? Our lives are just a borrowed pretext. That which we borrow to maintain our lives is merely so much dust. Life and death alternate like day and night. As you and I were observing transformation, it caught up with me. So why should I resent it? (Mair 1994: 169, translation modified)
> 予何惡? 生者, 假借也; 假之而生生者, 塵垢也。死生為晝夜。且吾與子觀化而化及我, 我又何惡焉? (18/46/21-2)

He is not attached to his human form and is unfazed even when a tree starts to grow out of him. This is simply another form that he has obtained, and he lets go of his habitual form without regret. Life and transformation are principal; the means to maintain them are secondary.

In another story from the "Inner Chapters" Ch. 6, four friends agree that each of them will take "nonbeing as his head, life as his spine, and death as his buttocks" (以無為首, 以生為脊, 以死為尻) and know "the oneness of life and death, of existence and nonexistence" (知生死存亡之一體, Mair 1994: 57–8). Later one of the friends, Sir Chariot, falls ill and another friend, Sir Sacrifice, goes to visit him, finding Sir Chariot heavily transformed:

> His back was all hunched up. On top were his five dorsal inductories. His chin was buried in his bellybutton. His shoulders were higher than the crown of his head. His neck bones pointed toward the sky. His vital yin yang breaths were all out of kilter. Yet his mind was at ease, as though nothing were amiss. (Mair 1994: 58)
> 曲僂發背, 上有五管, 頤隱於齊, 肩高於頂, 句贅指天。」陰陽之氣有沴, 其心閒而無事。(6/17/48–9)

Not only is he physically deformed but also his energies (*qi* 氣) are in disarray. Zhuangzi clearly defies traditional understandings that one should keep their body intact, and shows that the form of the body and even its intensive flows are less important than the flow or transformation itself. Although in other stories Zhuangzi stresses the importance of energies and vital breaths (one should "breathe from the heels," "listen with the energies," etc.), in this story he defies a (proto)Daoist self-cultivation through the energies, as Sir Chariot's spirit is still at ease in spite of all the physical and energetic disturbances. It may even be thought that the body, by deformation, returns to an intensive state that violates the rules of a fixed metric, moving that person toward an interpenetrating level of existence.[26]

Sir Chariot goes on to exclaim: "Great is the Creator of Things! She's making me all crookedy like this!" (偉哉! 夫造物者, 將以予為此拘拘也!). As in the previous response cited above, he does not resent it and explains:

> No, why should I resent it? Supposing that my left arm were transformed into a chicken, I would consequently go looking for a rooster that could call out the hours of the night. Supposing that my right arm were transformed into a crossbow, I would consequently go looking for an owl to roast. Supposing that my buttocks were transformed into wheels and my spirit into a horse, I would consequently mount upon them. What need would I have for any other conveyance? (Mair 1994: 58)
> 亡, 予何惡! 浸假而化予之左臂以為雞, 予因以求時夜; 浸假 而化予之右臂以為彈, 予因以求鴞炙; 浸假而化予之尻以為輪, 以神為馬, 予因以乘之, 豈更駕哉!(6/17/50–2)

Through imagination, Sir Chariot extends these bodily transformations into the realm of phantastic or surreal, where he imagines that an arm may transform into a chicken or crossbow. And if his buttocks transformed into wheels and spirit into horses, he could ride on them (making his name, Sir Chariot, quite literal). In this way, the transformation of his body could be taken much further, yet still would be in harmony with the transformation of things. He then explains transformation by timeliness (*shi* 時) and following or compliance (*shun* 順):

> Furthermore, what we attain is due to timeliness and what we lose is the result of compliance. If we repose in timeliness and dwell in compliance, sorrow and joy cannot affect us. This is what the ancients called emancipation: Those who are unable to win release for themselves are bound by things. Furthermore, things can not win out against heaven's duration. So why should I resent it? (Mair 1994: 58, tr. mod.)

且夫得者時也, 失者順也, 安時而處順, 哀樂不能入也。此古之所謂縣解也, 而不能自解者, 物有結之。且夫物不勝天久矣, 吾又何惡焉? (6/17/52–53)

Good things, or occurrences that suit our body, simply happen when time was ripe, with all previous events of the world making it so that it happened. Time itself brings about change, and one should not cling to a certain situation. When bad things, or occurrences that do not suit our body, happen, one should simply go along or comply with it—not through a stoic demonstration of strong will but by identifying oneself with the general transformation of all things, not merely with a particular form affected by those transformations (i.e., our person, our body and mind). Otherwise, things and forms would tie us into a knot (*jie* 結) so that we would become like a constricted place where flows do not pass well. We should untie it (*jie* 解), and only then will we be able to really understand (which is another meaning of the word *jie* 解[27]) ourselves and the surroundings. Either people are bound by things, or they set themselves free from them, by timeliness and compliance.

There is a problem for our description of the four friends' story. We present it as a good example of embodied knowledge, but embodied knowledge stresses the importance of emotions in that kind of knowledge. In this story, Sir Chariot says that for the one who has attained timeliness and compliance, "sorrow and joy cannot enter" (*aile buneng ru* 哀樂不能入). To solve this problem, a distinction can be made (cf. above, 4.11). The sorrow and joy mentioned here refer to a sorrow or joy arising from fixation, from being tied into a knot with certain things that pertain to a certain form of body and mind, to a certain fixed Umwelt (cf. above, 2.3). In that case the Spinozian description for basic affects applies (cf. above, 2.6): when one encounters things that do not fit one's form of body and mind, one becomes sad (i.e., one's power diminishes); and when one encounters things that fit one's form of body, one becomes happy (i.e., one's power grows). When one identifies with the overall transformation of things, they become untied from that form, and hence do not undergo this kind of sorrow or joy. It does not mean that emotion is cancelled or deprecated. It is only certain kinds or forms of emotions that are discarded: namely, the crude and mechanic affect. When one is fixed to a certain form, they undergo a sorrow or a joy, and these effects comprise, contract, or imply a lesser multiplicity and contain less things. If one has a full stomach, one is gratified. It is simply molecules of the food being integrated into the cells of a body, so that one is replenished and more vigorous. It is a simple joy. But it has the flip side that it may tie one excessively to certain forms of food. Take another form of joy, for example, receiving a reward. This creates joy, promoting a sense of vigor and accomplishment. Yet very little of the multiplicity of the world is contained in it, and even may tie one to a certain self-image. All of this is even clearer in case of sorrows. When one feels hungry, one becomes focused on obtaining food, feeling pain and sorrow until renourished. Or if one is insulted, one becomes focused on the offence and how to answer it. As in the case of food, it expresses a very small portion of the multiplicities and richness of the world. It is certainly necessary for survival, but this act of surviving easily ties one to a certain form that one wants to preserve. When one loosens attachment to a particular form, and identifies oneself with transformation, more things can be considered. That particular body and mind do not disappear, pains and gratifications are not annulled, but with this shift in attention come more things that matter, and joy and sorrow become more nuanced, rich, and include a greater multiplicity (in principle, the whole world). It is only joys and sorrows as crude and fixed forms that "cannot enter." Hence this claim about emotions in the *Zhuangzi* does not contradict the embodied account, for the joy and sorrow mentioned in the text are poor emotions, and one who has freed themselves from the "knot of things" would not feel anything. Their emotions are richer and comprise more things.

A similar story is then presented with the third and fourth friend, Sir Come and Sir Plow. Sir Come falls ill and Sir Plow goes to see him. Immediately, Sir Plow sends away the wailing relatives so they would "not disturb [or distress] transformation" (無怛化), then goes on to say:

> Then, leaning against the door, he spoke to Sir Come: "Great is the Transforming Creator! What next will he make of you? Where will he send you? Will he turn you into a rat's liver? Will he turn you into a bug's leg?"
>
> "The relationship of parents to a child," said Sir Come, "is such that he simply follows their commands, no matter which direction they may point him. The relationship of *yin* and *yang* to a man is no less important than that of parents to a child. If they urge me to die and I resist, that is my ill-temper. What fault of theirs is it? The Great Clod burdens me with form, toils me through life, eases me in old age, rests me in death. Thus, that which makes my life good is also that which makes my death good. Now, the Great Smelter casts his metal. If the metal were to jump up and say, 'You must make me into Excalibur!' the Great Smelter would certainly think that it was inauspicious metal. Now if I, who have chanced to take on human form, were to say, 'Man! I must remain a man!' the Great Transforming Creator would certainly think that I am an inauspicious man. Now, once I accept heaven and earth as the Great Forge, and the Transforming

Creator as the Great Smelter, I'm willing to go wherever they send me. Soundly I sleep; suddenly I awake."[28] (Mair 1994: 59, tr. mod.)

倚其戶與之語曰:「偉哉造物! 又將奚以汝為? 將奚以汝適? 以汝為鼠肝乎? 以汝為蟲臂乎?」子來曰:「父母於子, 東西南北, 唯命之從。陰陽於人, 不翅於父母, 彼近吾死而我不聽, 我則悍矣, 彼何罪焉! 夫大塊載我以形, 勞我以生, 佚我以老, 息我以死。故善吾生者, 乃所以善吾死也。今之大冶鑄金, 金踊躍曰『我且必為鏌鋣』, 大冶必以為不祥之金。今一犯人之形, 而曰『人耳人耳』, 夫造化者必以為不祥之人。今一以天地為大鑪, 以造化為大冶, 惡乎往而不可哉! 成然寐, 蘧然覺。」(6/17/54–60)

The scandal continues: the nonconformist sir Plow casually leans against the door, showing little concern for the purportedly serious situation, and infringes the prohibition to stand on the threshold (cf. above, 4.3). By standing on the threshold, he may even convey a meaning, a sense of liminality. In this as well as in the previous story, one of the characters is dramatically transformed. We gather from these stories that personal and interpersonal existence is defined not so much by specific forms but rather by a specific way of transformation.

The general process of transformation, taken as a whole, is given a name here (which is not very common in the Chinese tradition): Transforming Creator (*zaohua* 造化), Great Smelter (*daye* 大冶), or the Creator of Things (*zaowuzhe* 造物者). But this Transforming Creator is not beyond transformation, and it is not about the creation *of* transformation but about the creation *by* transformation. I claim that the name "Transforming Creator" denotes the whole of transformation as a creative agent. The "Great Smelter" is again the transformation itself, by which forms are "founded" and "smelted." The Creator of Things is not a Big Thing or *Summum Ens* beyond beings, but it is the Way, the *dao*, the general process of change and transformation that creates things. In this story, there seems to be a nearly religious attitude toward the Transforming Creator, but not as a being or an entity but namely as the Transformation itself, or *dao*. The friends do not transform themselves by venerating the Transforming Creator, but the other way around; they first identify themselves with the transformation, and go on to give occasion for the exaltation of Transformation.

This is a distinctive attitude toward change. In Platonism, the changing sensible world is a distorted representation of the unchanging ideas, and our task is to discard the former in order to better grasp the latter. In Buddhism, the changing and impermanent world is a source of suffering, and we should understand its irreality—that lack of independent subsistence. In Platonism the changing world is secondary and we strive for a truer primary world of ideas; it fades in the light of philosophical understanding. In Buddhism, the changing world is illusionary and it vanishes in an enlightened consciousness. But for Zhuangzi, change is true and real. The trick is that we should not identify ourselves with the outcome, at each moment, of the change (our actual state), but we should rather identify ourselves with the way we transform. Since this transformation is part of the overall Transformation, we will thus identify ourselves with the *dao*.

Superficially, the story of Sir Come and Sir Plow seems to describe a kind of transmigration—they seem to discuss where Sir Come would reincarnate after death. But the examples given—rat's liver, bug's leg—do not fit ordinary conceptions of transmigration where the "traffic" is between whole individuals, normally between humans, animals, and other living creatures. But here they discuss that the target might be a *part* of an animal or insect. The story does not give more details, but it may be supposed that Sir Come would not abide in that part with his personal (perhaps latent) consciousness of his "previous" life; it seems more probable that he just identifies himself with all Transformation, so that it doesn't matter much what forms or parts of forms it will take—they will always participate in the general process of transformation.

The hint to parts of organisms may also mean that the friends, in their self-identification, go beyond or beneath the identity of the global self, the integral I, and move toward the pre-individual parts and processes that generate the individual. This is the genetic ground of embodiment. Transformation is not merely a general or empty affirmation, as it takes place in a very concrete fashion, through precise genetic mechanisms. Beneath the constituted forms and individuals there is not directly a general transformation, but generative "molecular"[29] processes that produce those forms and individuals and through which the overall transformation manifests itself. The individual is developed from the pre-individual through a genetic process.

The story of four friends shows that embodied knowledge and action are not tied to a certain form, and yet are not random. This aligns with embodiment theory, but it is not very often focused upon. One's self-relation includes other things, processes, environments, and it changes with them. A self is not something actual and given, but it evolves through time and unfolds certain interpenetrating relations, actualizing and bifurcating its singularities. It is not fixed to an actual form, and yet the distribution of singularities prevents it from being completely random. Zhuangzi even takes it beyond the personal identity of being human. The field of individuation of "human" is also a certain form that can be traced into even greater interpenetration, so that what is now individuated as a human may be actualized also as rat's liver, for example.[30] And this transformation is the ultimate context of a contextualizing and embodying tendency in thought and action, which is, again, at the same time the maximum of decontextualization.

8.8 Free Roaming

"Sitting and forgetting" creates interruption, but in itself is not the most important thing. It gives access to the nuances of forces that we embody and to the more nuanced consciousness that is usually channeled into fixed and predetermined paths. This allows one to "roam freely and easily," as is translated the title of the 1st chapter of Zhuangzi (*xiaoyaoyou* 逍遙遊). Sitting and forgetting turns the mind into a mirror:

> Do not be a corpse for fame,
> Do not be a storehouse of plans,
> Do not be responsible for affairs,
> Do not be a proprietor of knowledge.
> Thoroughly embody unendingness and wander in nonbeginning.
> Thoroughly experience what you receive from heaven but do not reveal what you attain. Just be empty, that's all.[31] The mind of the ultimate man functions like a mirror. It neither sends off nor welcomes; it responds but does not retain. Therefore, he can triumph over things without injury. (Mair 1994: 70–1, tr. mod.)
> 無為名尸, 無為謀府, 無為事任, 無為知主。體盡無窮, 而遊無朕, 盡其所受於天, 而無見得, 亦虛而已。至人之用心若鏡, 不將不迎, 應而不藏, 故能勝物而不傷。(7/21/31–3)

Mind as a mirror became a common metaphor in the Chinese tradition, being employed later by Buddhists.[32] The focus of the metaphor is that a clear mirror is unbiased, so that it would reflect all things equally, as a clear mirror in good lightning mirrors everything in front of it, without selection or distortion. The second focus of the metaphor is immediate reaction, as whenever something is placed in front of the mirror, it immediately, without delay, is reflected by the mirror. The Zhuangzian practitioner's mind is supposed to be similar, giving adequate, unbiased, immediate responses to circumstances.

With this kind of mind, it is said that one can "ride the clouds":

> He rides on the clouds, drives a flying dragon, and wanders beyond the four seas. (Mair 1994: 7)
> 乘雲氣, 御飛龍, 而遊乎四海之外。(1/2/29)

> He rides the clouds, mounts the sun and moon, and wanders beyond the four seas. Since not even life and death have any transforming effect upon him, how much less do benefit and harm? (Mair 1994: 21)
> 乘雲氣, 騎日月, 而遊乎四海之外。死生无變於己, 而況利害之端乎! (2/6/72–3)

The metaphor of the air, wind, and clouds stresses the fact that the practitioner does not depend on fixed forms. Yet in some places even these airy metaphors are deemed too rigid:

> Master Lie could ride upon the wind whenever he pleased, drifting marvelously, and returning only after fifteen days. Although he was not embroiled in the pursuit of blessings and thus was able to dispense with walking, still there was something he had to rely upon. (Mair 1994: 5, translation slightly modified)
> 夫列子御風而行, 泠然善也, 旬有五日而後反。彼於致福者, 未數數然也。此雖免乎行, 猶有所待者也。(1/2/19–21)

Although Master Lie was more free than common mortals, he still was dependent on the impalpable but still material wind. One should go further:

> Supposing there were someone who could ride upon the truth of heaven and earth, who could chariot upon the transformations of the six vital energies and thereby go wandering in infinity, what would he have to rely on? (Mair 1994: 5)
> 若夫乘天地之正, 而御六氣之辯, 以遊無窮者, 彼且惡乎待哉!(1/2/21)

In the end, one should be free from all forms, even from the most rarefied ones like wind. Then one is freed from all forms and can dominate the interpenetrating energies (*qi* 氣) that give rise to forms. One then identifies oneself not with the forms but with their transformation. Being not only embodied but constantly embody-ing.

> Now you, sir, have a big tree and are bothered by its uselessness. Why don't you plant it in Nevernever Land with its wide, open spaces? There you can roam in nonaction by its side and sleep carefreely beneath it. (Mair 1994: 9)
> 今子有大樹, 患其無用, 何不樹之於無何有之鄉, 廣莫之野, 彷徨乎無為其側, 逍遙乎寢臥其下?(1/3/46–7)

Formed things that lend themselves to a certain use keep us attached to their functioning. We start to serve things, we are "thinged by things" (*wu yu wu* 物於物), we are tied into a knot by them. Uselessness, on the other hand, can offer respite from this slavery. It can provide the ultimate shelter. Goal-oriented activities provide "shelter" in the concrete sense of a house or in an extended sense of finding security with fellow people. But the most secure shelter is provided by the interpenetration of things (the "nothingness") that is open to transformations. This transforming being is called "roaming."

A free roamer depends on nothing, and nothing visibly depends on them. The roamer seems nearly formless, and hardly anything can be attributed to this person as their "own":

> In the government of the enlightened king," said Old Longears, "his merit covers all under heaven, but it seems not to be his own. His transforming influence extends to the myriad things, but the people do not rely on him. Whatever he does, no one mentions his name, since he causes everything to enjoy itself. He stands in unfathomability and wanders in nonexistence. (Mair 1994: 68)[33]
>
> 老聃曰:「明王之治, 功蓋天下而似不自己, 化貸萬物而民弗恃, 有莫舉名, 使物自喜, 立乎不測, 而遊於無有者也。」(7/20/14–15)

Roamers seem invisible, because they offer little resistance. Being one with the Transformation, each being's transforming already accords with them. While transforming, each thing "enjoys itself" (zi xi 自喜). In reality, no actual being can be so invisible, since being actual implies some resistance, opposition, and impermeability. The thing is that roamers have identified themselves not with their form, but with their transformation, and all transformations interpenetrate each other, forming the whole universe. In each transformation, the transformations of all other entities are implied. If the roamers are the whole universe, certainly they will not be seen, and nothing depends on them separately.

Zhuangzi offers another depiction of a free roamer:

> Duke Ai of Lu inquired of Confucius, saying, "In the state of Wey there was an ugly man called Nag the Hump. The men who lived with Nag doted on him so much that they could not stand to be away from him. Of the women who had seen him, more than ten petitioned their parents, saying, 'I would rather be his concubine than another man's wife.' No one had ever heard of him advocating anything; all he did was follow along with others. He did not occupy a lordly position whereby he could succor those in distress. He had no accumulated salary whereby he could fill people's stomachs. Furthermore, he was ugly enough to terrify all under heaven. He always followed along and never took the lead. And his knowledge did not extend beyond his immediate surroundings. Yet male and female alike congregated before him. Surely there must have been something that distinguished him from other men." (Mair 1994: 46)
>
> 魯哀公問於仲尼曰:「衛有惡人焉, 曰哀駘它。丈夫與之處者, 思而不能去也。婦人見之, 請於父母曰『與為人妻, 寧為夫子妾』者, 十數而未止也。未嘗有聞其唱者也, 常和而已矣。無君人之位以濟乎人之死, 無聚祿以望人之腹。又以惡駭天下, 和而不唱, 知不出乎四域, 且而雌雄合乎前。是必有異乎人者也。(5/13-14/31–5)

First, it should be mentioned that while Duke Ai of Lu is a historical figure, this story is completely fictional. The main character in this story, the free roamer Nag the Hump, is pictured to be physically deformed,[34] in an obvious effort to show that *forms* are not important. One should discard prejudice[35] in this respect. In the story, Nag the Hump is extremely attractive to everyone: women find him sexually attractive and ruler considers him to be an unsurpassable potential ruler.[36] His formless potency is felt by everyone around him, and they are attracted to it, everyone according to their specific actualizations and relevancies (e.g., sexuality, power). Duke Ai even tried to hand over his state to Nag the Hump, with the latter refusing and going away. This is one of the many stories to the theme "yielding the throne,"[37] where the ruler intends to give away his throne to a free roamer, but the latter refuses or disappears. A similar story is about Zhuangzi whom the ruler is said to have tried to enroll to his court; yet Zhuangzi refuses, bringing the comparison of a turtle that prefers to live and "drag its tail in the mud" rather than be dead, in an honored position in the ruler's temple. Riches and social status impede free roaming and force a person into tightly predefined forms and formalities.

Confucius (who in the following story is the mouthpiece of Zhuangzi) explains free roaming through two concepts: "wholeness of abilities" (*cai quan* 才全) and "potency takes no definite form" (*de buxing* 德不形):

> "What do you mean by wholeness of abilities?" asked Duke Ai.
> Confucius said: "Life and death, preservation and loss, failure and success, poverty and wealth, worthiness and unworthiness, slander and praise, hunger and thirst, cold and heat—these are all the transformations of affairs and the operation of destiny.
> Day and night they alternate before us, but human knowledge is incapable of fathoming their beginning. Therefore, we should not let them disturb our harmony, nor should we let them enter our Numinous Reservoir. If you let them interpenetrate in harmony and ease, without getting lost in what is pleasant, if you let them [alternate] day and night without interstice, and make spring with things, this is to receive and engender the timeliness in the heart-mind. This is what I mean by wholeness of one's abilities."
> "What do you mean by potency takes no definite form?"
> "Levelness is the maximum expansion of water at rest. We may use it as a model; when the internal is preserved, the external will remain unshaken as well. Potency is the cultivation of complete harmony. Though potency takes no form, things cannot separate from it." (Cf. Mair 1994: 47–8; Ziporyn 2009: 36–7; Watson 1968: 73–4)

> 哀公曰:「何謂才全?」仲尼曰:「死生存亡, 窮達貧富, 賢與不肖, 毀譽、饑渴、寒暑, 是事之變, 命之行也; 日夜相代乎前, 而知不能規乎其始者也。故不足以滑和, 不可入於靈府。使之和豫通而不失於兌, 使日夜無郤而與物為春, 是接而生時於心者也。是之謂才全。」「何謂德不形?」曰:「平者, 水停之盛也。其可以為法也, 內保之而外不蕩也。德者, 成和之修也。德不形者, 物不能離也。」(5/14/43–7)

While decontextualization or disembodiment strives for discrete and clear actualized forms, contextualization or embodiment moves toward the interpenetrating, the intensive, and virtual side of existence. Therefore it is said in the text that potency (*de* 德) does not have any prescribed or fixed form (e.g., a healthy body with vigorous *qi*) and yet things cannot separate from it. The virtual side will always remain an aspect of one's existence, or, according to the imagery of this story, one cannot separate themselves from someone who expresses the potency so well like Nag the Hump. It seems that Nag the Hump is a master of implication, as he explicates very little. Yet he is not dull in the ordinary sense; on the contrary, his non-expression is seen as the highest degree of expression since it is not channeled into certain fixed forms but maintains its state of latency and indeterminacy. In this way, he can take on any form. The roamer, or master of embodiment, is not tied to a form, but is in *trans*formation, in contact with his interpenetrating aspect. Potency itself has no form, and yet can transpire any form, including a handicapped form.

By de-forming the potency (in the sense of untying from fixed forms and even accepting a "deformed" body) one makes the ability whole, having complete possession of one's capacity for action. The ability is whole when one lets all kinds of events—both lucky and adverse—alternate "without interstice," without letting them to coagulate, to solidify, to reify into an intentional object onto which one would cling or which one would avoid with the same obstinacy. It is then said, with a nice metaphor, that one "makes spring with things" (*yu wu wei chun* 與物為春). That is, one touches the generative starting point of things and processes (their "springtime"), also engendering timeliness in one's own mind (*sheng shi yu xin* 生時於心), and becoming as timely and responsive as a mirror.

8.9 Knowing with Non-knowing

Zhuangzi exalts a special way of "not knowing" that refrains from fixed knowledge of particular forms:

Gnaw Gap asked Wearcoat about the Way. Wearcoat said, "If you
Rectify your physical form
    and unify your vision,
Heavenly harmony will arrive;
Gather in your knowledge
    and unify your understanding,
The spirit will come to take up its abode.
The Potency will beautify you;
The Way will reside in you.
You will look at things with the eyes
    of a newborn calf
  Who does not seek out their causes." (Mair 1994: 213–14, translation modified)
齧缺問道乎被衣，被衣曰：「若正汝形，一汝視，天和將至; 攝汝知，一汝度，神將來舍。德將為汝美，道將為汝居，汝瞳焉如新出之犢而無求其故!」(22/58/21–3)

Wearcoat describes a process of self-cultivation and its results: one must "rectify one's form" or perhaps simply "sit straight"; "unify the vision" or simply look at one spot; "gather in the knowledge" or be present to all perceptions and thoughts; and "unify the understanding," the calculating, or measuring intellect. This brings about "heavenly harmony," a spirit-like connection with the Potency and the Way. One will then reflect their surroundings as a mirror, or according to the metaphor used here, as a "newborn calf." It is stressed that what is characteristic about this kind of knowledge is that it does not inquire into the causes of things.[38]

The story takes another turn:

Before Wearcoat had finished speaking, Gnaw Gap had already fallen fast asleep. Wearcoat was greatly pleased and went away singing this song:

"His form is like a withered carcass,
His mind is like dead ashes;
He renders true his real knowledge,
and doesn't cling to reasoning.
So dim, so obscure,
In his mindlessness, you can't consult with him.
What kind of man is he?" (Mair 1994: 214, translation modified)
  言未卒，齧缺睡寐。被衣大說，行歌而去之，曰：「形若槁骸，心若死灰，真其實知，不以故自持。媒媒晦晦，無心而不可與謀。彼何人哉!」(22/58/23–25)

Wearcoat was saying "right things" about Gnaw Gap and the Way, but saying them is not the ultimate. Gnaw Gap drowses off or falls into a meditative state. Following Wearcoat's interpretation, Gnaw Gap has "form like withered carcass" and "mind like dead ashes": these phrases are used elsewhere in the *Zhuangzi* for meditative states (e.g., in Chapter 2; where "dried wood" appears instead of "carcass"; cf. above 8.3 and 8.6). This non-knowing is "real knowledge" (*shizhi* 實知) that does not cling to reasoning about the causes; it is a knowledge on the interpenetrating level, the numinous level (*ling* 靈) of the "spirits" (*shen* 神). Gap radiates potency but is "so dim and so obscure" (*meimeihuihui* 媒媒晦晦). Wearcoat cannot describe this kind or person, or bring him to clarity; therefore, he ends his praise with a rhetorical question.

There is another similar story in the same chapter:

> Resplendent Light inquired of Making-Being-Not-To-Be, saying, "Master, do you exist or do you not exist?" Not getting an answer to his question, Resplendent Light looked at the other's sunken, hollow appearance intently. For a whole day, he looked at him but couldn't see him, listened to him but couldn't hear him, groped for him but couldn't grasp him. "The ultimate!" said Resplendent Light. "Who else could attain such a state? I can make nonbeing to be, but I cannot make nonbeing not to be. And when it comes to making being not to be, how could one arrive at that?" (Mair 1994: 220, tr. mod.)
>
> 光曜問乎無有曰：「夫子有乎, 其無有乎?」光曜不得問, 而孰視其狀貌, 窅然空然, 終日視之而不見, 聽之而不聞, 搏之而不得也。光曜曰：「至矣! 其孰能至此乎! 予能有無矣, 而未能無無也, 及為無有矣, 何從至此哉!」(22/60/65–68)

Here the Resplendent Light perhaps embodies the intelligence acquired through sitting and forgetting. He says that he can "make nonbeing to be" (*you wu* 有無): he can bring nonbeing or the virtual into being, provides an access to the virtual interpenetration inside being. He is faced with a character called *Wuyou* 無有, which normally would mean simply "Nonbeing," but in this context it could be interpreted rather as "making being not to be." This could be interpreted as the complementary aspect to the "making nonbeing to be." Making all being not to be could mean that the virtual interpenetration is explicitly integrated with the actual juxtaposed existence, loosening knots and fixations in the latter. The intermediary task is to "make nonbeing not to be" *wuwu* 無無. This would be the task of refraining from taking nonbeing as being or the virtuality as actuality, or—in Western traditional terms—from treating being as a being. In the face of "Making-Being-Not-To-Be" there is nothing to be grasped (he appears sunken and hollow); there is no juxtaposed piece of knowledge to be obtained. It is the maximum of deactualization or counter-actualization. And this very impossibility of reducing virtuality to actuality rejoices the enlightened knowledge or the Resplendent Light.

It is true that actualization proceeds from the interpenetrating or formless toward actualized forms, and deactualization from actualized forms to the interpenetrating or formless. Those who attain it do not discuss it:

> From formlessness to form, from form to formlessness—this is known to all men in common, but not something to which one who will attain the Way attends. This is something which is discussed by the masses of men in common, but he who attains it does not discuss it, and those who discuss it do not attain it. Even the clear-sighted do not encounter it, so better to remain silent than dispute over it. The Way cannot be heard, so better to stop up your ears than listen for it. This is what is meant by the great obtainment. (Mair 1994: 217)
> 不形之形, 形之不形, 是人之所同知也, 非將至之所務也, 此眾人之所同論也。彼至則不論, 論則不至。明見無值, 辯不若默。道不可聞, 聞不若塞。此之謂大得。」(22/59/41–3)

This reflects the saying of *Laozi* §56, cited twice in the *Zhuangzi* (in Chs. 13 and 22): "the one who knows, does not speak; the one who speaks does not know" (知者不言, 言者不知). This comes dangerously close to a self-destroying position. Non-knowledge is posited as an ideal, but how can one consider it as something valuable? And is it not a kind of knowledge, after all, a certain knowledge that reacts *against* certain other knowledge?

Instead of a simple opposition between knowing and not knowing: for example, knowing the date of death of Confucius, and ignoring that fact, there is a deeper distinction between different levels of interpenetration of knowledge. On the one hand, there is the juxtaposed, actual knowledge where mental "pieces" stand one next to another; another is the interpenetrating, virtual knowledge where all mental parts interpenetrate each other. It leads to a paradox: in one sense, such knowledge cannot be expressed in words juxtaposing each other, and there is no distinct content to be conveyed. Therefore, one should remain silent. But on the other hand, the interpenetrating knowledge cannot be unexpressed, but it will express itself in each and every word and deed. Indeed, an obstinate silence would mean an attachment to a certain actual form; and if this form is taken together with the forms that it excludes (i.e., speaking), it would be kept apart from it, it would juxtapose with it; and hence it would still be in the realm of the juxtaposing and actual.

In a third story on the same topic, personalized aspects of Daoist practices of embodied knowledge are depicted discussing the Way. Exalted Purity (*Taiqing* 泰清) goes to different persons, asking about the Way. Infinity (*Wuqiong* 無窮) answers that he does not know. "Non-action" (*Wuwei* 無為) gives a positive answer: the Way can be valued or despised, constrained or scattered. "Non-beginning" (*Wushi* 無始) gives some negative descriptions:

> The Way cannot be heard, for what is heard is not the Way; the Way cannot be seen, for what is seen is not the Way; the Way cannot be spoken, for what is spoken is not the Way. Do you know that what forms forms has no form? The Way does not correspond to any name. (Mair 1994: 219, translation modified)
> 道不可聞, 聞而非也; 道不可見, 見而非也; 道不可言, 言而非也。知形形之不形乎? 道不當名。(22/60/62–3)

This is close to the beginning of the *Laozi*: "the Way that can be talked about is not the constant Way" (*dao kedao fei changdao* 道可道非常道). There is the patent paradox: this truth is also *said* and should thus be considered shallow. Yet it is possible that a different kind of speaking is involved here, which hints rather than denotes (cf. above, 2.10).

Exalted Purity, in his discussion with Non-beginning, asks rhetorically: "Then not to know is to know? To know is not to know? Who knows the knowing of not knowing" (Mair 1994). This may again seem a blatant paradox, but Non-knowing (*feizhi* 弗知) and "not to know" (*bu zhi* 不知) are two distinct concepts. Non-knowing is not simply being without knowledge, but refers to the interpenetrating level of knowledge (and a corresponding interpenetrating level of being). While disembodied knowledge is on the level of the actual and juxtaposing, embodied knowledge is on the level of the virtual and interpenetrating. Embodied knowledge is the generative base for disembodied knowledge, because every knowledge and form of being is unfolded from a certain interpenetrating or "enfolded" state. For example, a multicellular organism unfolds from an embryo; an idea unfolds from a certain intuition. The actualized state is the anchoring point of the virtual, so that actualized structures and sequences help to "ground" the actualization process, sending new confirmations or challenges for further actualizations. The fact that two tissues come into contact may induce further cell differentiations, and without this actual contact, further unfolding from the virtual does not take place. The fact that someone has actualized certain distinctions and concepts creates new questions and problems that require additions, reworkings, and deletions to the initial ideas. Non-knowing indicates this virtual or interpenetrating aspect that is the unceasing reservoir of further actualizations. It is some clear knowledge that is in communication with its obscure background, the non-known, from which it has been carved out. It acknowledges the obscure background that is the constitutive condition of every clear focus on it.

New actualizations and unfoldings require a return to the virtual and enfolded. One cannot have a new idea without having in a sense dismantled old forms and "melted up" previous knowledge. Even more fundamentally, in every moment of continuing existence one makes reference to their interpenetrating side, to a "pure memory" (Deleuze 1994: 79–84), on the background of which the actual state acquires meaning and force.

The previous subsections traced the foundation of being into the interpenetrating. The previous two subsections show how in a parallel way Zhuangzi traces understanding to the interpenetrating. "Non-knowing" is *not* not knowing but an interpenetrating knowledge. It takes the implicitness of embodied knowledge to the maximum; it refuses to recontextualize or reterritorialize knowledge into any distinguishable actual form. Confucius with his embodied implicit knowledge still also expressed this knowledge in specific ritual actions and teachings, but the Zhuangzian free-roamers do not do anything special and do not teach anything. Their level of interpenetration is on a higher level than Confucius', above the human form (or above any form) and on the level of the whole nature.

8.10 Zhuangzian Ideas as Reflection on a Skill

Zhuangzi's ideas can arise spontaneously from reflection on a certain skill. Seemingly without direct influence from the *Zhuangzi*, very similar ideas pop out in contemporary practitioners. Let us take the example of Michael Grab, the founder of "Gravity Glue," who arranges stones on top of each other, creating beautiful and seemingly impossible structures. Putting stones on each other is a "minor art" that fits perfectly into the Zhuangzian series of cicada-catchers and butchers. It is a skill that does not have a direct utilitarian value, or is not limited to it, and that also does not belong to the established forms of art like gallery painting or sculpture.

Grab brings out similar phases as Zhuangzi: (1) "I began balancing rocks through somewhat of a whim in the summer of 2008 while exploring Boulder Creek in Boulder, CO, USA."[39] Then, (2) "over years of practice"[40] he has attained (3) an intuitive understanding of stones, he feels their "vibrations or "clicks," as the surfaces move against one another."⁴¹ It is, for him, also a meditative practice (which is a "natural byproduct" of stone balancing): "In order to feel the smallest 'clicks', it helps to breathe slowly, clear the mind, and relax, while remaining alert."⁴² In Zhuangzian terms, this would be his "mind-fasting" through which he matches his "heaven" to the "heaven" of his stones: "You must get to know the rocks you are working with. Some rock characters will coordinate better with others, vice versa, back, forth, right, left, up, or down." He has an embodied, intuitive, and very nuanced understanding of the stones he uses—just as Cook Nail has of the ox of Carpenter Praise of the wood.

Just as in case of Wheelwright Flat (cf. 8.2), words are not adequate to render his skill that is "beyond words." Through this practice, Grab becomes intensely sensitive to his wider surroundings, "Most prominent being wind, tides, sunsets … Spring snow run-offs, moonrises. For me it is all a very direct relationship with reality. Here and Now." In this way he extends his subjectivity: "It's about dissolving boundaries between self and environment. One must BEcome⁴³ the balance in order to realize such a thing in a complicated equation of rocks!" And his practice is emergent, it is born in a particular context, with the stones and surroundings he finds out there, and it is not completely predictable: "Also a beautiful aspect of playing with nature is the chaos element. The unpredictability. Conditions that force one to adapt in order to continue. It keeps the practice slightly beyond control, and therefore fresh and challenging." He calls it his "yoga practice"⁴⁴ or his "therapeutic ritual."⁴⁵ In this way he develops his embodied existence embedded in a context. This kind of practice allows everyone "to seek their own 'still-point' or inner silence" (cf. Confucius' "emptiness" in 4.10), and in this way "this art allows one to freely be themselves, manifesting their own particular vibration into a 3D world." This even leads him to join the transformation of things like the four friends in 8.7. In the interviewer's words: "Both honoring nature and the importance of time spent by himself Grab believes that the ephemeral nature of the balance encourages contemplations of non-attachment, beauty and even death."⁴⁶

From this contemporary parallel between Grab and Zhuangzi's characters, we can see that Zhuangzian ideas may arise spontaneously from practicing a minor art, and there seems to be a natural progression in this process, the "third phase" of which involves a phase transition in subjectivity and being-in-the-world. This process involves a meditative element, but the main purport of this embodied self-cultivation is not art itself, nor meditation in itself, but the "free and easy wandering" attained in this process. Therefore, it does not matter so much, through what kind of art one has obtained the "way." What matters is the extended subjectivity and identification with the general transformation of things. The swimmer might not be good at woodcutting or stone-placing, and the woodcutter might not be good at swimming or stone-placing, but their respective minor art has opened a door for "free and easy wandering." This is not a finished and unchanging state, on the contrary, it is a heightened sensibility to context, to things, beings, persons, environments; it is the ability to appreciate and adapt to change and to its feedback. It is joyful.

8.11 Zhuangzi and Decontextualization

The *Zhuangzi* is a powerful philosophical text that sets up concepts, conceptual structures, and conceptual characters. And we should note the undeniable paradox that all these wonderful elaborations on embodied existence and knowledge are expressed in language and put down in a written text, i.e., in a disembodying and decontextualizing media (we can read this text over 2000 years later, in a different place). But it would be a mistake to think that a more "genuinely" embodied thought would not use language or writing. As we saw above, an embodied and embedded existence does not mean to be identical to one's body and context. On the contrary, every embodied being is already self-transcending and context-transcending; it is different from itself and from its surroundings, and integrates this difference, thereby always changing and transforming.

The difference between "embodied" and "disembodied" knowledge is rather of degree than of nature: seemingly even the most disembodied thought is ultimately grounded in an embodiment, and seemingly even the most thorough immersion in the body is already transcending itself and hence "disembodied" to an extent. Embodiment and disembodiment refer, first of all, to two different tendencies: toward the context and toward decontextualization, both of which have their merits and demerits: immersion in a context can become oppressive, whereas decontextualization can lead to self-alienation, to an impoverished life in abstract, symbolic and imaginary forms. Or in a slightly different way, embodiment can be seen as the generative ground of the existence, an interpenetrating level of life, and disembodied or decontextualized tendencies serve the function of bringing certain forms into greater clarity, making them more "external," "juxtaposed," i.e., pursuing the actualization process of a certain *part* or *aspect* of existence (e.g., establishing clear juridical laws, making tools for greater efficiency in crafts like the compass and square in carpentry), that can then also help the embodied existence (e.g., in a society with a rule of and by the law its members can transform more freely, integrate and differentiate in a more nuanced, multiple, variated way).

If we look closer, there is already a disembodied or self-transcending aspect in the "first phase" (and second phase is its prolungation), and there is always an embodied or returning-to-self aspect in the "second phase," because it works on bodily capacities. But relatively speaking, the first phase is more about immediate embedded existence in given abilities and surroundings and the "second phase" is more about self-transcendence, disembodiment, decontextualization, self-alienation. In the second phase, by developing a special skill, they undo their previous self-evidences, decompose their bodies. When I am still learning to swim, I do not yet know how to move my body in the water, so that its previous habits, acquired on land, are not sufficient, and I have to decompose them and develop new habits. They put themselves into new situations and environments (in water, in dialogue with a cicada or an ox or a tree, etc.). After this disembodied and decontextualized phase, it becomes possible to reintegrate the body and the context on a new level, where the practitioners understand the relevant articulations of other things, beings and environments, and are able to compose their own body with them, so as to be very sensitive to the changes in them, and find an adequate response and behavior, in a new embodiment.

This new embodiment of the "third phase" has in a certain way *englobed* in itself the disembodiment and decontextualization. It already implies a radical cut with the habitual, acquired bodily and mental forms and habits. The practitioners leave their already actualized form behind and become "integrated with the Great Interpenetration" and are able to transform with the all-encompassing transformation of things. This is the maximum of both embodiment and disembodiment, because it can be argued that an ordinary disembodied use of language, symbols, rules, definitions, etc. does not take disembodiment far enough, and still depends on the aims, goals, preferences, intentions of the one using them. To become *really* "disembodied," one has to cut even these links as much as possible. Of course, those links can never be completely severed, and the embodied grounding can never be entirely eliminated, but in this process of "forgetting" them, the transformation of things shines through more clearly. Therefore it is a more nuanced *embodiment* that comes out of this extreme *disembodiment*. With this, the *Zhuangzi* is another "ramification" or utmost developments of the Chinese embodied thought.

8.12 Conclusion

Zhuangzi takes embodied premises to their furthermost consequences. The most interesting parts of the *Zhuangzi* in this respect are the "skill stories" about masters in a craft or skill (wheelwrights, carpenters, butchers, swimmers, cicada-catchers, etc.). In these stories, the aspects of existence and knowledge as embodied, embedded, extended, enacted, emotive, etc. come most vividly to the fore. Those aspects that in the disembodied account (e.g., in Aristotle's *Metaphysics*) were deemed "good" and superior, like the knowledge of causes and ability to explicate in language and teach to others, are defiantly denounced by Zhuangzi—his characters explicitly say they do not know why they are able to do what they do, and neither are they able to put it into words or teach it to others. On the contrary, non-speaking and not-knowing are presented as "good" and superior. A Zhuangzian "not knowing" is not merely the ignorance of some facts or principles but it is an interpenetrating form of knowing, the parts of which are not made rigid, fixed, separated from the whole reserve of knowledge, abstracted from the context and embodiment.

This is not simply about attaining a mastery in a specific art, but there is a soteriological aspect to it: through their art, practitioners are able to transform their own subjectivity and their being in the world. This seems to be the natural outcome of a dedication to a practice, as we saw from the contemporary practice of "gravity glue" by Michael Grab. The practice becomes more than just an art or *technē* (*shu* 術) and becomes a way (*dao* 道). It involves forms of meditation (that for Grab is a "natural byproduct" of his practice) as forms of counter-actualizations, i.e., practices where established bodily and mental forms are dissolved (see Yan Hui's "sitting and forgetting" in 8.6), so that one gains access to the more interpenetrating levels of reality, from where those forms are actualized, generated. In this way, Zhuangzian practitioners are able to "roam freely": they still have a certain psychophysical form, but they affirm their transformation and are not overly attached to the products of this process (see the story about four friends in 8.7).

The skill stories typically follow a tripartite sequence: they start from a certain givenness, exercise their skill, and finally "forget" themselves in the performance. This is a familiar process for anyone who has practiced some skill, and is found in the examples of Cook Nail, Carpenter Praise, and the swimmer. After mastering the skill, one can match the articulations of one's own body and mind to things, beings, or environments. One's behavior becomes extremely sensitive to its concrete context it is embedded in, and does not impose on it some rigid, fixed, pre-established, universal, unchanging rule or form.

Instruments and materials in those stories can be taken as examples of the extendedness of knowledge. It is interesting to note the similarities and differences with Confucius and Mozi. Confucius developed important aspects of his behavior with the help of ritual items (jade tablet, zither), with which he conveyed embodied and contextual meaning, and Mozi made references to tools (e.g., carpentry utensils like compass and square) in order to convey a decontextualized and disembodied meaning (with a compass practically anyone and anywhere can draw perfect circles). Zhuangzi, on the one hand, like Mozi, mostly refers to tools that indeed have a practical purpose (knife, chisel, etc.), but on the other hand, like Confucius, his attention is not so much on the practical and utilitarian outcome but in self-cultivation. This is most clear in 8.4, where mechanical efficiency is explicitly discarded as also turning the mind into a "machine."

The embodied and enacted approach is paradoxically clearest in Yan Hui's meditation of "sitting and forgetting," where he "sloughs off" his body (8.6). Yet it is precisely in this meditation practice that one's own body and its relation to other things and beings become the most nuanced and refined. When one's mind contemplates itself and one's power of being, it becomes less attached to particular psychosomatic forms that one has actualized and acquired. By "discarding" the body, Yan Hui is much more "in" his body, and by "forgetting" rituals and music, he becomes free from social conventions or forms. He reaches the virtual or interpenetrating level of being, from which all forms unfold and actualize. Yan Hui is still anchored in actuality, he continues to exist as an actual human being, but he is not attached to human forms, and due to this he is capable of responding most adequately to the feedback that he receives from the things, beings, and environments.

This kind of contextualizing and embodying attitude takes the Way itself as its context and "body." A body expresses certain singularities that are unfolded in actual form as a human being and as a certain individual. But those virtual singularities in their feedback with actualized forms (like a "mirror," see 8.8) are constantly evolving and changing. Furthermore, they interpenetrate with singularities of other things, beings, and processes. Zhuangzian masters identify themselves not with forms but with transformation. This is expressed in a powerful way in the story of four friends (see 8.7). In a sense, the maximum of contextualization here leads to a maximum of decontextualization, in the sense that those friends are completely free from attachment to any form or context and are perfectly joyful when they change.

From the gnoseological side, this access to a more interpenetrating level of being is paralleled with a kind of knowledge that belongs to that interpenetrating level. It is called "not-knowing" (see 8.9). It is a knowledge that is obscure and dark because it does not actualize anything. Yet, it is not imprecise, random, or crazy. It involves the knowledge of the singularities that from our perspective interpenetrate each other but that in themselves are perfectly distinct.[47]

Earlier in this book it was shown how embodiment-like ideas can arise from a ritualistic background in different ages and places (Confucians, Kurankos, Hasidis). In this chapter it was shown how reflection on a skill can lead to similar ideas (Zhuangzi, Michael Grab): how intuitive understanding of the material is obtained, how one is freed from attachment to forms and feels connected to the environment.

The *Zhuangzi* is another example of how contextualized and embodied thought and practice are drawn to their furthermost consequences, so that the "context" becomes the "de-context" itself, or transformation.

9

Conclusion

This project distinguishes between two tendencies in knowledge and its progression: decontextualizing-disembodying and contextualizing-embodying. The former has been dominant in the Western tradition for a long time, and the latter has been proposed more recently in scientific and philosophical discussions.

Embodiment Theory (ET) is an important research project for investigating contextualizing tendencies of knowledge with its interconnected topics of embodiment, embeddedness, enactivity, extendedness, emotivity, implicitness, and a few others. ET has been constituted in opposition to the dominant Western understanding of cognition as disembodied, abstract, theoretical, ready-made, cold, and explicit. Chapter 2 presents some central topics of ET and shows how the disembodying tendency can be reinterpreted against the backdrop of embodiment. While embodiment is basic and gives meaning, disembodiment may emancipate some from certain social and intellectual oppressive contexts.

Chapter 3 gives historical and cultural background from ancient Greece and China that explains why tendencies toward decontextualizing prevailed in Greece, and tendencies toward contextualizing, in China. Ritualistic background is central to Chinese tradition, as well as two other traditions—Kurankos of Sierra Leone and Hasidism of Eastern Europe—that seem to warrant the impression that a reflection on rituals can give rise to similar contextualizing and embodying ideas.

The main body of the book (Chapters 4–8) shows that ET is a good framework from which to approach Chinese philosophy. Chapter 4 gives an ET interpretation of Confucius' *Analects*. Chapters 5 and 6 describe two contrary tendencies toward a disembodied theory, the Mohists and Legalists, respectively. Chapters 7 and 8 present two developments or ramifications based on an embodied understanding of knowledge and existence, taken from the *Record of Music* and *Zhuangzi*. They give an idea, how far an embodied ontology and epistemology can be taken.

Western and Chinese mainstream philosophical traditions differ in respect to the importance attributed to disembodied tools and to embodied aspects (starting from Confucius' *Analects*, discussed in Chapter 3). The Chinese philosophical tradition incorporates important parts of disembodied thought, or tendencies toward disembodiment, through the Mohists and Legalists (discussed in Chapters 4 and 5), although it was reserved mostly to the sphere of government and social engineering, while technical innovation was mostly outside the concerns of philosophy.

The *Record of Music* and the *Zhuangzi* present some of the furthest developments of embodied thinking. The *Record of Music* develops an account of epistemology, ethics, and ontology, while the *Zhuangzi*, among other topics, presents several stories where the logic of embodiment is most clearly stated.

In the *Zhuangzi*, ideas of embodiment are taken to the extreme, and it leads to a maximum of disembodiment; his maximum immersion in a context leads to a liberation from actualized contexts and forms, to a general trans-formation. In this way, our initial idea of opposing embodiment and disembodiment, contextualization and decontextualization, mutates into identifying two *directions* or aspects in any body and context, toward engaging or disengaging, toward virtual interpenetration or actual juxtaposing. Juxtaposing ideas are a constant lure, so the complementary direction toward interpenetration has to be emphasized. It helps to better *contextualize* the decontextualizing direction. The actualized forms become emancipatory and valuable only when taken in their transformation and self-transcendence.

Notes

Chapter 1

1. For a couple of centuries, the royal science was very successful, relating terrestrial and celestial motions in Newton's laws, extending them in Einstein's theory, uniting a large number of different phenomena (e.g., electricity and magnetism, which were then later brought together with weak and strong interaction), etc. At the same time, it tended to discard or downplay non-linear phenomena and systems far from equilibrium. In reaction to this, from the middle of the twentieth century new theoretical methods and concepts were introduced (e.g., chaos theory, dissipative structures, self-organization) that tried to deal with these previously overlooked aspects of reality (and that can be brought fruitfully together with the Embodiment Theory that we are going to discuss below).
2. Many early Greek philosophers were also important mediators of scientific and technological knowledge from Egypt and Mesopotamia (whereas in the Chinese context that we are going to explore later, this played little role); and even though these endeavors were very different from contemporary science, they perhaps favoured the tendency toward abstract, mediated, decontextualized knowledge.
3. For instance, one of the leading modern proponents of ET, Antonio Damasio, has written on Spinoza, see Damasio (2003). Also Gilles Deleuze emphasizes the embodied basis for creating higher forms of knowledge: the "common notions" are formed through bodily interactions with a thing or an environment (he likes to bring the example of learning to swim), see Deleuze (1988) and (2007).
4. See, for instance Nietzsche's (spuriously edited) *Will to Power* § 636 (1967: 339–40) and "On the Despisers of the Body" of the *Thus Spoke Zarathustra* (2006: 22–4).
5. Dermot Moran says that while Husserl's role in establishing the embodiment-thinking is acknowledged, it is still largely underestimated (Moran 2017: 28).
6. For example: the history of Chinese thought (Sivin 1995; Emerson 1996; Lewis 2006; Jullien 2007; Sommer 2008; Hutton 2018), medicine (Kuriyama 1999; Hsu 2007), Daoism (Schipper 1994; Despeux 2005; Kohn 2006), senses (Geaney 2002; Sterckx 2003), emotions (Zhang 2007), power (Zito and Barlow 1994), skills (Lai and Chiu 2019; Lai 2022b), activity (Valmisa 2021), extended cognition (Lai 2022b). See also National Taiwan University Press' book series called "Body and Nature" (身體與自然) that has a volume edited by Shunde Yu (2015), directly concerning questions of embodiment in Western and Chinese traditions.

7 The present book discusses philosophical texts; such important topics as medicine and elaborate Daoist body techniques are not treated here. Mutual refreshment between ET and Chinese philosophy, notably Confucianism, has been emphasized by Bongrae Seok (2013).
8 Hegel's own goal was concrete knowledge where the opposition between embodiment and disembodiment would be sublated, but he was unable to appreciate that Confucius points in the same direction.

Chapter 2

1 I use the term "embodied needs" to avoid both the idea that there might be needs unrelated to body and also the reductionism that all needs can be *explained* by bodily needs. On the one hand, all of our subjective life is related to the state of our body, but on the other hand we should avoid establishing body and mind as two different substances (and reducing one to the other). A state of hunger or loneliness is both "bodily" and "spiritual."
2 See Heidegger (1996) and how the being-toward-death donates meaning in general. The anticipated destruction of meaning by death is the very basis of having some meaning.
3 Cf. Chinese *gāo* 高, lit. "high," and *dī* 低, lit. "low": *gāoxìng* 高興 "glad," *qíngxùdī* 情緒低 "depressed."
4 In Estonian, for instance, *parem käsi* means both "right hand" and "better hand."
5 See, in particular his analysis of Being-in-the-world, Being-together, Attunement, Care, Facticity, and Historicity. Heidegger shows how the "ontic" spatiotemporal and social determinations are based on a more primordial Being-in-the-world, Being-Together, and Being-toward-death, and how these determinations are not extrinsic to the existence but belong to its very core.
6 Merleau-Ponty (1945: 180–1) remarks on the ease with which organists are able to adapt themselves to different organs that can be very different from each other in their physical makeup. A few hours of practice are sufficient for an organist to be able to play on a new organ. Keys, stops, and pedals are placed at different places and distances, but the organist has the "feeling" how to play organs, and is able to adapt to the actual instrument. They meet the organ on a more interpenetrating level.
7 For instance, among primates, crouching is a sign of submission, and drumming on the chest is a show of pride and strength. These behaviors are apparent even among juvenile primates.
8 Cf. Wittgenstein's question in "On Certainty" §9: "Now do I, in the course of my life, make sure I know that here is a hand—my own hand, that is?" (1969: 3).

9   And in case of certain dysfunctions the patient in fact has to activate the whole body in order to find a part of it: for instance, on the order to raise the hand, she first moves all of the body parts and only then is able to focus on the hand separately (see Merleau-Ponty 1945: 140–3).
10 References to Merleau-Ponty's *Phenomenology of Perception* are to the French original; those page numbers can be found at the margins of the English translation of Merleau-Ponty (2012).
11 Colombetti argues that "affectivity" is a broader term than emotion; I accord it, but since I do not intend to present a special detailed study of affectivity, I may at places use them interchangeably.
12 Spinoza's fundamental affects should not be confused with the modern research into basic affects. They are not building blocks of other affects, and are not really distinct from them: all other affects are finer modulations of them, bifurcations in the affective phase-space. Although it may be difficult to detect joy or sorrow in every affect, it is still true that all the affective life takes place on the background of our ontological striving and of the essential precariousness of this endeavor.

   Giovanna Colombetti (2014) argues that the term "basic affects" is not good: there are no primitive affects, from which others would be made of like building blocks, and no discrete set of basic affects in contrast to other affects can be drawn. Indeed, she shows how arbitrarily the most common number of six was arrived at: an earlier proposition by Silvan Tomkins included nine basic affects, but Paul Ekman, who used photographs in his experiment, in case of three simply did not have photographs that would meet the criteria of his experiment, and so he discarded them. And even the nine affects of Tomkins was an arbitrary selection (2014: 38–9). Jaak Panksepp, who distinguished seven basic affects, shows how they partially use the same neurological structures and neurotransmitters, and can be distinguished only from a certain aspect. He presents them neither as building blocks nor completely discrete.
13 This is also the idea in Hanna and Maiese (2009); this cultivation of emotions is made possible by the hierarchical structures from more basic emotions to second, third, etc. order emotions.
14 For example, Maiese (2011: 204–18) shows how psychopathy in reality is not about egoism but about the inability to make longer temporal projects, a disturbance rooted in bodily problems (psychopaths do not inhibit action after punishment but, on the contrary, reinforce it).
15 This self-relation should not be considered in any reified form, as a self *qua* self, a self attributed to oneself *as* self. The reified self or self *qua* self is built upon more basic self-relation, as a totality created, as Deleuze and Guattari say, "in one corner" (*à côté*): "the subject is produced as a […] residuum alongside the desiring-machines" (Deleuze and Guattari 1983: 17). I agree with Hutto that at the very

basic level it is not necessary to posit a reified self, even a minimal one, some kind of "ownership," and I take the self-relation discussed here to be compatible with Hutto's "selflessness" of his "radical enactivity" (see Hutto and Satne 2017; Hutto and Ilundáin-Agurruza 2018).

16 The unconscious forms a whole with the conscious (in the narrow sense of the term), so that both can be taken together as a global system, that by convention can be called consciousness, because there is a concomitant knowing (*con-scientia*) also in the unconscious (in a certain sense, the conscious in the narrow sense of the term is a concomitant to the unconscious, so that actually the unconscious would be that "with" which or "in accompaniment with" which we know).

17 For our purposes here we don't need to make finer distinctions between affects and feelings. For some possible ways of distinguishing them, see Damasio (1994: 127–64), Maiese (2011), Colombetti (2014).

18 In the sense of Deleuzian larval subjects that contemplate themselves and what they contract in their synthesis (Deleuze 1994: 70–9).

19 Martin Heidegger, one of the forerunners of embodiment theory, made attunement (*Stimmung*) the ontological mode of *Dasein* and care (*Sorge*) one of the core dimensions of his fundamental ontology in his *Being and Time* (Heidegger 1996: 126–31, 169–212; cf. Colombetti 2014: 11–13).

20 For pre-reflective consciousness, see Sartre (1956: l-lvi), cf. Miguens, Preyer, and Morando (2019), and Smith (2020: §3.2).

21 For the notion of constraints, see Deacon (2011).

22 If not, we perceive it as a pathology, e.g., psychosis or also autism and schizophrenia, where the immediate being-together or habitual give-and-take "dancing" with others is impaired.

23 By hot and cold knowledge, I refer to temporal modality. It is different from, although related to, Ball and Vincent's (1998) definition of those terms, where "hot" refers to experiential and "cold" to formal knowledge. My usage does not focus on the distinction formal/informal; but of course, formal knowledge is indeed "slower," because it is more mediated.

24 "[T]he mind travels unceasingly over the interval comprised between its two extreme limits, the plane of action and the plane of dream" (Bergson 1990 [1896]: 172).

Chapter 3

1 Certainly, both tendencies were present in both cultures; hence the speculative claim here is about the relative dominance. Also, the discussion is distinct from body-mind dualism question (see Raphals 2015). One can distance from the immediate both holistically and dualistically.

2   In contrast, early Chinese philosophers paid little attention to scientific queries, with the exception of Mohists, who represented namely a decontextualizing current.
3   Of course, we should not forget that only adult, free local males were citizens, while women, foreigners, and slaves were excluded, so that only perhaps a tenth of the population had citizenship.
4   The jurors in Athens, chosen by lots, were several hundred or even thousand people.
5   "Whether fees were originally paid [at Plato's Academy—M.O.] is not certain, but in most schools of the Hellenistic period they were, and contributions were probably expected from members for the upkeep of the school" (Lloyd and Sivin 2002: 107).
6   When Spinoza reworked his initial draft of "Ethics" into a "geometric" presentation (using axioms, propositions, corollaries, etc.), it was probably motivated by the same concern for making his text as unassailable as possible, not simply for success in competition with other schools as in Antiquity but for personal safety of the author.
7   Although such criticism did exist: e.g., in the story about the first philosopher, Thales, who is said to have stumbled into a well while staring at the stars, and laughed at by a Thracian maid who says that Thales may know distant stars but is ignorant about what is by his feet; or in the "Clouds" of Aristophanes, where Socrates is been ridiculed as a vain theorizer. Yet the same Thales, according to another story, demonstrated his practical acumen, when he predicted a good olive harvest and made big money by renting all the oil presses. And Socrates, who in Plato's dialogues preconizes a theory of ideas, was engaged in discussions with different people, addressing practical topics about a good behavior and good life of a citizen, which he demonstrated both by bravery as a soldier and later by not escaping his death penalty.
8   Of course, the Greek world also developed sophisticated academic commentarial tradition that may have become quite dogmatic, pedantic, and estranged from the everyday life. This is a common fate or phase of many philosophical traditions in any culture.
9   For references, see Fung (2020), Fraser (2020c), Graham (1989).
10 For a bibliography on ET and rituals, see Kundtová Klocová and Geertz (2019).
11 The Chinese term for "Confucian" is *ru* 儒, which linguistically contains no reference to the name of Confucius and the *ru* has existed before him. The Chinese character has three components: a man, rain, and roots; hence one of the hypotheses is that originally they were some kind of rain-makers, sorcerers. Later it came to be identified with a scholar, and since the classical scholarship (in terms of arts to be mastered, rituals to be followed, and classical texts to be known)

was defined by Confucius and his followers, so this scholar was also a Confucian. Confucius himself seems to have "self-consciously identified himself with a Ru tradition, but also sought to differentiate the 'gentleman's Ru'" (Csikszentmihalyi 2004: 16). This tradition englobed a rich variety of traditions, practices, and ideals, and it is important to bear in mind the plurality of it (Csikszentmihalyi 2004: 18).

12 Eno's views are not uncontested and remain minoritarian. According to the dominant view political aspirations were at the core of Confucius' teaching. For example, Yuet Keung Lo says that "For Confucius, applied knowledge means political service […]. Clearly, Confucius taught with the express purpose of training political and diplomatic talents" (Lo 2014: 77).

13 Rituals often involve deliberate archaisms (remember Eno's remark on early Confucians above or think of Catholic priests who even today use clothes of the Roman Empire) and in this way they have a decontextualizing effect. But usually this is presented as integration into a certain sacred context.

14 All the simple page numbers in this subsection refer to this article.

15 Also Nietzsche in his *Genealogy of Morals* II.1–3 (1994: 35–9) speaks about the problem of how to make a people to keep promises and create a memory for it, and how it was solved by inflicting pain, "writing" into the flesh. This topic is developed by Gilles Deleuze and Félix Guattari in *Anti-Oedipus* III.1. (1983: 139–45).

16 Cf how Lu Jiuyuan 陸九淵 (1139–93), the founder of heart-mind branch of Song dynasty Neo-Confucianism, said that "'Six Classics' are comments on me; I am a comment of the 'Six Classics'" (《六經》註我,我註《六經》, Lu 1992: 254) and "If while learning you know the root, then the 'Six Classics' are my comments and footnotes" (學苟知本,《六經》皆我註腳, Lu 1992: 251–2).

17 Cf. Chan Buddhism that is said to be a "special transmission outside the scriptures."

18 Again, they can be compared to the Chan "encounter dialogues." It should be noted that Buber was aware of Eastern traditions and had himself commented on Zhuangzi, for example (see Buber 1957: 31–58; Herman 1996).

19 "[M]odern Jewish philosophy finds fertile ground and stimulation for thought in the variety of rituals and synagogue liturgies that mark the Jewish festivals" (Kepnes 2004: 242).

Chapter 4

1 This chapter is based on Ott (2017).
2 Confucius' name appears only once in Book 10, at the very beginning.
3 The very fact that a ritual manual containing general prescripts was attributed to a concrete historical figure, Confucius, is in line with the ET attitude: instead of general rules to be followed, there are particular models to be imitated.

4   In the following references to the *Analects*, there are given, first, the chapter and paragraph, and then after the semicolon, the page number in Slingerland's translation (2003a). If the last reference is not given, the translation is mine.
5   The Chinese originals are from the *Chinese Text Project*, http://ctext.org/analects.
6   The divergent trends in Greek and Chinese medicine are especially clear in the fate of pulse taking (Kuriyama 1999: 17–108). Pulse was very important for diagnostics in both traditions. In China it developed into a refined method of checking pulse at three locations on both wrists and at two levels of depth for taking information about different aspects of the body. But in Greece the question arose about the objective underpinnings of the pulse. And by today, measurable heart rate is the only characteristic of pulse that remains. This is a good representative for the general tendency to reduce phenomena to their spatiotemporal being, to the maximum of actualization and metrization.
7   In Slingerland's translation, "assumed a changed expression" and "assume a solemn expression." The word "solemn" does not appear in the text, although from extratextual knowledge we may suppose that it is the right description.
8   Of course, Confucius was a conservative when it came to rituals and customs, and the fact that he accepted silken cap instead of linen one is only a minor detail (see Sarkissian 2014: 109–10). Yet his emphasis on contextual knowledge can allow for modifications to happen during the course of time. He is certainly not against the change as such: "Standing on the bank of a river, the Master said, 'Look at how it flows on like this, never stopping day or night!'" (9.17; 92).
9   Mercedes Valmisa has developed this topic of adaptive behavior at length in her book *Adapting. A Chinese Philosophy of Action* (2021).
10 For example, in Estonia you should not shake hands over the threshold.
11 This saying is not about Confucius but about Gongshu Wenzi, a worthy minister in Wei. This description of his behavior, given by his student, expresses a truly lofty ideal, and Confucius, who comments on it, expresses his astonishment or disbelief (cf. Slingerland 2003a: 159).
12 The most general ethical rules, e.g., the categorical imperative (that the maxim of your behavior could become a general law) or the golden rule (do to others what you want them to do to you), are formal and acquire meaning and content from the context at hand.
13 This does not necessarily mean being "spineless," because certain social contexts (a tyranny, for instance) might themselves be unadaptive to a wider order of things, to the *dao*. The *Analects* contain plenty of denunciations by Confucius of his contemporary social order.
14 In the traditional educational setting it meant also that the teacher may have required more inflexibly rote learning from beginners and allowed more flexible dealings with more advanced students (cf. Lai 2006b).

15 This is what made the representational robots, criticized by Rodney Brooks (1999), so clumsy.
16 This was made clearer in the subsequent Confucianism: the *Mencius* opens with this topic, when Mencius bashes king Hui of Liang, who asks him how to bring profit (*li* 利) to the kingdom.
17 The following part of this subsection is based on my article "Contextualising and decontextualising knowledge: extended knowledge in Confucius, Mozi and Zhuangzi" (Ott 2022). I am grateful to the publisher for the permission to reproduce parts of the article.
18 In fact, Confucius most probably never served as an envoy to a foreign state, and this piece is one of the evidences that the descriptions in Book 10 were originally general precepts that were only later attributed to Confucius.
19 Indeed, the very choice of "old rituals" served as a critique of many contemporary cultural forms.
20 This leads to a generalized self-reflection (*fan* 反) in Mencius.
21 Following the golden rule, it cannot even be said with absolute certainty, for example, that you should not kill other person, since you would not want to kill or be killed yourself. In some cases, self-sacrifice may be warranted, and in other cases killing persons may be justified. Although Confucians called for a lenient government (cf. *Analects* 2.3), they usually did not condemn capital punishment—nor did Mohists, who laboriously demonstrated that to kill a robber is not to kill a person, 殺盜人非殺人也 《墨子·小取》.
22 Karyn Lai is speaking of Daoism, but it is equally applicable to Confucianism (cf. Lai 2006a: 58).
23 In the article referred to, Shun leaves the *le* untranslated, lest a fixed English equivalent would hinder a nuanced understanding of the term.
24 In Carl Gustav Jung's (1971) theory the human psyche tends to develop, in the course of life, aspects that are less pronounced in the beginning, so that under ideal conditions a person in a sense finally changes into his/her opposite. This is the phenomenon of "enantiodromia" or becoming-opposite. The previous dominant characteristics do not go away, so that the outcome is not a simple opposite of the initial situation but a more nuanced, richer personality. It must be noted that Jung was also directly influenced by the Chinese *yin-yang* thought.

Chapter 5

1 I shall omit the Disputers because for our present purposes most of their relevant aspects are already covered by Mohists, and also because not much information is available on the Disputers and even the exact character of their endeavor is not

clear; and at least some of them might have been simply entertainers, as Chris Fraser (2020c) argues about Gongsun Long. Of course, already the categorization into schools is a controversial topic: while Mohists did indeed form a self-conscious school or society, the Disputers did not form any coherent school with certain ideas and methods, and they were grouped together and given a common name only retrospectively.

2. Yet, the Zhou kings lasted surprisingly long: their power was seriously weakened already in 771 when their capital was sacked, but they survived for another half a millennium, until 256 BC. This was thanks to their ritual and symbolic power (cf. above, 3.3), and Yuri Pines (2009) has showed that this was an important factor that kept alive the idea(l) of political unity that was finally realized by Qin Shi Huangdi in 221 BC and later renewed by other dynasties after periods of disunity.

3. In the following discussion about Mozi, I include also the Later Mohists, who came much later and were active in fourth–third centuries BC.

4. The *Mozi* explicitly opposes Confucian ritualism (see especially chapters "Against Confucians" and "Against Music") because it is hypocritical and onerous to the society:

> Moreover, they use various elaborate rites and music to delude people. They use prolonged mourning and false grief to deceive relatives. They introduce fate and cause poverty, and live in idleness. They turn their backs on what is fundamental and abandon their duties, finding contentment in idleness and pride. (Johnston 2010: 353, 355, tr. modified)
> 且夫繁飾禮樂以淫人，久喪偽哀以謾親，立命緩貧而高浩居，倍本棄事而安怠傲。《非儒下》

This abandonment of the fundamentals in favor of rituals and music may become lethal to the common people:

> The people have three hardships: to be hungry and not find food; to be cold and not find clothing; to be weary and not find rest. These three things are great hardships for the people. If this is so, then suppose we strike the great bells, beat the sounding drums, strum lutes, blow pipes, and brandish shields and battle-axes. Will this enable the people to find the materials for food and clothing? I certainly don't think this will ever be so. (Johnston 2010: 309).
> 民有三患飢者不得食寒者不得衣勞者不得息三者民之巨患也。然即當為之撞巨鍾、擊鳴鼓、彈琴瑟、吹竽笙而揚干戚民衣食之財將安可得乎即我以為未必然也。《非樂上》.

5. The Chinese originals for *Mozi* are from Chinese Text Project. http://ctext.org/mozi.

6. Mohists admit that also an idea and a ready-made form may serve as standards: "The idea, the compasses, a circle, all three may serve as standard" (Explanation to A 70; Graham 1976: 316).

7   A somewhat later part of the *Mozi* (in Chapters 40–5) where Mohist logic is developed. Fraser (2020a) dates it to the first half of the third century BC.
8   With the help of fossil fuels, we had for some time the impression that everyone can be better off and that there can be luxury for free, but now we see how human luxury has deprived other species, and of course, the resources are distributed very unevenly also among humans.
9   Or, according to the translation of W. P. Mei: "there was strife among the strong and struggle among the weak." https://ctext.org/mozi/identification-with-the-superior-iii.
10 Although the Mohists also counteracted this historical process by aiding weaker states against the stronger ones, and thus somewhat slowed the process of China's unification into one big hierarchical system.
11 This idea was indeed developed by later Legalist thinkers and politicians into outright authoritarian and totalitarian models of state.
12 Mozi himself did not spell out what this dependence would mean concretely. The Confucian Mengzi (372–289 BC) brought forth the idea that the mood of the Heaven can be gauged from the mood of the population, and if the population is not content, it means that the ruler is inept, and that Heaven is not satisfied with him, eventually legitimizing a coup.
13 In case of the Canons and Expositions I follow the sequence established by Graham (1976). C refers to Canons and E to Expositions. Usually, the Canon gives a terse meaning of the defined notion, and the Exposition gives a somewhat longer explanation, at times offering examples.
14 Of course, I do not pretend that Confucius and Mozi were bound to only one strategy of teaching; it is only for the sake of exposition that I bring out the embodied knowledge from Confucianism and disembodied knowledge from Mohists as dominant tendencies in their respective traditions. After all, Confucius most probably also used tools in his teachings, like the ancient classics (*Odes*, *Documents*, etc.), although, of course, his interest laid elsewhere, in embodying the ancients' example. In principle, when you have understood the Mohist Canon, you may throw it away, but you should never throw away Confucian classics, from which ever-deeper implicit meanings can be unfolded. And this, in turn, can of course lead to intellectual conformism. On the other hand, we can be quite sure that Mo Di (and at least some of his followers) had a strong personal charisma and appeal; otherwise the Mohist school would not have become so strong and persisted for so long. From stories about Mohists we can see that they indeed tried to embody and live up to their ideals of all-encompassing love, helping the weaker, etc.
15 And the "disputers" (*bianzhe* 辯者) or followers of the "School of Names" (*mingjia* 名家) against whom the Mohists find themselves at the defensive also do not seem to make formal investigations into the *a priori* reasoning. It does not

connect up with a *technē* of reasoning, but at places it connects up with the direct opposite of it, becoming a tool of obstructing reasoning or "common sense," for purposes of self-cultivation like in the case of *chan*-buddhist *gong-an* 公案 (and already their predecessors described in the *Zhuangzi* might have some mystical aims) or also for simple entertainment (Fraser 2020c).

Chapter 6

1. It is not completely clear what did it mean concretely. Did he have a kind of a law school? Did he teach people rhetoric? Indeed, he is considered also a forefather of the "school of names" or "debaters."
2. https://ctext.org/lv-shi-chun-qiu/li-wei.
3. In citations, first chapter is indicated, then to the first or second volume of Wenku Liao's translation (Liao 1939, 1959, respectively), and page numbers of those volumes. Wade-Giles romanization has been changed to pinyin. The Chinese text is from Chinese Text Project. https://ctext.org/hanfeizi. A bilingual edition with Wenku Liao's translation is available at http://www2.iath.virginia.edu/exist/cocoon/xwomen/texts/hanfei/tpage/tocc/bilingual.
4. Traditional paragons of benevolent ancient rulers.
5. Traditional paragons of evil rulers, respectively the last ruler of Xia and Shang dynasty.
6. For an idea how to transform Han Feizi's system so that the place of the ruler would be indeed empty, see Ott (2013).
7. The binome with these two words, *pusu* 樸素, means "simple," "unsophisticated," "unadorned" in modern Chinese. The two words appear together in *Laozi* §19 "to show simplicity and keep to the uncarved" *jiansu, baopu* 見素抱樸.
8. *Du* 度 appears only once in the *Analects*, in Chapter 20, which is probably of later origin; *shu* 數 appears five times, but not in the sense of a precise quantity.
9. Han Feizi is said to have united the theories of two former Legalists: the laws, patterns, or rules (*fa* 法) of Shang Yang 商鞅 (390–338 BC), and the methods (*shu* 術) of Shen Buhai 申不害 (395–337 BC). This kind of "method" is precisely something that Zhuangzi looks down upon, as we shall see below.
10. One important difference between Legalist and Greek decontextualized thought is that the Chinese Legalists were mostly focused on government and state management and not in epistemology or natural sciences like Greek philosophers. Mohists had a similar interest in language and logic as the mainstream Greek philosophy. But Legalists were discredited after the Qin dynasty, and Mohists lost one of their important *raison d'être*, which was to help smaller states against bigger ones, because after the unification there was no one left to offer their help to, and probably the state authorities did not like such potentially subversive brotherhoods.

Chapter 7

1. This is something that also the Legalists propounded. One should not be like a man of Song who once saw a rabbit bump into a tree stump, killing itself, and started to wait at the stump for another free meal, expecting another rabbit to do the same, and forgoing tilling his fields (Han Feizi, Ch. 49). Yet the Legalists required written laws which obviously cannot be changed very often. This contradiction could be solved by distinguishing different tempos of change: laws should change *slowly, seldom*.
2. It is quite possible that people joined Mohist brotherhood for quite other reasons that may have been deeply emotional. But here we are concerned only with their philosophical justification.
3. See https://ctext.org/lv-shi-chun-qiu/da-yue.
4. The English translations are mostly from Cook (1995) (which is not a translation of the complete text) and have been sometimes modified; the Chinese text is from the Chinese Text Project, https://ctext.org/liji/yue-ji (its accompanying translation by James Legge is also consulted). The first reference is to the articulation of the text of the *Record of Music*, the second is to Cook's translation, and the third is to the articulation of the text in Cook's translation.
5. On the lines of this distinction between "heaven's nature" and "human nature's desires" the Song dynasty philosophers drew a distinction between "heavenly veins" (*tianli* 天理, a notion that appears in the same passage cited here) and "human desires" (*renyu* 人欲). About the issue of translating the *li* as "veins" (like the veins in a jade or marble), see Ott (2020).
6. More precisely, to the "ritual body" *gong* 躬; see Sommer (2008) and (2012).
7. As it is said in the *Zhuangzi* Chapter 20, that one must "thing things, and not let oneself to be thinged by things" (物物而不物於物).
8. In China, drums were used to signal attack and gongs to signal retreat.
9. This is also the title of two chapters in the "*Guanzi*" 管子 that together with the "Inward Training" (*Neiye* 內業) form a distinct block in that compilation of texts.
10. I leave aside the question whether this and other correspondences reflect any real historical practices or whether they are completely theoretical constructs. In any case, it shows an awareness that music influences people's minds and the desire to purposefully use it to mold the society.
11. Traditionally, they were categorized according to the material they were made of, or the material of their most characteristic part. The list given at that point of the *Record of Music* is heterogeneous; in addition to the categorization according to material (stone, silk, bamboo), there are also "bells" and "drums" that would belong to metal and skin instruments, respectively. In addition, there were also

instruments of gourd (e.g., mouth organ, *sheng*), wood (a tiger-shaped rattle), and clay (e.g., *xun*, ocarine).

12 For some examples of how emotions and different keys are paired, see *Characteristics* … 2009.

13 Chinese thinkers did also that, and developed an increasingly accurate idea of mathematical correlations in music, arriving at the correct mathematical definition of equal temperament before the West, by Zhu Zaiyu (1536–1611) in 1584.

14 For example, in the Soviet Union Music Academies there was a quota for composers on how many works in minor key they could compose; certainly, it had to be less than a half, because music in minor key could reduce the energy of the Soviet person, and this energy had to be expressed and sustained with music in major key.

15 In Ott (2019), I relate these concepts to Deleuze's concepts of intensities and virtual, respectively.

16 A Western analogue would be the veins in a block of marble, a simile that Leibniz liked.

17 A parallel passage can be found in the *Xunzi* that Knoblock (20.8) translates as follows: "As a general rule, when lewd music rouses, it is a rebellious spirit that is the response, and where that spirit achieves full representation, disorder is born. When correct music stirs men, it is an obedient spirit that is the response, which, when completely represented, gives birth to order" (凡姦聲感人而逆氣應之, 逆氣成象而亂生焉; 正聲感人而順氣應之, 順氣成象而治生焉, Xunzi 1999: 659). It should be noted, however, that *ni* and *shun* have a wider meaning than "rebellious" and "obedient"; and for general philosophical reasons I do not find it suitable to translate *chengxiang* 成象 as "achieve full representation," because *xiang*, an image or symbol, does not refer to the order of representation, but rather of presentation or actualization (e.g., when the *yin-yang* duality, according to *Xici*, proceeds to form "four symbols," *sixiang* 四象, that denote very generally the next level of actualization). "To take shape" would be a better translation.

18 Cook interprets the text in an abstract sense. Guidi (2005: 85) takes a more concrete approach that the passage refers to particular ceremonies, and translates: "When correct sounds stimulate man, a spirit-energy of concord responds to it; when the spirit of concord takes form, harmonious music is produced; the leader of the chant and the followers echo each other harmoniously, all round, oblique, curved or straight things return to their roles" ("[Quando] i suoni corretti stimolano l'uomo, risponde ad essi uno spirito-energia di concordia; [quando] lo spirito di concordia prende forma, viene prodotta la musica armoniosa; chi conduce il canto e chi lo segue si echeggiano [armoniosamente]; ogni [cosa o essere] rotondo, obliquo, curvo o diritto rientra nel suo ruolo"), where the things referred to seem to be the utensils of rituals and dances.

19 For counter-actualization or counter-effectuation, see Deleuze (1990: 157, 168), Deleuze and Guattari (1987: 159–60), Shults (2014: 135), Philippe (1999: 61), and Ott (2019).
20 Indeed, the word *gui* 歸, "to return," in several texts does have exactly this meaning.
21 In Spinozian terms, it would be a mere partial joy, a "tickle," *titillatio*, cf. above, 4.11.
22 In Spinozian terms, this would be an integral joy or felicity, *hilaritas*; see *Ethics* IIIp11sc.
23 For a parallel in contemporary world, you may think, for example, of the military parades commemorating a past victory and inculcating pride and courage, or the Holy Week procession, commemorating Jesus' life events and exhorting penitence.
24 The Chinese text is from the Chinese Text Project, https://ctext.org/xunzi.
25 Henri Bergson has an interesting treatment of grace in his *Laughter* (2008 [1900]) that is intimately related to his philosophy of duration. A gracious or nimble act or movement is such whose parts interpenetrate each other, continue each other, whereas a clumsy movement seems to be composed of separate pieces that do not seem to fit well together. Duration or temporal existence also requires a blending or interpenetration of moments with each other that forms the continuity of time or duration. Of course, it also requires an aspect of differentiation, by which the next moment distinguishes itself from the whole of the past—it is what Bergson called *élan*. We shall treat integration and differentiation below in this chapter. For grace and dexterity, see also Bernstein et al. (1996).
26 Think of the solemn and boring ceremonies we all have gone through. The boredom is important part of it; it trains your patience and obedience.
27 Knoblock parses the phrases differently and translates: "Music joins together what is common to all; ritual separates what is different" (Xunzi 1999: 661).
28 I propose this reading of *liu* 流, which literally means "to flow" (and can connote licentiousness). From the context we know that the negative side of music must be related to an excess of integration. This would be homogeneity where the distinctions between elements (here, people) are reduced to a minimum. Cook has "reckless abandon," Legge "weak coalescence," Guidi "one lets oneself to be carried away by emotions" ("ci si lascia trascinare [dai sentimenti]," 2005: 71).
29 This phrase renders *li* 離, "to depart; distant, separate." Cook has "estrangement," Guidi "disunite" ("ci si disunisce," 2005: 71).
30 Empirically it can be argued that music and ritual have both functions: there are distinctions in the music (people play different instruments, sing different voices, etc.), and there is cohesion in the rituals (see Konvalinka *et al.* 2011 for research on the cohesion between performers of rituals and people who are related to them and who watch the ritual). But at least for the authors of the *Record of Music*, in case of music the aspect of integration is more prominent, and in case of rituals that of differentiation.

31. For example, in an atom there are, on the one hand, differentiations between nucleus and the electrons, and between configurations of electrons; on the other hand, it has its cohesion. In a society there must be some "vertical" distinctions between parents and children, "horizontal" distinction between trades and occupations, etc.; on the other hand, it must also have enough integration so as to be counted as *a* society.
32. Cf. *Analects* 3.4: "When it comes to ritual, it is better to be spare than extravagant" (Slingerland 2003a: 18; cf. above, 4.8).
33. There is an important minimalist trend in modern music: La Monte Young, Arvo Pärt, and many others, whose aesthetics relates to the ideas described here. The Chinese literati, with their minimalism, may also wish to oppose themselves to the art forms of common people, where music is loud and "filled," paintings are extremely colorful (cf. the "bland" landscape ink-painting of the literati, and some popular Daoist temple), etc. And perhaps their "empty" music needs a background of "filled" music to be fully appreciated; perhaps the Confucian minimalist music requires a background of filled popular music. And applying the principles of the *Record of Music* itself, it could be argued that you need different music for different persons and for one person at different moments, in order for it to remain contextually adequate.
34. Cf. François Jullien's *In Praise of Blandness* (2004a).
35. This was the idea behind John Cage's 4'33" that is composed entirely of pauses. The "music" we hear during that piece consists of all the sounds that are audible in the room. The stillness of the piece turns everything into music.
36. If ghosts leave the impression of a spatiotemporal entity, we understand that they are ghosts from the fact that they do not obey the ordinary spatiotemporal rules.
37. Guidi translates: "The music, in its action, depends on Heaven; the *li* in its regulating capacity, depends on Earth" ("La musica, nella sua azione, dipende dal Cielo; il *li*, nella sua capacità regolatrice, dipende dalla Terra," 2005: 75).
38. In more correctly Deleuzian terms the intensities that interpenetrate or implicate each other should be distinguished from the virtual where differential relations perplicate each other, but for the present purposes we can keep the intensive and the virtual together.

Chapter 8

1. This chapter will not enter into the question of authorship. The name *Zhuangzi* refers to the eponymous personality that figures in the book, and the authors of the text, without regard to the real persons who composed the text. The passages chosen here (both from "Inner" and "Outer" chapters) are of rather similar tonality

and it is not so important whether it was the historical Zhuangzi himself who authored them or someone else.

2. The beginning, until the question "Are the sages still alive?" is from Mair and the rest from Watson (wheelwright's translated name is maintained from Mair).

3. The Chinese text is from Chinese Text Project, http://ctext.org/zhuangzi. The references are to *Zhuangzi Yinde* edition (Zhuangzi 1986): chapter, page, line.

4. Person's names in the *Zhuangzi* are a topic on their own. There are fictionalized historical figures like Duke Huan or Confucius, and there are figures with playful or phantastic names, like Flat in this story. On the one hand, all characters of the Chinese writing have a meaning, and hence also personal names are meaningful. So the playful names in *Zhuangzi* do not sound so outlandish to the Chinese (and indeed, in most translations, they are left untranslated). On the other hand, it is clear that Zhuangzi often plays with the names, sometimes creating further paradoxes, like here. See also below Praise, 8.5.

5. There are other such examples in the *Zhuangzi*, where there is a tension between the name and the trade, e.g., a carpenter called Stone (4.4).

6. Or, according to another interpretation, he has to adjust the spokes in a very precise way: "If the spokes are loose, they'll fit sweet as a whistle but the wheel won't be solid. If they're too tight, you won't be able to insert them no matter how hard you try. To make them neither too loose nor too tight is something you sense in your hand and feel in your heart" (Mair 1994: 129).

7. Of course, by depicting all this Zhuangzi himself is giving an account of practice, but it is precisely *embodied*, and since the word "theory" has been traditionally considered disembodied, then in order to avoid confusion it is better to be cautious with the use of this notion in case of an embodied account of knowledge.

8. Of course, it may seem ironic that this Zhuangzian story itself appears in a written book …

9. Incidentally, the "uselessness" (*wuyong* 無用 or *wusuoyong* 無所用) is also a major theme in the *Zhuangzi*. But it is not so much about the lack of (direct) utility (although this theme is also present in the "big words" of Zhuangzi in the first chapter) than about the "uselessness" of a thing, being or person *itself*: a garbled tree can live out its lifespan and not be cut down, a disabled person is not conscripted to the army and hence does not have to risk his life in war. And the idleness is not due to the exploitation of slave labor, but to the inner freedom from attachment to actualized forms, both sensible *and* mental.

10. Other similar characters (e.g., the master swimmer we shall discuss below) even explicitly state that they do not know the "why" or the "cause" of their art; hence they only know that it is "so" (*ran* 然), but not what "makes it so" (*suoyiran* 所以然).

11. Cf. Leibniz' analogy of "veined block of marble" (1996: 4).

12 Deleuze in his lectures on Spinoza (see Deleuze 1977–81) also brings the example of learning to swim. Billeter (2002) makes an important case of such kind of learning processes, his favorite example being learning to ride a bicycle. This accords with Deleuze's emphasis on "apprenticeship," in contrast to "learning" (Deleuze 1994: 164–7).
13 For Zhuangzi's notion of *ming*, see Raphals (2022) and (2003).
14 Forgetting is an important topic in the *Zhuangzi* and we will come back to it below; see 8.6.
15 There are different interpretations of that place; several commentators understand it in this way that the person balanced those balls at the end of a stick. But a stick is not mentioned in the text and it is impossible to balance five balls on top of a stick. Although the impossible can't be ruled out in case of Zhuangzi, according to more minimal interpretation, in the beginning the person trained himself with the balls, juggling them, before he was able to stand still and completely focus his attention. According to Karyn Lai, "it was a common practice for cicada catchers to use poles with sticky adhesive at one end" (Lai 2022a: 327).
16 Hubert Dreyfus has linked Heidegger's authentic (*eigentlich*) existence to the acquisition of skill: (1) An initial banal and public setting, the everydayness (*Man-selbst*) that serves as a backdrop for any activity; (2) development of skill through four (2017 [2000]: 29–33) or five (2014 [1985]: 30–6) stages; until (3) one has become an expert and "has mastered the discriminations that constitute his skill, he can respond to the situation in a more subtle way than a non-expert can" and "a fully authentic Dasein can manifest an even higher kind of primordial understanding. As a cultural master he can take up marginal possibilities in his culture's past in way that enables him to change the style of a whole generation and thereby disclose a new world" (Dreyfus 2017 [2000]: 44).
17 Victor Mair has proposed an emendation from *sheng* 生 "life" to *xing* 性 "nature" that has the radical "heart." It is plausible, since the use of radicals was fluctuating in old times. But it can be understood also without this emendation. Burton Watson has "life of the spirit" (1968: 134).
18 Note that his name is Praise: it can be interpreted as a second-order praise(worthiness) that one attains after having discarded praise, or as an irony.
19 Often this place is translated that male gibbon will mate with female gibbon, and bucks with does, etc. But this would not be strange and worth mentioning in this context. The text would make more sense if the reference was to similar, but not identical species (as it literally is in the text). A gibbon would still prefer a macaque over a beautiful human being.
20 This deeper understanding of themselves may be expressed in their statements that they do not know who they are or why they are doing what they do, but in their case, this not-knowing is not a drawback (as it would be on the second stage of

knowledge), but an advantage: it shows that they have integrated everything so well that there is no need to take an external, objectifying attitude and state something *of* this situation. Some of those characters in fact speak of their knowledge, but they do it in a different way: their speaking is an *expression* of their situation itself. Emphasis is less on denotative and more on phatic and poetic aspects of their speech-act.

21   In Spinoza's terms, these masters form "common notions" with those things and environments (see *Ethics* IIp38–40, Spinoza 2002: 265–8; and Deleuze's interpretation in 1988 and 2007). They form an extended subjectivity.

22   As in English, in Chinese as well "dissection" can have both bodily and mental connotations: cf. different graphs for the word *bian*: 辯 "argue" and 辨 "distinguish," where one has in its middle part "speech" and the other "knife."

23   On the example of "Huainanzi" Ch. 12, where the same story appears, many interpreters emend 大通 to 化通. In my citation I follow the received version.

24   "When mind observes itself and its power of activity, it is joyful, the more so the more distinctly it imagines itself and its power of activity" (*cum mens se ipsam suamque agendi potentiam contemplatur, laetatur; et eo magis, quo se suamque agendi potentiam distinctius imaginatur, Ethics,* 3p53, Spinoza (2002: 305), translation slightly modified).

25   Cf. the "simply sitting in meditation" (*shikantaza* 只管打坐) of the Japanese Sōtō zen school.

26   Sir Chariot in his deformation as if becomes an embryo again. "[T]here are 'things' that only an embryo can do, movements that it alone can undertake or even withstand (for example, the anterior member of the tortoise undergoes a relative displacement of 180 degrees, while the neck involves the forward slippage of a variable number of proto-vertebrae). The destiny and achievement of the embryo is to live the unlivable, to sustain forced movements of a scope which would break any skeleton or tear ligaments" (Deleuze 1994: 215).

27   The whole story of cook Nail can be taken as a visualization of this character 解: you have "horns" on the left and "knife" and "ox" on the right. So, being free from the knot of things and forms can be exemplified as the cutting of an ox. And if you remember, cook Nail also encountered difficult places where the sinews etc. of the ox formed as if knots, and he was able to untie them, without ever touching a thing, but always moving in the nothingness that is at the heart of all things and events, as their virtual or interpenetrating side.

28   In Mair's interpretation the last phrases are taken to be an external description of Sir Come: "Suddenly he slept / suddenly he awoke."

29   It is a term used by Gilles Deleuze and Félix Guattari in their *Anti-Oedipus* (see Deleuze and Guattari 1983); it designates the level of desire-production that is beneath the "molar" level of constituted forms.

30 It may be useful to remark that individuation should not be judged according to its end product, that is, fully formed individuals. Individuation proceeds from pre-individual through a field of individuation and intensive actualization processes to form a fully constituted individual.
31 We encountered this topic of emptiness while discussing Confucius, in 4.8.
32 For example, in the famous contest between Shenxiu and Huineng: "mind is like a clear mirror" (心如明鏡臺), and "the mirror is originally clean and pure" (明鏡本清淨). Cf. Yampolski (1967).
33 This section is related to government and to the idea that the ruler rules without ruling, by not-doing (*wuwei* 無為), an idea already present in the *Analects* of Confucius (see above, 4.11), and later developed by Han Feizi (cf. 6.5). But it is a separate topic in its own right (see also Ott 2013). It is also related to a long tradition in the Chinese political theory of reminding the rulers that they do not own the world or the "all below Heaven" (*tianxia* 天下).
34 In the *Zhuangzi* there are several stories of accomplished persons who are physically disabled; also remember the story of four friends, some of whom became heavily distorted.
35 In Zhuangzi's times, there were quite a few prejudices toward handicapped persons. People may have suspected that the person had committed some crime and was mutilated in punishment, or that Heaven itself did not like the person, so that they were born disabled.
36 A similarly attractive personality is pictured by Pier Paolo Pasolini in his book (1969) and movie (1968) *Teorema* (see Pasolini 1992). The main character Angelo is not disabled, but he is equally attractive to everyone (and to each in a different way) and has a similar transformative influence on them.
37 The paradigmatic mythical figure behind this Leitmotiv is the ancient ruler Yao, who did not hand the throne to his son, but to Shun, the capable minister. There were some historic cases trying to imitate it, but usually they did not end well.
38 The roamer presumably does not indulge in remembering or planning. This is very different from the knowledge of causes as the highest form of knowledge in Aristotle.
39 https://wonderfulengineering.com/heres-the-secret-behind-how-this-guy-can-balance-rocks-in-any-arrangement/.
40 http://beautifuldecay.com/2014/02/25/michael-grab-balances-rocks-impossible-ways/.
41 http://gravityglue.com/about.
42 *Ibid.*
43 In BEcoming, being and becoming are united; it is to be in what comes.
44 *Ibid.*
45 https://www.demilked.com/gravity-glue-stone-balancing-michael-grab/.

46 http://beautifuldecay.com/2014/02/25/michael-grab-balances-rocks-impossible-ways/.
47 Cf. Deleuze's distinction that virtual is distinct and obscure, and actual is clear and confused (Deleuze 1994: 213–14). The virtual differential relations and singular points are distinct, but they are in obscurity. The actual forms are clear, but they are confused—like in Leibniz's example the sound of the sea is formed from a myriad of "small perceptions" that we cannot perceive distinctly, but that are confused into a general impression, which is our clear perception of the sound of the sea.

References

Aizawa, Ken 2014. "Extended Cognition." Lawrence Shapiro (ed.). *The Routledge Handbook of Embodied Cognition*. London-New York: Routledge, 31–8.

Ames, Roger; Dissanayake, Wimal; Kasulis, Thomas P. (eds.) 1994. *Self as Person in Asian Theory and Practice*. New York: SUNY Press.

Anderson, Michael; Richardson, Michael; Chemeroa, Anthony 2012. "Eroding the Boundaries of Cognition: Implications of Embodiment." *Topics in Cognitive Science*, 4, 717–30.

Aristotle 1908. *Metaphysics*. Tr. by W. D. Ross. http://classics.mit.edu/Aristotle/metaphysics.1.i.html (accessed February 28, 2018).

Aristotle 1998. *Metaphysics*. Tr. by Hugh Lawson-Tancred. London: Penguin.

Ball, Stephen; Vincent, Carol 1998. "'I Heard It on the Grapevine': 'hot' knowledge and school choice". *British Journal of Sociology of Education*, 19:3, 377–400.

Barbieri, Marcello 2003. *The Organic Codes. An Introduction to Semantic Biology*. Cambridge: Cambridge University Press.

Bechtel, William; Graham, George (eds.) 1998. *A Companion to Cognitive Science*. Malden, MA: Blackwell.

Bergson, Henri 1990 [1896]. *Matter and Memory*. New York: Zone Books.

Bergson, Henri 2008 [1900]. *Laughter. An Essay on the Meaning of the Comic*. Rockville: Arc Manor.

Bermúdez, José Luis 2022. *Cognitive Science: An Introduction to the Science of the Mind*, 4th ed. Cambridge: Cambridge University Press.

Bernstein, Nicholai; Latash, Mark; Turvey, Michael 1996. *Dexterity and Its Development*. New York-London: Psychology Press.

Billeter, Jean-François 2002. *Leçons sur Tchouang-tseu*. Paris: Allia.

Bly, Benjamin Martin; Rumelhart, David E. (eds.) 1999. *Cognitive Science*. San Diego: Academic Press.

Brooks, Rodney 1999. *Cambrian Intelligence. The Early History of the New AI*. Cambridge, MA-London: MIT Press.

Buber, Martin 1948. *Hasidism*. New York: Philosophical Library.

Buber, Martin 1957. *Pointing the Way. Collected Essays*. New York: Harper & Brothers.

Buchanan, Brett 2009. *Onto-ethologies: The Animal Environments of Uexküll, Heidegger, Merleau-Ponty, and Deleuze*. Albany: SUNY Press.

Characteristics of Musical Keys 2009. http://biteyourownelbow.com/keychar.htm (accessed March 30, 2024).

Chemero, Anthony 2009. *Radical Embodied Cognitive Science*. Cambridge, MA: MIT Press.

Clark, Andy 1997. *Being There. Putting Brain, Body, and World Together Again*. Bradford: Bradford Books.
Clark, Andy 2008. *Supersizing the Mind. Embodiment, Action, and Cognitive Extension*. New York: Oxford University Press.
Clark, Andy; Chalmers, David 1998. "The Extended Mind." *Analysis*, 58 (1), 7–19.
Colombetti, Giovanna 2014. *The Feeling Body. Affective Science Meets the Enactive Mind*. Cambridge, MA: MIT Press.
Cook, Scott 1995. "'Yue Ji' 樂記—Record of Music: Introduction, Translation, Notes, and Commentary." *Asian Music*, 26 (2), 1–96.
Crossley, Nick 2004. "Ritual, Body Technique, and (Inter)subjectivity." Kevin Schilbrack (ed.). *Thinking through Rituals. Philosophical Perspectives*. New York-London: Routledge, 31–51.
Csikszentmihalyi, Mark 2004. *Material Virtue. Ethics and the Body in Early China*. Leiden: Brill.
Csikszentmihalyi, Mihalyi 2014. *Flow and the Foundations of Positive Psychology*. Dordrecht: Springer.
Damasio, Antonio 1994. *Descartes' Error: Emotion, Reason, and the Human Brain*. New York: Putnam.
Damasio, Antonio 2003. *Looking for Spinoza: Joy, Sorrow, and the Feeling Brain*. San Diego: Harcourt.
Dawson, Michael 2014. "Embedded and Situated Cognition." Lawrence Shapiro (ed.). *The Routledge Handbook of Embodied Cognition*. London-New York: Routledge, 59–67.
Deacon, Terrence 2011. *Incomplete Nature*. New York: W. W. Norton & Company.
DeLanda, Manuel 2002. *Intensive Science and Virtual Philosophy*. London-New York: Bloomsbury.
DeLanda, Manuel 2004. "Material Complexities." Neil Leach, David Turnbull, Chris Williams (eds.). *Digital Tectonics*. Chichester: Wiley.
Deleuze, Gilles 1977–1981. *Sur Spinoza*. https://www.webdeleuze.com/cours/spinoza (accessed February 20, 2024).
Deleuze, Gilles 1988. *Spinoza, Practical Philosophy*. Tr. by Robert Hurley. San Francisco: City Lights Books.
Deleuze, Gilles 1990. *The Logic of Sense*. New York: Columbia University Press.
Deleuze, Gilles 1994. *Difference and Repetition*. New York: Columbia University Press.
Deleuze, Gilles 2007. *On Spinoza*. Lectures at Vincennes. http://deleuzelectures.blogspot.com/2007/02/on-spinoza.html (accessed April 15, 2018).
Deleuze, Gilles; Guattari, Félix 1983. *Anti-Oedipus. Capitalism and Schizophrenia I*. Minneapolis: University of Minneapolis Press.
Deleuze, Gilles; Guattari, Félix 1987. *A Thousand Plateaus. Capitalism and Schizophrenia II*. Minneapolis: University of Minneapolis Press.

Despeux, Catherine 2005. "Visual Representations of the Body in Chinese Medical and Daoist Texts from the Song to the Qing Period (Tenth to Nineteenth Century)." *Asian Medicine*, 1 (1), 10–52.

De Vignemont, Frédérique 2018. "The Extended Body Hypothesis. Referred Sensations from Tools to Peripersonal Space." Albert Newen, Leon de Bruin, Shaun Gallagher (eds.). *The Oxford Handbook of 4E Cognition*. Oxford: Oxford University Press, 389–403.

De Vignemont, Frédéric 2021. "Peripersonal Perception in Action." *Synthese*, 198, 4027–44.

Doris, John 2002. *Lack of Character: Personality and Moral Behavior*. Cambridge: Cambridge University Press.

Dreyfus, Hubert 2014. "From Socrates to Expert Systems. The Limits of Calculative Rationality (1985)." Mark A. Wrathall (ed.). *Essays on the Phenomenology of Everyday Perception and Action*. Oxford: Oxford University Press, 25–43.

Dreyfus, Hubert 2017. "Could Anything Be More Intelligible than Everyday Intelligibility? Reinterpreting Division I of *Being and Time* in the Light of Division II (2000)." Mark A. Wrathall (ed.). *Background Practices. Essays on the Understanding of Being*. Oxford: Oxford University Press, 27–44.

Dupuy, Jean-Pierre 2009 [1994]. *On the Origins of the Cognitive Science. The Mechanization of the Mind*. Cambridge, MA: MIT Press.

Durt, Christoph; Fuchs, Thomas; Tewes, Christian (eds.) 2017. *Embodiment, Enaction, and Culture. Investigating the Constitution of the Shared World*. Cambridge, MA-London: MIT Press.

Eliade, Mircea 1961. *The Sacred and the Profane: The Nature of Religion*. Tr. by Willard R. Trask. New York: Harper Torchbooks.

Emerson, John 1996. "Yang Chu's Discovery of the Body." *Philosophy East and West*, 46 (4), 533–66.

Emmeche, Claus 2011. "Organism and Body: The Semiotics of Emergent Levels of Life." Claus Emmeche, Kalevi Kull (eds.). *Towards a Semiotic Biology. Life is the Action of Signs*. London: Imperial College Press, 91–111.

Emmeche, Claus; Kull, Kalevi 2011. *Towards a Semiotic Biology. Life Is the Action of Signs*. London: Imperial College Press.

Eno, Robert 1990. *Confucian Creation of Heaven. Philosophy and the Defense of Ritual Mastery*. New York: SUNY Press.

Eno, Robert 2010. "Legalism." https://scholarworks.iu.edu/dspace/handle/2022/23454 (accessed January 28, 2022).

Eno, Robert 2015. "The Analects of Confucius. An Online Teaching Translation." http://hdl.handle.net/2022/23420 (accessed July 12, 2022).

Fodor, Jerry 1975. *The Language of Thought*. New York: Thomas Y. Crowell Company.

Fraser, Chris 2015. "Mohist Canons." http://plato.stanford.edu/entries/mohist-canons/ (accessed May 28, 2016).

Fraser, Chris 2020a. "Mohism." https://plato.stanford.edu/entries/mohism/ (accessed January 15, 2022).
Fraser, Chris 2020b. "Influence of Social Origins on Mohist Thought." https://plato.stanford.edu/entries/mohism/social.html (accessed January 15, 2022).
Fraser, Chris 2020c. "Shool of Names." https://plato.stanford.edu/entries/school-names/ (accessed July 10, 2022).
Fung, Yiu-ming (ed.) 2020. *Dao Companion to Chinese Logic*. Cham: Springer.
Gallagher, Shaun 2013. "The Socially Extended Mind." *Cognitive Systems Research*, 25–6: 4–12.
Gallagher, Shaun 2014. "Phenomenology and Embodied Cognition." Lawrence Shapiro (ed.). *The Routledge Handbook of Embodied Cognition*. London-New York: Routledge, 9–18.
Gallagher, Shaun 2023. *Embodied and Enactive Approaches to Cognition*. Cambridge: Cambridge University Press.
Gallagher, Shaun; Schmicking, Daniel (eds.) 2010. *Handbook of Phenomenology and Cognitive Science*. Dordrecht: Springer.
Geaney, Jane 2002. *On the Epistemology of the Senses in Early Chinese Thought*. Honolulu: University of Hawai'i Press.
Gibson, James 2015 [1979]. *The Ecological Approach to Human Perception*. New York-London: Psychology Press.
Graham, Angus 1976. *Later Mohist Logic, Ethics, and Science*. Hong Kong: The Chinese University Press.
Graham, Angus 1989. *Disputers of the Tao. Philosophical Argument in Ancient China*. Chicago-La Salle: Open Court.
Guidi, Alessandro 2005. *Lo Yueji. Il pensiero musicale nella Cina antica*. Bologna: CLUEB.
Hadot, Pierre 1995. *Philosophy as a Way of Life. Spiritual Exercises from Socrates to Foucault*. Oxford: Blackwell.
Hall, David; Ames, Roger 1987. *Thinking through Confucius*. New York: SUNY Press.
Hall, David; Ames, Roger 1998a. *Thinking from the Han: Self, Truth, and Transcendence in Chinese and Western Culture*. New York: SUNY Press.
Hall, David; Ames, Roger 1998b. "Chinese Philosophy." In *Routledge Encyclopedia of Philosophy*. https://www.rep.routledge.com/articles/chinese-philosophy/v-1/ (accessed September 5, 2016).
Hanna, Robert; Maiese, Michelle 2009. *Embodied Mind in Action*. Oxford: Oxford University Press.
Hegel, Georg Wilhelm Friedrich 1892. *Lectures on the History of Philosophy*. London: Kegan Paul.
Heidegger, Martin 1967 [1962]. *What Is a Thing*. South Bend: Gateway Editions.
Heidegger, Martin 1996 [1927]. *Being and Time*. New York: SUNY Press.
Herman, Jonathan 1996. *I and Tao: Martin Buber's Encounter with Chuang Tzu*. New York: SUNY Press.

Hoffmeyer, Jesper 1996. *Signs of Meaning in the Universe*. Bloomington-Indianapolis: Indiana University Press.
Hoffmeyer, Jesper 2008. *Biosemiotics. An Examination into the Signs of Life and the Life of Signs*. Scranton, PA: University of Scranton Press.
Hsu, Elisabeth 2007. "The Experience of Wind in Early and Medieval Chinese Medicine." *The Journal of the Royal Anthropological Institute*, 13, S117–S134.
Hurley, Susan 1998. *Consciousness in Action*. Cambridge, MA: Harvard University Press.
Hurley, Susan 2001. "Perception and Action: Alternate Views." *Synthese*, 129, 3–40.
Husserl, Edmund 1970. *The Paris Lectures*. The Hague: Nijhoff.
Hutto, Daniel; Ilundáin-Agurruza, Jesús 2018. "Selfless Activity and Experience: Radicalizing Minimal Self-Awareness." Published on Academia.edu on April 14.
Hutto, Daniel; Myin, Eric 2013. *Radicalizing Enactivism. Basic Minds without Content*. Cambridge, MA: MIT Press.
Hutto, Daniel; Myin, Eric 2017. *Evolving Enactivism. Basic Minds Meet Content*. Cambridge, MA: MIT Press.
Hutto, Daniel; Satne, Glenda 2017. "Continuity Skepticism in Doubt: A Radically Enactive Take." Christoph Durt, Thomas Fuchs, Christian Tewes (eds.). *Embodiment, Enaction, and Culture. Investigating the Constitution of the Shared World*. Cambridge, MA-London: MIT Press, 107–27.
Hutton, Eric 2018. "Extended Knowledge and Confucian Tradition." J. Adam Carter, Andy Clark, Jesper Kallestrup, S. Orestis Palermos, Duncan Pritchard (eds.). *Extended Epistemology*. New York: Oxford University Press, 177–94.
Jackson, Michael 1983. "Knowledge of the Body." *Man*, 18 (2), 327–45.
Jacobson-Maisels, James 2016. "Embodied Epistemology: Knowing through the Body in Late Hasidism." *The Journal of Religion*, 96 (2), 185–211.
Johnston, Ian 2010. *The Mozi. A Complete Translation*. New York: Columbia University Press.
Jones, David 2008. *Confucius Now. Contemporary Encounters with the Analects*. Chicago: Open Court.
Jullien, François 2004a. *In Praise of Blandness*. Cambridge, MA: MIT Press.
Jullien, François 2004b. *Treatise on Efficacy*. Honolulu: University of Hawai'i Press.
Jullien, François 2007. *Vital Nourishment*. New York: Zone Books.
Jung, Carl Gustav 1971. "Psychological Types." *Collected Works of C. G. Jung*. Vol. 6. 2nd ed. Princeton: Princeton University Press.
Jung, Hwa Yol 2011. *Transversal Rationality and Intercultural Texts. Essays in Phenomenology and Comparative Philosophy*. Athens, OH: Ohio University Press.
Kasulis, Thomas 2002. *Intimacy or Integrity. Philosophy and Cultural Difference*. Honolulu: University of Hawai'i Press.
Kepnes, Steven 2004. "Ritual Gives Rise to Thought: Liturgical Reasoning in Modern Jewish Philosophy." Kevin Schilbrack (ed.). *Thinking through Rituals. Philosophical Perspectives*. New York-London: Routledge, 230–43.

Knoblock, John 1994. *Xunzi. A Translation and Study of the Complete Works. Vol 3.* Stanford: Stanford University Press.

Kohn, Livia (ed.) 2006. *Daoist Body Cultivation. Traditional Models and Contemporary Practices.* St. Petersburg, FL: Three Pines Press.

Kohn, Livia 2014. *Zhuangzi. Text and Context.* St Petersburg, FL: Three Pines Press.

Konvalinka, Ivana *et al.* 2011. "Synchronized Arousal between Performers and Related Spectators in a Fire-Walking Ritual." *PNAS*, 108 (20), 8514–19.

Kull, Kalevi 2000. "An Introduction to Phytosemiotics: Semiotic Botany and Vegetative Sign Systems." *Sign Systems Studies*, 28, 326–50.

Kundtová Klocová, Eva; Geertz, Armin W. 2019. "Ritual and Embodied Cognition." Risto Uro, Juliette J. Day, Richard E. Demaris, Rikard Roitto (eds.). *The Oxford Handbook of Early Christian Ritual.* Oxford: Oxford University press, 74–94.

Kuriyama, Shigehisa 1999. *The Expressiveness of the Body and the Divergence of Greek and Chinese Medicine.* New York: Zone Books.

Lai, Karyn 2006a. *Learning from Chinese Philosophies: Ethics of Interdependent and Contextualised Self.* Aldershot: Ashgate.

Lai, Karyn 2006b. "*Li* in the *Analects*: Training in Moral Competence and the Question of Flexibility." *Philosophy East and West*, 56 (1), 69–83.

Lai, Karyn 2007. "Understanding Change: The Interdependent Self in Its Environment." *Journal of Chinese Philosophy*, 34 (1), 81–99.

Lai, Karyn 2014. "*Ren* 仁: An Exemplary Life." Amy Olberding (ed.). *Dao Companion to the Analects.* Dordrecht: Springer, 83–94.

Lai, Karyn (ed.) 2022a. *Knowers and Knowledge in East-West Philosophy.* London: Palgrave Macmillan.

Lai, Karyn 2022b. "Performance and Agency in the *Zhuangzi*." Kim-chong Chong (ed.). *Dao Companion to the Philosophy of the Zhuangzi.* Cham: Springer, 661–82.

Lai, Karyn; Chiu, Wai Wai (eds.) 2019. *Skill and Mastery. Philosophical Stories from the Zhuangzi.* Lanham: Rowman and Littlefield International.

Lakoff, George; Johnson, Mark 1980. *Metaphors We Live By.* Chicago: Chicago University Press.

Landrum, Lisa 2015. "Before Architecture: Archai, Architects and Architectonics in Plato and Aristotle." *Montreal Architectural Review*, 2, 5–25.

Legge, James 1885. "Sacred Books of the East, Volume 28, Part 4: The Li Ki." Available online: http://ctext.org/liji/yue-ji (accessed February 15, 2018).

Leibniz, Gottfried Wilhelm 1996. *New Essays on Human Understanding.* Tr. by Peter Remnant, Jonathan Bennett. Cambridge: Cambridge University Press.

Lewis, Mark Edward 2006. *The Construction of Space in Early China.* New York: SUNY Press.

Li, Zehou 2010. *The Chinese Aesthetic Tradition.* Honolulu: University of Hawai'i Press.

Liao, Wenku 1939. *The Complete Works of Han Fei Tzu* 韓非子: *A Classic of Chinese Legalism.* Vol. 1. London: Probsthain.

Liao, Wenku 1959. *The Complete Works of Han Fei Tzu* 韓非子: *A Classic of Chinese Political Science*. Vol. 2. London: Probsthain.
Liu, Johanna 2014. "Art and Aesthetics of Music in Classical Confucianism." Vincent Shen (ed.). *Dao Companion to Classical Confucian Philosophy*. Dordrecht: Springer, 227–44.
Lloyd, Geoffrey; Sivin, Nathan 2002. *The Way and the Word. Science and Medicine in Early China and Greece*. New Haven: Yale University Press.
Lo, Yuet Keung 2014. "Confucius and His Community." Amy Olberding (ed.). *Dao Companion to the* Analects. New York: Springer, 55–79.
Lu Xiangshan 陸象山 1992. *Collected Works of Lu Xiangshan*. 陸象山全集 Beijing: Zhonghua shudian. 北京: 中國書店.
Maiese, Michelle 2011. *Embodiment, Emotion, and Cognition*. Basingstoke: Palgrave.
Maiese, Michelle 2014. "Body and Emotion." Lawrence Shapiro (ed.).*The Routledge Handbook of Embodied Cognition*. London-New York: Routledge, 231–9.
Maiese, Michelle; Hanna, Robert 2019. *The Mind-Body Politic*. Cham: Palgrave Macmillan.
Mair, Victor 1994. *Wandering on the Way. Early Taoist Tales and Parables of Chuang Tzu*. New York: Bantam Books.
Massumi, Brian 2005. "Fear." *Positions*, 13 (1), 31–48.
Mengzi 2008. *Mengzi. With Selections from Traditional Commentaries*. Tr. by Bryan Van Norden. Indianapolis-Cambridge: Hackett.
Merleau-Ponty, Maurice 1945. *Phénoménologie de la perception*. Paris: Gallimard.
Merleau-Ponty, Maurice 2012 [1945]. *Phenomenology of Perception*. Tr. by Donald A. Landes. London-New York: Routledge.
Moran, Dermot 2017. "Intercorporeality and Intersubjectivity: A Phenomenological Exploration of Embodiment." Christoph Durt, Thomas Fuchs, Christian Tewes (eds.). *Embodiment, Enaction, and Culture. Investigating the Constitution of the Shared World*. Cambridge, MA-London: MIT Press, 23–46.
Nakamura, Hajime 1964. *Ways of Thinking of Eastern Peoples*. Honolulu: East-West Center Press.
Newen, Albert; Bruin, Leon de; Gallagher, Shaun 2018. *The Oxford Handbook of 4E Cognition*. Oxford: Oxford University Press.
Nietzsche, Friedrich 1967. *Will to Power*. Edited With Commentary By Walter Kaufmann. New York: Vintage Books.
Nietzsche, Friedrich 1994. *On the Genealogy of Morality*. Tr. by Carol Diethe. Cambridge: Cambridge University Press 1994.
Nietzsche, Friedrich 2006. *Thus Spoke Zarathustra. A Book for All and None*. Cambridge: Cambridge University Press.
Noë, Alva 2004. *Action in Perception*. Cambridge, MA: MIT Press.
Noë, Alva; Thompson, Evan (eds.) 2002. *Vision and Mind. Selected Readings in the Philosophy of Perception*. Cambridge, MA: MIT Press.

Olberding, Amy 2007. "The Educative Function of Personal Style in the 'Analects.'" *Philosophy East and West*, 57 (3), 357–74.

Ott, Margus 2013. "Chinese Refreshment for Contemporary Political Thought: *wúwéi*, Care, and Democracy." *International Journal of Area Studies*, 8 (1), 36–50.

Ott, Margus 2017. "Confucius' Embodied Knowledge." *Asian Studies*, 5 (2), 65–85.

Ott, Margus 2019. "Deleuze and Zhuangzi: Actualization and Counter-actualization." *Asian Studies*, 7 (1), 315–35.

Ott, Margus 2020. "Deleuzian (Re)interpretation of Zhu Xi." *Asian Studies*, 8 (2), 281–310.

Ott, Margus 2021. "Constraint and Li, Work and Qi: Deacon and Zhu Xi." *Chinese Semiotic Studies*, 17 (2), 237–54.

Ott, Margus 2022. "Contextualising and Decontextualising Knowledge: Extended Knowledge in Confucius, Mozi and Zhuangzi." Karyn Lai (ed.). *Knowers and Knowledge in East-West Philosophy. Epistemology Extended*. Cham: Palgrave Macmillan, 293–318.

Panksepp, Jaak; Biven, Lucy 2012. *The Archaeology of Mind: Neuroevolutionary Origins of Human Emotion*. New York: W. W. Norton & Company.

Pasolini, Pier Paolo 1992. *Theorem*. London: Quartet Encounters.

Philippe, Jonathan 1999. "Nietzsche and Spinoza: New Personae in a New Plane of Thought." Jean Khalfa (ed.). *Introduction to the Philosophy of Gilles Deleuze*. London-New York: Continuum, 50–63.

Pines, Yuri 2000. "Disputers of the 'Li': Breakthroughs in the Concept of Ritual in Preimperial China." *Asia Major*, 13 (1), 1–41.

Pines, Yuri 2009. *Envisioning Eternal Empire. Chinese Political Thought of the Warring States Era*. Honolulu: University of Hawai'i Press.

Polanyi, Michael 1962. *Personal Knowledge. Towards a Post-Critical Philosophy*. London: Routledge.

Puett, Michael 2002. *To Become a God: Cosmology, Sacrifice, and Self-Divinization in Early China*. Cambridge, MA-London: Harvard University Asia Center for the Harvard-Yenching Institute.

Raphals, Lisa 2003. "Fate, Fortune, Chance, and Luck in Chinese and Greek: A Comparative Semantic History." *Philosophy East and West*, 53 (4), 537–74.

Raphals, Lisa 2015. "Body and Mind in Early China and Greece." *Journal of Cognitive Historiography*, 2 (2), 132–82.

Raphals, Lisa 2022. "The *Zhuangzi* on *Ming* (命)." Kim-chong Chong (ed.). *Dao Companion to the Philosophy of the Zhuangzi*. Cham: Springer, 217–33.

Rizzolatti, Giacomo; Arbib, Michael 1998. "Language within Our Grasp." *Trends in Neuroscience*, 21, 188–94.

Robins, Dan 2010. "The Later Mohists and Logic." *History of Philosophy and Logic*, 31, 247–85.

Ruyer, Raymond 1946. *Éléments du psycho-biologie*. Paris: Presses Universitaires de France.

Sarkissian, Hagop 2010. "Confucius and the Effortless of Virtue." *History of Philosophy Quarterly*, 27 (1), 1–16.
Sarkissian, Hagop 2014. "Ritual and Rightness in the *Analects*." Amy Olberding (ed.). *Dao Companion to the Analects*. Dordrecht: Springer, 95–116.
Sarkissian, Hagop 2017. "Situationism, Manipulation, and Objective Self-Awareness." *Ethical Theory and Moral Practice*, 20, 489–503.
Sartre, Jean-Paul 1956. *Being and Nothingness*. New York: Philosophical Library.
Schilbrack, Kevin 2004. "Ritual Metaphysics." Kevin Schilbrack (ed.). *Thinking through Rituals. Philosophical Perspectives*. New York-London: Routledge, 131–51.
Schipper, Kristofer 1994 [1982]. *The Taoist Body*. Berkeley: University of California Press.
Schön, Donald 1983. *The Reflective Practitioner. How Professionals Think in Action*. New York: Basic Books.
Seok, Bongrae 2013. *Embodied Moral Psychology and Confucian Philosophy*. Lanham: Lexington Books.
Shapiro, Lawrence (ed.) 2014. *The Routledge Handbook of Embodied Cognition*. London-New York: Routledge.
Shonkoff, Sam Berrin 2017. "Sacramental Existence and Embodied Theology in Buber's Representation of Ḥasidism." *Journal of Jewish Thought and Philosophy*, 25, 131–61.
Shults, LeRon F. 2014. *Iconoclastic Theology: Gilles Deleuze and the Secretion of Atheism*. Edinburgh: Edinburgh University Press.
Shun, Kwong-loi 2017. "*Le* in the *Analects*." Paul Rakita Goldin (ed.). *A Concise Companion to Confucius*. Oxford: John Wiley & Sons, 133–47.
Sivin, Nathan 1995. "State, Cosmos, and Body in the Last Three Centuries B.C." *Harvard Journal of Asiatic Studies*, 55 (1), 5–37.
Slingerland, Edward 2003a. *Confucius' Analects with Selections from Traditional Commentaries*. Indianapolis-Cambridge: Hackett.
Slingerland, Edward 2003b. *Effortless Action: Wu-Wei as Conceptual Metaphor and Spiritual Ideal in Early China*. Oxford: Oxford University Press.
Slingerland, Edward 2008. *What Science Offers the Humanities: Integrating Body and Culture*. Cambridge: Cambridge University Press.
Slingerland, Edward 2013. "Body and Mind in Early China: An Integrated Humanities-Science Approach." *Journal of the American Academy of Religion*, 81 (1), 6–55.
Slingerland, Edward 2018. *Mind and Body in Early China. Beyond Orientalism and the Myth of Holism*. New York: Oxford University Press.
Slingerland, Edward; Chudek, Maciej 2011. "The Prevalence of Mind–Body Dualism in Early China." *Cognitive Science*, 35, 997–1007.
Sommer, Deborah 2008. "Boundaries of the *Ti* Body." *Asia Major*, 21 (1), 293–324.
Sommer, Deborah 2010. "Concepts of the Body in the Zhuangzi." Victor Mair (ed.). *Experimental Essays on Zhuangzi*, 2nd ed. Dunedin: Three Pines Press, 212–28.
Sommer, Deborah 2012. "The Ji Self in Early Chinese Texts." Jason Dockstader, Hans Georg Möller, Günter Wohlfart (eds.). *Selfhood East and West: De-constructions of Identity*. Nordhausen: Traugott Bautz, 17–45.

Spinoza, Baruch 2002. *Complete Works*. Indianapolis-Cambridge: Hackett.
Stanislavski, Konstantin 2010. *An Actor's Work on a Role*. Tr. by Jean Benedetti. London and New York: Routledge.
Sterckx, Roel 2003. "Le Pouvoir du Sens: Sagesse et Perception Sensorielle en Chine Ancienne." François Jullien (ed.). *Cahiers d'Institut Marcel Granet* 1. Paris: Presses Universitaires de France, 71–92.
Stjernfelt, Frederik 2007. *Diagrammatology*. Dordrecht: Springer.
Strejcek, Brendan; Zhong, Chen-Bo 2014. "Morality in the Body." Lawrence Shapiro (ed.). *The Routledge Handbook of Embodied Cognition*. London-New York: Routledge, 220–30.
Suzuki, D. T. 1996. *Zen Buddhism: Selected Writings of D. T. Suzuki*. New York: Doubleday.
Thelen, Esther; Smith, Linda B. 1996. *A Dynamic Systems Approach to the Development of Cognition and Action*. Cambridge, MA-London: MIT Press.
Thompson, Evan 2007. *Mind in Life. Biology, Phenomenology, and the Sciences of Mind*. Cambridge, MA-London: Belknap Press.
Thompson, Kirill Ole 2017. "Relational Self in Classical Confucianism: Lessons from Confucius' *Analects*." *Philosophy East and West*, 67 (3), 887–907.
Treffert, Darold A. 2009. "The Savant Syndrome: An Extraordinary Condition. A Synopsis: Past, Present, Future." *Philosophical Transactions of the Royal Society B: Biological Sciences*, 364 (1522): 1351–7.
Turvey, Michael; Fonseca, Sergio 2009. "Nature of Motor Control: Perspectives and Issues." *Advances in Experimental Medicine and Biology*, 629, 93–123.
Turvey, Michael T.; Shaw, Robert E.; Reed, Edward S.; Mace, William M. 1981. "Ecological Laws of Perceiving and Acting: In Reply to Fodor and Pylyshyn." *Cognition*, 9 (3), 237–304.
Uexküll, Jakob von 1926. *Theoretical Biology*. New York: Harcourt, Brace & Co.
Uexküll, Jakob von 1957. "A Stroll through the Worlds of Animals and Men: A Picture Book of Invisible Worlds." Claire H. Schiller (ed. and tr.). *Instinctive Behaviour: The Development of a Modern Concept*. New York: International Universities Press, 5–80.
Valmisa, Mercedes 2021. *Adapting. A Chinese Philosophy of Action*. Oxford: Oxford University Press.
Van Norden, Bryan 2002. "Introduction." Bryan Van Norden (ed.). *Confucius and the Analects. New Essays*. Oxford: Oxford University Press, 3–36.
Van Norden, Bryan 2019. "Mencius." *Stanford Encyclopedia of Philosophy*. https://plato.stanford.edu/entries/mencius/ (accessed April 15, 2024).
Varela, Francisco; Thompson, Evan; Rosch, Eleanor 1991. *The Embodied Mind. Cognitive Science and Human Experience*. Cambridge, MA: MIT Press.
Virág, Curie 2014. "Early Confucian Perspectives on Emotions." Vincent Shen (ed.). *Dao Companion to Classical Confucian Philosophy*. Dordrecht: Springer, 203–26.
Wang, Robin 2010. "The Virtuous Body at Work: The Ethical Life as *Qi* 氣 in Motion." *Dao* 9 (3), 339–51.

Ward, Dave; Stapleton, Mog 2012. "Es Are Good: Cognition as Enacted, Embodied, Embedded, Affective and Extended." Fabio Paglieri (ed.). *Consciousness in Interaction: The Role of the Natural and Social Environment in Shaping Consciousness.* Amsterdam: John Benjamins, 89–104.

Watson, Burton 1968. *The Complete Works of Chuang Tzu.* New York: Columbia University Press.

Wilson, Robert A.; Foglia, Lucia 2015. "Embodied Cognition." *Stanford Encyclopedia of Philosophy.* http://plato.stanford.edu/entries/embodied-cognition/ (accessed December 19, 2018).

Winston, Kenneth 2005. "The Internal Morality of Chinese Legalism." *Singapore Journal of Legal Studies* (2): 313–47.

Wittgenstein, Ludwig 1969. *On Certainty.* Oxford: Basil Blackwell.

Wong, David 2014. "Cultivating the Self in Concert with Others." Amy Olberding (ed.). *Dao Companion to the Analects.* Dordrecht: Springer, 171–97.

Xunzi 1999. *Xunzi.* Tr. by John Knoblock. Beijing: Foreign Language Press.

Yampolski, Philip 1967. *The Platform Sutra of the Sixth Patriarch.* New York: Columbia University Press.

Yu, Shunde (ed.) 2015. *Shentigan de zhuanxiang* (Changing Directions in Bodily Feeling). Taibei: Taibei chuban zhongxin.

Zahavi, Dan 2003. *Husserl's Phenomenology.* Stanford: Stanford University Press.

Zhang, Yanhua 2007. *Transforming Emotions with Chinese Medicine. An Ethnographic Account from Contemporary China.* New York: SUNY Press.

Zhuangzi 1986. *Zhuangzi yinde.* Shanghai: Shanghai guji chubanshe.

Ziporyn, Brook 2009. *Zhuangzi. The Essential Writings with Selections from Traditional Commentaries.* Indianapolis-Cambridge: Hackett.

Zito, Angela; Barlow, Tani E. (eds.) 1994. *Body Subject, and Power in China.* Chicago: University of Chicago Press.

Index

English concepts:
 4EA 10, 30
 actual 15, 26, 28, 53, 56, 67, 97, 115, 123, 137, 138, 156, 157, 159, 165, 168, 172, 173, 174, 175, 180, 184, 186, 204
 actuality 27, 138, 172, 173, 180
 actualized, actualization 25, 26, 27, 53, 54, 70, 101, 134, 137, 138, 155, 156, 157, 159, 165, 169, 170, 173–5, 177–81, 184, 191, 197, 200, 203
 affective, affectivity 5, 6, 10, 17–19, 21, 27, 30, 32, 70, 118, 187
 contextual, contextualized, contextualization, contextualism 1, 2, 5, 6, 27, 28, 30, 31, 35, 36, 39, 40, 44, 47, 49, 60, 63, 67, 68, 74, 80, 85, 87, 90, 106, 110–14, 117, 138, 141, 143, 146, 155, 157, 160, 165, 170, 180, 181, 183, 184, 191, 192, 199; *see also* decontextualized, recontextualize
 counter-actualize, counter-actualization 123, 173, 178, 198
 deactualization 173
 decontextualized, decontextualization 1–3, 5, 6, 7, 9, 16, 27, 28, 30, 31, 34, 36, 39, 48, 49, 64, 65, 77–81, 83, 88, 90, 102, 105–8, 110, 112–14, 138, 143, 154, 155, 157, 160, 166, 170, 177, 178, 180, 183, 184, 185, 189, 190, 192, 195; *see also* contextual, recontextualize
 differentiation 7, 18, 29, 101, 129, 130, 139, 174, 198, 199
 disembedded 83
 disembodied, disembodiment 3, 5, 6, 8, 9, 16, 18, 25–8, 30, 34, 53, 56, 64, 75, 77–9, 83, 87, 89–91, 96, 105, 107–9, 113, 121, 135, 147, 153, 157, 159, 170, 174, 177–80, 183, 184, 186, 194, 200

 embedded, embeddedness 5, 6, 10, 13, 14, 24, 30, 44–7, 54–7, 60, 63, 78, 96, 110, 113, 118, 119, 121, 129, 138, 141, 150, 176, 177–80, 183
 embodied, embodiment 3–16, 18–31, 34, 36, 40, 41, 43–7, 49, 51–3, 56–60, 62, 63, 68, 72–5, 78, 79, 86, 87, 89, 90, 92, 97, 99, 108–11, 113–15, 117, 121, 123, 129, 135, 136, 138–43, 145–7, 150, 153, 155–60, 162, 163, 165–7, 170, 172, 174–81, 183–6, 188, 194, 200
 emergence 5, 19, 20, 30, 45, 46, 68–9, 75, 78, 90, 151, 176
 enactive, enactment 5, 6, 10, 14, 15, 19, 30, 39, 43, 57, 58, 60, 74, 78, 96, 113, 123, 125, 127, 138, 141, 179, 180, 183, 188
 explicit(ness) 6, 7, 10, 16, 24–6, 28, 29, 32, 34, 35, 42, 46, 49, 68, 72, 77, 78, 79, 85, 87, 89–91, 93, 94, 97, 107, 110, 113, 129, 134, 144, 145, 183
 extended, extendedness 5, 6, 10, 15–17, 22, 23, 27, 30, 60, 62, 63, 75, 78, 113, 141, 151, 154, 179, 180, 183, 185, 192
 flexibility, flexible 20, 57, 57, 75, 130, 138, 191
 flow 19, 24, 72, 74, 122, 123, 130, 136, 138, 139, 148, 151, 156, 157, 161, 162, 191, 198
 golden rule 63, 64, 82, 112, 154, 191, 192
 implicit(ness) 5–7, 23–5, 30, 40, 41, 43, 44, 60, 68, 72, 73, 78, 87, 90, 97, 129, 144, 146, 175, 183, 194
 inflexible 73, 191
 integration 7, 29, 70, 71, 129, 130, 139, 150, 190, 198, 199
 intensive, intensity 26, 27, 56, 62, 67, 78, 123, 156, 157, 161, 170, 197, 199, 203

interpenetrate, interpenetration 5, 15, 21, 24–7, 29, 39, 53, 58, 111, 117, 121, 123, 131, 134, 135, 137–9, 141, 148, 154, 156, 157, 159, 161, 165, 167–70, 172–5, 177–81, 184, 186, 198, 199, 202
interpersonal 56, 119, 134, 164
juxtapose, juxtaposition 5, 15, 25–7, 29, 53, 60, 123, 137, 138, 172–4, 177, 184
metrical 26, 56, 155–7, 161; *see also* topological
other-relation 5, 30, 64, 152, 154, 160; *see also* self-relation
recontextualize, recontextualization 64, 65, 148, 175; *see also* contextual, decontextualized
representation 3, 10, 15, 26–8, 127, 164, 192, 197
revirtualization 123
ritual 6, 13, 23, 28, 31, 36–40, 42–9, 51–6, 60–3, 66, 67, 69, 71–5, 77, 78, 83, 85, 88, 97, 110, 113, 114, 117, 119, 126, 127–31, 133–40, 151, 152, 175, 176, 180, 181, 183, 189, 190–3, 196–9
sandwich model 10, 14, 15, 59, 115
self-cultivation 6, 23, 33, 34, 37–40, 43, 46, 52, 58, 60, 63–6, 68, 70–3, 101, 114, 115, 119, 137, 139, 150, 152, 157, 161, 171, 176, 180, 195
self-relation 5, 18, 21, 30, 64, 165, 187, 188; *see also* other-relation
singularity 26, 27, 29, 53, 54, 56, 59, 74, 75, 149, 155–7, 165, 180, 181, 204
Summum Ens 164
topological 26, 53, 155, 157; *see also* metrical
Umwelt 4, 13, 123, 154, 162
virtual, virtuality 56, 67, 101, 137–9, 155, 157, 170, 172–5, 180, 184, 197, 199, 202, 204

Chinese concepts:
an 安, 'calm', 'ease', 'safety', 'tranquil', 'enjoy oneself', 'sequrely', 'contentment' 59, 98, 103, 106, 128, 133, 149, 193
benti 本體, 'root rhizomatic body' 138
bie 別, 'distinction', 'different' 114, 128, 138
caiquan 才全, 'completeness of abilities' 169, 170
dao 道, 'Way', 'doctrine', 'course', 'system', 'policy' 37, 56, 69, 84, 95, 98, 99, 101, 103, 110, 120, 125, 126, 130, 132, 144, 147–9, 152, 171, 173, 174, 179
daye 大冶, 'Great Smelter' 164; cf. *zaohua* 造化 and *zaowuzhe* 造物者
de 德, 'charisma', 'virtue', 'potency' 72, 82, 108, 124, 125, 130, 169–71
dong 動, 'move', 'movement', 'motion', 'motivation', 'stir' 74, 115, 119, 120, 122–4, 129, 130, 133, 134, 147
fa 法, 'law', 'norm', 'model', 'rule', 'standard' 39, 79, 81, 82, 86, 91–3, 96, 97, 102, 105, 106, 170, 195; *see also* Legalism
fan 反, 'come back', 'return', 'introspection', 'reflection'; 'conflict', 'negation' 67, 93, 96, 116, 125, 133, 150, 167, 192
fen 分, 'distribution', 'lot', 'role', 'partition' 84, 122, 123
hua 化, 'transformation', 'to become' 116, 138, 158, 160, 161, 163, 164, 168
he 和, 'harmony' 29, 69–71, 84, 122, 124–6, 128, 130–2, 137, 138, 168, 170, 171
jian'ai 兼愛, 'all-inclusive care', 'encompassing love' 82
jie 解, 'cut', 'separate', 'loosen', 'untie', 'understand' 147, 162, 202
jing 靜, 'stillness', 'calm' 115, 134, 153
jixin 機心, 'mechanical mind' 152
junzi 君子, 'exemplary person', 'gentleman', 'noble person', 'superior man' 37, 57, 59, 67, 73, 86, 117, 125, 130, 132; *see also xiaoren* 小人
le 樂, 'joy', 'pleasure', 'delight', 'happiness', 'enjoying' 70, 71, 75, 119, 124, 127, 128, 162; *see also yue* 樂, 'music'
li 利, 'benefit', 'utility', 'usefulness', 'profit' 79, 82, 86, 98, 101, 104, 110, 167, 192
li 禮, 'ritual', 'propriety' 37, 39, 54, 56, 73, 74, 109, 114, 117, 126, 128,

129–31, 133, 134, 137, 138, 193; see also *le* 樂, 'music'
li 理, 'veins' 112, 116, 117, 121–4, 130, 139, 147, 148, 196; see also *qi* 氣, 'energy'
ling 靈, 'numinous' 170, 172
ming 命, 'fate', 'inevitability', 'necessity', 'destiny' 'mandate', 'task', 'command', 'messenger' 61, 71, 106, 126, 148, 149, 156, 164, 170, 193
ni 逆, 'go against' 122, 127, 197; see also *shun* 順
qi 氣, 'energy' 55, 57, 119, 121, 122, 124, 139, 153, 160, 161, 166, 167, 197; see also *li* 理, 'veins'
qing 情, 'feelings', 'core feeling', 'emotional core', 'emotion', 'attitude' 99–101, 109, 115, 124–126, 129, 137, 186
ren 仁, 'humaneness' 56, 109; see also *yi* 義
se 色, 'demeanor', 'hue', 'color', 'expression', 'countenance', 'beauty' 52–5, 57, 59, 60, 130, 154
shen 神, 'spirit', 'spiritual' 137, 147, 149, 150, 152, 153, 161, 171, 172
shensheng 神生, 'spiritual life' 152
shi 時, 'time', 'timeliness', 'hours', 'occasion' 56, 57, 110, 147, 153, 161, 162, 170
shifei 是非, 'right and wrong' 106, 109
shizhi 實知, 'real knowledge' 171, 172
shu 術, 'skill', 'art', 'method' 95, 105, 106, 119, 153, 179, 195
shun 順, 'go along', 'comply', 'follow', 'obey', 'flexibility' 71, 122, 130, 161, 162, 197; see also *ni* 逆
tianli 天理, 'Heavenly veins', 'natural grain' 116, 147, 148, 196
tianzhi 天志, 'Heaven's intention' 81
tong 同, 'identical', 'unify', 'same', 'together' 29, 84, 89, 114
tong 通, 'interpenetration', 'connect' 117, 120, 158, 159, 170, 202
wang 忘, 'forgetting' 125, 153, 158
weiqi 圍棋 (jp. *go*) 65
wen 文, 'refinement', 'elegance', 'culture', 'writings', 'form', 'pattern', 'civil' 73, 81, 112, 115, 124, 132–135, 137

wuwei 無爲, 'effortless action' 72, 94, 107
wuxing 五行, 'five phases' 33, 128
wuyuwu 物於物, 'thinged by things' 167, 196
xiaoren 小人, 'small person', 'petty person', 'little man' 59, 86, 125, 130; see also *junzi* 君子
xiaoyao 逍遙, 'roam', 'roam freely' 166, 167
xinshu 心術, 'arts of the heart/mind' 119
yi 義, 'appropriateness', 'righteousness' 56, 59, 81, 85, 86, 103, 109; see also *ren* 仁
yi 儀/義, 'standard', 'principle' 79, 84
yue 樂, 'music' 54, 66, 114, 117, 119, 122, 124, 126, 127, 128–34, 137, 138, 193; see also *li* 禮 'ritual' and *le* 樂, 'joy'
zaohua 造化, 'Transforming Creator' 164; cf. *daye* 大冶 and *zaowuzhe* 造物者
zaowuzhe 造物者, 'Creator of Things' 164; cf. *zaohua* 造化 and *daye* 大冶
zhi 制, 'designing', 'construct', 'regulator', 'restrain' 99, 125, 127, 138
zhi 智, 'wise', 'wisdom' 94, 96, 106, 109
zixi 自喜, 'enjoy oneself' 168
zuo 作, 'create', 'make' 129, 134, 137, 138
zuowang 坐忘, 'sitting and forgetting' 158

Schools:
  Aristotelianism 34, 43, 89
  Buddhism (*fojia* 佛家) 4, 68, 164, 166, 190, 195
  Confucians, Confucianism or *ruism* (*rujia* 儒家) 4, 6, 7, 23, 36–8, 46, 47, 57–60, 63–6, 70, 78, 82, 83, 85–8, 91, 92, 97, 98, 100, 103, 104, 109–11, 114, 122, 133, 138, 140, 150, 154, 157, 181, 186, 189, 190, 192–4, 199
  Daoists, Daoism (*daojia* 道家) 4, 47, 65, 114, 158, 161, 174, 185, 186, 192, 199
  Disputers (*bianzhe* 辯者) 36, 77, 192–4

Epicureans 34
Hasidis 6, 40, 43–7, 49, 60, 181, 183
Legalists (*fajia* 法家) 4, 6, 7, 28, 36, 47, 49, 65, 75, 77, 79, 85, 90, 91–3, 95, 96, 98, 99, 101, 104, 105, 107, 108, 111, 113, 114, 152, 183, 184, 194–6
Mohists (*Mojia* 墨家) 4, 6, 28, 36, 39, 47, 49, 65, 75, 77–9, 81–3, 85–90, 108, 110, 112–14, 152, 154, 183, 184, 189, 192–6
Neo-Confucianism 122, 139, 190
Neo-Mohists 86
Platonism, platonic 34, 80, 81, 164
Stoicism 32, 34, 162
Ruists; *see* Confucians

Personal names:
Ames, Roger 55
Aristotle 143–6, 179, 203
Baal Shem Tov; *see* Eliezer, Israel ben
Bezalel 43–5
Binmou Jia 賓牟賈 132
Bob the Z 18
Brooks, Rodney 20, 192
Buber, Martin 40, 43–5, 190
Chalmers, David 17
Clark, Andy 17
Cohen, Hermann 47
Colombetti, Giovanna 118, 187
Confucius 孔子 4–8, 23, 35, 37, 38, 42, 49, 51, 53–63, 66, 68, 69, 71, 73, 74, 86–8, 90, 97, 104, 107, 108, 110, 112, 114, 125, 132, 138, 148–52, 154, 157, 158, 168, 169, 173, 175, 176, 180, 183, 184, 186, 189–92, 194, 200, 203
Csikszentmihalyi, Mihalyi 72, 136
Deacon, Terrence 15
Deleuze, Gilles 2, 185, 187, 190, 197, 201, 202, 204
Deng Xi 鄧析 91
Dreyfus, Hubert 201
Driesch, Hans 20
Duke Huan of Qi 齊桓公 100, 101, 141–3, 158, 200
Eliezer, Israel ben (*also* Baal Shem Tov) 43
Empedocles 33
Eno, Robert 37, 38

Euclid 32, 33
Grab, Michael 8, 175, 176, 179, 181
Guattari, Félix 2, 187, 190, 202
Hall, David 55
Han Feizi 韓非子 7–9, 92–105, 107, 108, 124, 126, 127, 195, 196, 203
Hanna, Robert 17, 18
Hegel, Georg Wilhelm Friedrich 6, 186
Heidegger, Martin 3, 63, 186, 188, 201
Husserl, Edmund 3, 22, 185
Hutton, Eric 23
Jackson, Michael 40–2
Johnson, Mark 12
Kasulis, Thomas 65, 75
Kepnes, Steven 47
Kuriyama, Shigehisa 52
Lakoff, George 12
Lin, Fang 林放, disciple of Confucius 66
Liu, De 劉德 114
Lloyd, Geoffrey 32
Lu, Jia 陸賈 111
Lu, Jiuyuan 陸九淵 190
Maiese, Michelle 17, 187
Mao, Chang 毛萇 114
Mencius 孟子 7, 39, 64, 73, 109–12, 138, 192
Merleau-Ponty, Maurice 3, 4, 155, 186, 187
Moses 43–5
Mozi 墨子 23, 78, 79–84, 88, 90, 97, 112–14, 151, 154, 180, 193, 194
Nietzsche, Friedrich 3, 185, 190
Otto 17
Pines, Yuri 39, 193
Plato 26, 32, 35, 189
Polanyi, Michael 23, 72
Pythagoras 121
Rosch, Eleanor 4
Ruyer, Raymond 15
Sartre, Jean-Paul 3, 29
Schilbrack, Kevin 45
Schön, Daniel 25
Shapira, Kalonymus Kalmish 40, 43, 44
Shun, Kwong-loi 信廣來 70, 75
Sima Niu 司馬牛, disciple of Confucius 67

Slingerland, Edward 5, 55
Smith, Linda 19
Spinoza, Baruch 3, 18, 133, 158, 159, 185, 187, 189, 201, 202
Thelen, Esther 19
Thompson, Evan 4
Uexküll, Jakob von 4, 154
Varela, Francisco 4
Wang, Chong 王充 36
Wang, Fuzhi 王夫之 36
Wang, Yangming 王陽明 70
Wong, David 72
Xunzi 荀子 7, 23, 39, 109, 112–14, 126–8, 138, 197
Yan, Hui 顏回, disciple of Confucius 59, 66, 69, 73, 74, 157–60, 179, 180
Zahavi, Dan 22
Zhu Xi 朱熹 72
Zhuangzi 莊子 2, 8, 17, 22, 23, 70, 124, 136, 141, 144, 146, 150, 152, 154, 155, 157–61, 165, 166, 168–70, 172, 175, 176, 179–81, 190, 195, 199–201, 203
Zigong 子貢, disciple of Confucius 64, 68, 71, 152
Zixia 子夏, disciple of Confucius 52
Zizhang 子張, disciple of Confucius 74

Texts:
Analects (*Lunyu* 論語) 4–6, 35, 51, 53, 55, 56, 59, 64, 68, 74, 75, 86, 87, 97, 104, 122, 130, 135, 183, 184, 191, 192, 195, 203
Annals of Lü Buwei (*Lüshi chunqiu* 呂氏春秋) 91, 114
Changes (*Yi* 易) 38
Documents (*Shu* 書) 39, 194
Elements (of Euclid) 32, 33
Laozi 老子 101, 173, 174, 195
Mencius (*Mengzi* 孟子) 111, 192
Mozi 墨子 78, 81, 83, 85, 90, 110, 193, 194
Neo-Mohist Canons 85
Odes (*Shi* 詩) 38, 68, 126, 194
Record of Music (*Yueji* 樂記) 7, 8, 49, 59, 114, 115, 118–22, 125, 128, 129, 132, 135, 138, 139, 183, 184, 196, 198, 199
Rites (*Li* 禮) 38, 114
Spring and autumn Annals (*Chunqiu* 春秋) 38
Sunzi 孫子 5
Xunzi 荀子 112, 114, 128, 197
Zhuangzi 莊子 44, 49, 140, 141, 144, 146, 150–3, 160, 163, 173, 175, 177–9, 181, 184, 195, 196, 200, 203

www.ingramcontent.com/pod-product-compliance
Lightning Source LLC
Chambersburg PA
CBHW052108300426
44116CB00010B/1578